Telling Stories

Georgetown University Round Table on Languages and Linguistics Series
Selected Titles

Crosslinguistic Research in Syntax and Semantics: Negation Tense and Clausal Architecture
RAFFAELLA ZANUTTINI, HÉCTOR CAMPOS, ELENA HERBURGER, PAUL H. PORTNER, EDITORS

Discourse and Technology: Multimodal Discourse Analysis
PHILIP LEVINE AND RON SCOLLON, EDITORS

Educating for Advanced Foreign Language Capacities
HEIDI BYRNES, HEATHER D. WEGER-GUNTHARP, KATHERINE SPRANG, EDITORS

Language in Our Time: Bilingual Education and Official English, Ebonics and Standard English, Immigration and Unz Initiative
JAMES E. ALATIS AND AI-HUI TAN, EDITORS

Language in Use: Cognitive and Discourse Perspectives on Language and Language Learning
ANDREA E. TYLER, MARI TAKADA, YIYOUNG KIM, AND DIANA MARINOVA, EDITORS

Linguistics, Language, and the Professions: Education, Journalism, Law, Medicine, and Technology
JAMES E. ALATIS, HEIDI E. HAMILTON, AND AI-HUI TAN, EDITORS

Linguistics, Language, and the Real World: Discourse and Beyond
DEBORAH TANNEN AND JAMES E. ALATIS, EDITORS

Little Words: Their History, Phonology, Syntax, Semantics, Pragmatics, and Acquisition
RONALD P. LEOW, HÉCTOR CAMPOS, AND DONNA LARDIERE, EDITORS

TELLING STORIES:
Language, Narrative, and Social Life

Deborah Schiffrin, Anna De Fina, and Anastasia Nylund, Editors

Georgetown University Press
Washington, DC

Georgetown University Press, Washington, D.C. www.press.georgetown.edu

Library of Congress Cataloging-in-Publication Data

Georgetown University Round Table On Languages and Linguistics (2008).
Telling stories : language, narrative, and social life / Deborah Schiffrin, Anna De Fina and Anastasia Nylund, editors.
p. cm. — (Georgetown University Round Table on languages and linguistics series)
Papers based on those presented at the 2008 Georgetown University Round Table On Languages and Linguistics (GURT).
Includes bibliographical references and index.
ISBN 978-1-58901-629-3 (pbk. : alk. paper)
1. Discourse analysis, Narrative—Congresses. 2. Narration (Rhetoric)—Congresses. 3. Storytelling—Congresses. 4. Sociolinguistics—Congresses. 5. Psycholinguistics—Congresses. I. Schiffrin, Deborah. II. De Fina, Anna. III. Nylund, Anastasia. IV. Title.
P302.7.G48 2008
401′.41—dc22 2009024105

♾ This book is printed on acid-free paper meeting the requirements of the American National Standard for Permanence in Paper for Printed Library Materials.

15 14 13 12 11 10 9 8 7 6 5 4 3 2
First printing

Printed in the United States of America

Contents

Illustrations

Tables

Figures

Acknowledgments

Telling Stories is the outcome of the 2008 Georgetown University Round Table in Languages and Linguistics (GURT), titled *Telling Stories: Building Bridges among Language, Narrative, Identity, Interaction, Society, and Culture.* We could not have put together such a stimulating and high-quality collection of papers without the effort of all those who contributed to the success of the conference. Indeed, GURT 2008 provided narrative analysts from all over the world with an opportunity to present and discuss their work. Thus we are indebted to all those who helped us organize this edition of GURT.

In particular, we would like to thank Georgetown's Faculty of Language and Linguistics and the Linguistics Department for their generous support. We also want to acknowledge the work of all the students who volunteered to assist us in the many tasks related to the conference. Of special note is Jermay Jamsu, our webmaster and master of other electronic issues, and Inge Stockburger, whose calm demeanor qualifies her as an event planner if she ever decides to leave linguistics (hopefully she won't)! Special thanks go to Manela Diez, who devoted her efforts to resolve the innumerable small and big problems that come with the organization of an event of this kind. GURT simply could never happen without her. And of course we are grateful to the many student volunteers who managed registration, book displays, technology, copying, displaying posters, and so on. Finally, we would like to thank our colleagues for undertaking the review of abstracts: Cecilia Castillo Ayometzi, Michael Bamberg, Ellen Barton, Mike Baynham, Colleen Cotter, Nikolas Coupland, Norbert Dittmar, Mark Freeman, Alexandra Georgakopoulou, Marjorie Goodwin, Cynthia Gordon, John Haviland, David Herman, Barbara Johnstone, Christina Kakava, Kendall King, Michael Lempert, Luiz Paulo Moita Lopes, Galey Modan, Ana Relano Pastor, Sabina Perrino, Rob Podesva, Aida Premilovac, Branca Ribeiro, Natalie Schilling-Estes, Amy Shuman, Elizabeth Stokoe, Deborah Tannen, Joanna Thornborrow, Andrea Tyler, and Ruth Wodak.

Introduction

DEBORAH SCHIFFRIN AND ANNA DE FINA
Georgetown University

NARRATIVES ARE FUNDAMENTAL to our lives. We dream, plan, complain, endorse, entertain, teach, learn, and reminisce by telling stories. They provide hopes, enhance or mitigate disappointments, challenge or support moral order, and test out theories of the world at both personal and communal levels. Given this broad swath of uses and meanings, it should not be surprising that narratives have been studied in many different disciplines: linguistics, literary theory, folklore, clinical psychology, cognitive and developmental psychology, anthropology, sociology, and history. And in the past few years, we find that narrative has become part of the public imagination and has provided ways of categorizing more and more genres and social practices.

When we first envisioned the theme of the Georgetown University Round Table 2008, we wanted its primary focus to be the linguistic study of narrative, especially as it has developed within discourse analysis and sociolinguistics. However, as suggested by our conference theme and subtitle—building bridges among language, narrative, identity, interaction, society and culture—studying the language of narrative took us far afield to other concerns: the construction of self and identity; the differences among spoken, written, and mediated narrative discourse; the role that small and big (e.g., life) stories play in everyday social interactions; and the contribution of narrative to social status, and to roles and meanings within institutional settings as varied as therapeutic and medical encounters, education, politics, media, and marketing and public relations.

What we envisioned bore fruit. The oral presentations, organized panels, workshops, and posters became a forum for building interconnections among language, narrative, and social life. Of course publishing every presentation, each worthy of publication, was impossible. After a general call for written versions of the presentations, peer reviews led us to the subset of submissions that appear in this volume. As the reader can see in the remainder of the introduction, the individual chapters in this volume are united by several underlying themes.

The volume begins with three very different, but ultimately interconnected and important, contributions from the three Georgetown University Round Table plenary addresses, by William Labov (a linguist), Richard Bauman (an anthropologist and folklorist), and Jerome Bruner (a psychologist). Each contribution evokes some of the same underlying themes: the moral order, remediation of a story, the "master discourses" of Western culture. For example, the moral order underlies Labov's search for a rationale or cause of unexpected violence and the ability to predict or foresee the course of life; Bauman examines the use of tall tales that involve deception for personal gain, while also endorsing canonical myths and master stories of public negotiation; and Bruner highlights how legal efforts to curtail digressions hark back to the narratives that provide the foundational myths for Western culture and the backbone of Western civilization.

We begin by double-voicing chapter 1, by Labov, "Where Should I Begin?" He examines the preconstruction of several stories: How do storytellers know where to begin? How can omissions be as critical to the story's outcome as what has been included? In chapter 2 Bauman also addresses beginnings, but rather than focusing on the starting point of a narrative itself, he examines a technological beginning—the use of sound recordings of narratives in the late 1800s and early 1900s. These recorded narratives highlight individual trickery, along with the use of common features of American oral storytelling and a general "country" style. In chapter 3 Bruner harks back to cultural beginnings, looking at the narrative mode as the primordial tool for making sense of existence and as the most traditional repository of collective norms and mores.

In the remainder of this introduction, keeping in mind that each chapter relates in numerous ways to our overall themes, we suggest a few connections among the chapters as well as links to the three plenary contributions. Labov's focus on the moral order of actions and reactions from specific characters in the story world suggests a connection to positioning theory and the repercussions of narrative form and function (including self-disclosure) for identity construction.

In chapter 4, "Positioning as a Metagrammar for Discursive Story Lines," Rom Harré provides a theoretical model for the important relationship between positioning and story lines, both of which are crucial for identity. What he proposes is that beliefs about rights and duties to perform certain types of acts determine how social interactions contribute to a story line. These beliefs form a metagrammar that transcends the rules and conventions constituting the grammar (i.e., the shared knowledge of a set of rules and conventions) of an unfolding story line.

Another direction in positioning theory is taken by Alan Hansen and his colleagues, who in chapter 5—"'Ay Ay Vienen Estos Juareños': On the Positioning of Selves through Code Switching by Second-Generation Immigrant College Students"—examine how second-generation Mexican immigrants use code switching, especially in reported speech in both small and long narratives, to manage self and other identities. They show that bilingual code switching has an especially important role in constructing a mother-in-law as the "biggest enemy." Although the mother-in-law was prefigured as an antagonist before her appearance in narrative form, a switch to Spanish and the physical pounding of hand and fist on the table emphasized her as a domestic antagonist.

Identity is also at the center of chapter 6, by Leor Cohen, "A Tripartite Self-Construction Model of Identity." Building on an interactionist and social constructionist social psychological model of identity, Cohen analyzes a narrative of a first-year

Ethiopian Israeli female college student during a focus group session in a language learning program. He shows how elements of personal, collective, and relational orientations are negotiated by the storyteller and how they interrelate with each other, thus adding cogent support for the argument that identities are not cognitive structures but are carefully constructed in discourse.

Another analysis of immigrant identity, Gabriella Modan and Amy Shuman's "Narratives of Reputation: Layerings of Social and Spatial Identities," chapter 7, proposes a reassessment of orientation and the role of place in narrative, taking as data a series of stories narrated by an Israeli immigrant during an interview focused on his perceptions about his multiethnic neighborhood. The authors argue that the presence, absence, or level of detail of orientation serves as a strategy to include or exclude the listener as an in-group member. They also show how place relates to identity construction in narrative, discussing how deictic shifts contribute to creating or disallowing certain subject positions for narrators and their stories.

We have moved from narrative and the moral order, to narrative beginnings, to positioning theory and other approaches to the study of the connections between narrative and identity. The contributions from Michael Bamberg and Malavika Shetty lead us to public media that alter the channels through which we hear, see, and absorb a version of experience, thus remediating again the way a narrative is put forth. Shetty's "Identity Building through Narratives on a Tulu Call-in TV Show," chapter 8, examines how social constructs like gender, caste, and class can be constituted and reproduced through narrative. By analyzing the show *Pattanga,* Shetty shows how narratives are used on TV to politically and culturally define a Tulu identity. She illustrates, for example, how traditional narratives are introduced and co-narrated in order to strengthen a sense of collective membership and to emphasize community achievement and claim the dignity of the Tulu language. Telling a narrative on the show also becomes an occasion—especially for women and lower-caste viewers—to propose changes in their role relationships, and hence facets of their identities. Thus, canonical and traditional Tulu narratives in a public format became a resource to project and create a different persona.

Continuing the focus on remediation, in chapter 9 Bamberg analyzes a television interview with the erstwhile U.S. presidential candidate John Edwards, shortly after he had acknowledged a previously unknown extramarital relationship. Bamberg deconstructs the multimodal facets of the interview, as well as the complex of interactional and situational levels of context, in order to address two interrelated keys to identity: self-disclosure and authenticity. By bringing together a repertoire of discursive tools, Bamberg shows that Edwards's performed disclosures depended on both verbal and nonverbal devices that refocused the attention of the viewing audience from the characters within a story world to the inner mental entity of a narrative self for which a broad, diverse, and distant audience came to feel empathy.

Following up on Bamberg's discussion, in chapter 10 Alexandra Georgakopoulou questions the associations among identity, reflection, and self-disclosure typical of biographical approaches to narrative that, according to her view, stem from excessive reliance on interviews. Using data from an ethnographic study of adolescent interaction in a London middle school, she compares how narratives contribute to identity claims in conversational exchanges between the adolescents and in interviews, and she finds significant differences both in the way stories are used for identity work in the two contexts and in the sequential placement of stories with respect to identity claims. She concludes that reflection and self-disclosure should be seen as relatively de-essentialized and multidimensional, rather than absolute, concepts that come with different possibilities in different contexts.

A similar criticism to traditional views of identity is expressed in chapter 11, by Jarmila Mildorf, "Negotiating Deviance: Identity, Trajectories, and Norms in a Graffitist's Interview Narrative." Mildorf argues against a tendency in life stories research to focus on what she calls "integrative" life trajectories, and for the need to look at life stories created around identities associated with deviance and crime. She presents the case study of her interviews with a graffiti writer in the city of Stuttgart and shows how the interviewee himself strives with the conflicting needs to present a coherent life story, to confront negative perceptions of graffiti writing, and to emerge as an authentic representative of his youth culture.

Continuing on the theme of narrative and identity, but from strikingly different perspectives, in chapter 12 Lars Christer Hydén and Linda Örulv show how people with Alzheimer's disease have cognitive and linguistic difficulties that impede the telling of stories that might contribute to identity work. By comparing multiple tellings of the same story, these researchers illustrate how a narrator with the disease used strikingly different communicative resources when telling a narrative to three different audiences. In one telling, for example, chronology was downplayed in exchange for thematic development and variety more typical of longer life stories than of those focusing on one experience.

Also highlighting the importance of situating a narrative in its particular constellation of contextual features is chapter 13, by Jenny Mandelbaum, "The Management and Import of Concurrent and Intervening Actions during Storytelling in Family 'Ceremonial' Dinners." Her analysis reminds us that not only can listeners alter the design of a narrative, but they can also become coauthors, transform relational and interpersonal matters, and reshape the larger activities in which they are embedded. On the basis of more than forty naturally occurring videotaped ceremonial family dinners, Mandelbaum uses a close analysis of conversation and turn taking to show how narratives may be constructed from beginning to end during the intervention of other activities that overlap with, interrupt, or possibly challenge the integrity (cf. truth, authenticity) of another's story.

Although the raw material of narrative is often open to different interpretations, most narratives are not openly tested for truth and authenticity. In the next two chapters, however, we turn to narratives that are deeply concerned with questions of truth, tellability, and the moral order. Both Isolda E. Carranza and Laura Felton Rosulek unpack how the legal system demands that one version of events be privileged over another. As they both show, heteroglossia, or multiple voicing, has a role in the legal process in assigning truth and authenticity to only one version of what happened.

In chapter 14 Carranza shows how truth and authorship are shaped in the course of the path taken by witnesses' depositions within the institutional meanders of the justice system. Using data from a very large corpus of oral criminal trials for homicide in a large city of a Spanish-speaking country, she focuses on the multilateral character of storytelling in institutions and the complexity of the entextualization, decontextualization, and recontextualization processes. Thus the genre known as a deposition (by a witness or defendant) is part of a story trajectory that results from a network of social positions and their specific power relations, which play a crucial role in the administration of criminal justice.

In another courtroom study, "Legitimation and the Heteroglossic Nature of Closing Arguments," chapter 15, Rosulek examines differing versions of "reality" in closing arguments during criminal trials. Instead of searching for truth or authenticity itself, she uses a Bakhtinian perspective to show how multiple voices allow conflicting versions of events at the center of trials. Her contribution, based on data from official transcripts of the closing arguments in eighteen felony trials in a state district court in the Midwestern United States, along with Carranza's, adds to our understanding of the varying linguistic strategies (in different countries and during different facets of a trial) used by lawyers to make their cases.

The last two chapters return to context and focus more explicitly on narratives across the media. Along with Bamberg's and Shetty's chapters, which use data coming from television shows, these final chapters push the boundary of remediation a bit further.

In chapter 16, "Multimodal Storytelling and Identity Construction in Graphic Narratives," David Herman contends that structuralist narratology failed to come to terms with two dimensions of narrative: the referential or world-creating potential of stories; and the issue of medium-specificity, or the way storytelling practices, including those bearing on world creation, might be shaped by the expressive capacities of a given semiotic environment. The focus of the chapter is on how discursive patterns provide cues to cognitive processes that create mental models. Herman studies multimodal stories, specifically three graphic narratives, and shows how the medium in which these narratives are told has a constitutive influence on how messages are encoded and most surely on story reception as well.

In chapter 17, "The Role of Style Shifting in the Functions and Purposes of Storytelling: Detective Stories in Anime," Fumiko Nazikian takes mediated narratives as data to illustrate the discursive functions of two Japanese verb ending forms, *desu/masu* and *da*. Specifically, she argues that such forms have different roles in the construction of point of view in narrative. By analyzing the *Detective Conan* anime stories, she shows that the *da* form is used to mark a switch from an ongoing event to narrated events, and to create vivid images in the mind of the other participants as if they were in the narrated scene. Conversely, the *desu/masu* form is also associated with discourse-organizational and interactional effects. In particular, in the detective stories the protagonist resorts to this form to underscore his authority and the legitimacy of his hypotheses about events leading to crimes.

This collection of seventeen contributions provides a small but significant window into some of the themes that, in our view, will define research on narrative in the coming years. Some of these themes have already started taking center stage—for example, the diversification of methodological tools, concepts, and contexts in the study of identities in narratives. Others are relatively new, such as the investigation of how mediated communication has changed storytelling practices and our conception of narrative. Yet other questions were already central to narrative research but have taken new directions—for instance, the study of how narratives participate in the construction of the moral order, and the different roles that truth and deception play in varying social practices. What emerges from the chapters in this book is a common emphasis on contexts and practices, a close attention to differences rather than an assumption of homogeneity. These elements confirm a welcome opening up of the field to the realities of postmodern societies.

1

Where Should I Begin?

WILLIAM LABOV
University of Pennsylvania

THE QUESTION THAT FORMS the title of this chapter has been asked by most of us as we are just about to deliver a narrative. It is not put to the listener but is directed inwardly, to the self as author of the narrative. Whether or not the question is formulated explicitly, it must be answered by everyone who tells a story.

The answer may seem obvious: "Begin at the beginning." But how does the storyteller discover that beginning? And is there more than one possible beginning for any given story? The pursuit of these questions will tell us something more about how narratives are constructed through the prior construction of a causal chain of events. It will also show how the transformation of events in the interests of the teller is facilitated by his or her decision on where to begin.

An answer to "Where shall I begin?" requires a process of *narrative preconstruction* (Labov 2006), which must precede the delivery of any narrative of personal experience. An explication of that process begins with the concept of *reportability.* Given the fact that narratives occupy more conversational space than most turns at talk, it appears that certain events and sequences of events carry enough social interest to justify that occupation, whereas others do not.[1] The normal narrative is centered upon a *most reportable event:* the event that is the least common and has the greatest consequences for the life chances of the actors involved. But a report of the most reportable event is not itself a narrative. Consider the turn of talk:

(1) Jacob Schissel: My brother stuck a knife in my head.

This utterance is not a narrative. It is treated by the listener as an *abstract,* indexing the existence of a narrative in which is the most reportable event. It is normally followed by a request for that narrative:

(2) WL: How'd that happen?

The answer to this question is usually the narrative itself, which is more than a description of the most reportable event: It is a request for the causes of the most reportable event, or an accounting of it. Even when (2) takes a less explicit demand for an accounting, "What happened?" the narrator understands it as a request for more than a string of events, but a sequence that satisfies the demand for *credibil-*

ity. The fundamental dynamics of narrative construction are built on the inverse relationship between reportability and credibility: the more reportable an event, the less credible (Labov 1997). A narrative may be dismissed by listeners if it is not deemed reportable, with the responses "So what?" "Et puis?" "Y que?" and their equivalents. It may also be dismissed as a fabrication unworthy of attention if the causal accounting delivered by the narrator is considered inadequate.[2] A certain amount of attention must then be given to establishing the credibility of the most reportable event. If we identify the most reportable event as e_0, the narrator must identify some prior event e_{-1} that answers the question, "How did e_0 happen?" and stands in a causal relationship to e_0. This is a recursive process. Given e_{-1}, a prior event e_{-2} is required that stands in a causal relationship to it and answers the question "How did e_{-1} happen?"

Any answer to the question "Where shall I begin?" requires a termination of that recursive process. Narrative preconstruction can be terminated when it encounters an event e_n with no immediate or obvious cause. This may be termed the *initiating event,* because it initiates the chain that leads to the most reportable event. As we will see, this initiating event may be viewed as mysterious and puzzling or as trivial and unimportant. An answer to the question, "How did (e_{-n}) happen?" would be "I don't know. We were only, . . ." followed by a description of ordinary behavior. We will call this behavior the *initial matrix* i_0, for which the question "Why did you do that?" would be heard as foolish or inappropriate. Given the identification of the most reportable event e_0, the causal sequence $e_{-1} \ldots e_{-n}$, and the initial matrix i_0, the narrator can begin the process of *narrative construction.*

In the framework for narrative construction developed in Labov and Waletzky (1967), the first building block is the "orientation," which provides information on the time, the place and the actors involved in the narrative.[3] It also provides information on what the actors are doing in this ordinary situation: behavior that is expected and needs no explanation. The orientation is built upon the initial matrix i_0.

Narrative preconstruction necessarily precedes narrative construction. It does not have a unique termination. As we examine various narratives of personal experience, it will appear that the choice of e_n and i_0, arresting the causal chain at a particular link in the sequence, is not strictly determined. The decision on where to begin is a major element in the construction of the narrative in the interests of the teller. At first glance, the orientation section of the narrative is only a domain of factual information, with less evaluative material than any other section. Yet location of this orienting information determines more than anything else the assignment of praise and blame for the causal sequence that leads to the most reportable event.

The Norwegian Sailor

In several analyses of narrative structure, I have dealt with Harold Shambaugh's account of the Norwegian sailor. Shambaugh, a thirty-one-year-old resident of Columbus, Ohio, had traveled widely in the service. In a discussion of the use of common sense, he mentioned several occasions when quick reactions were called for, including one in South America.[4]

(3) (What happened in South America?)

a Oh I w's settin' at a table drinkin'
b And uh this Norwegian sailor come over
c an' kep' givin' me a bunch o'junk about I was settin' with his woman.
d An' everybody settin' at the table with me were my shipmates.
e So I jus' turn' aroun'
f an' shoved 'im,
g an' told 'im,
h I said, "Go away,
i I don't even wanna fool with ya."
j An' nex' thing I know I'm layin' on the floor, blood all over me,
k An' a guy told me, says, "Don't move your head.
l Your throat's cut."

Listeners generally agree that the most reportable event e_0 is the cutting of Shambaugh's throat by the Norwegian sailor. As in most effective narratives of personal experience, we learn about this in the same way that the narrator does, the information delivered in clause l. The event e_0 itself occurs just before clause j. If we were dealing with a purely temporal reconstruction, it would appear as (4). Here the sequence of events proceeds backwards in time, moving from the most reportable event e_0 to the initiating event e_3. The past perfect is used for this purpose, the English tense that is specific to reverse movement in time.

(4) Temporal reconstruction of "The Norwegian Sailor."

e_0 This Norwegian sailor cut my throat.
e_{-1} I had refused to listen to him.
e_{-2} He had complained that I was sitting with his woman.
e_{-3} He had come over to the table where I was sitting
i_0 I was sitting with my shipmates drinking

But the temporal events do not necessarily show the causal links that are related to credibility. We can capture the necessary preconstruction as a sequence of causes if these events are related with the subordinate conjunction *because,* as in (5).

(5) Causal preconstruction of "The Norwegian Sailor."

e_0 This Norwegian sailor cut my throat.
e_{-1} because I refused to listen
to his complaint
that I was sitting with his woman
e_{-2} because he came over and complained
i_0 when everyone at the table where we were sitting
were my shipmates

(5) provides is a simpler set of connections. The violent act e_0 was caused by Shambaugh's refusal e_{-1}, As the arrow indicates, that refusal was the result of the event e_{-2} that the complaint was embedded in a matrix that contained no justification for it. The initiating event, the Norwegian sailor's complaint, is seen as inexplicable and irrational.[5]

The construction of the narrative on the basis of preconstruction (5) is shown as (6). In the actual construction, complaints and refusals are both shown as multiple events. The quasi-modal *kept* implies a repeated series of complaints condensed into b, c and the refusal e_{-1} is expanded into the five clauses e, f, g, h, i, which may have been interspersed with the repeated complaints.[6] The importance of the location of the orientation for the narrative is underlined by the elaboration of the orienting material in clause d.

(6) Narrative construction of "The Norwegian Sailor."

(OR = orientation; CA = complicating action; EV = evaluation)

OR	i_0	a	Oh I w's settin' at a table drinkin'
CA	e_{-2}	b	And uh this Norwegian sailor come over
		c	an' kep' givin' me a bunch of junk about I was settin' with his woman.
OR	d		An' everybody settin' at the table with me were my shipmates.
CA	e_{-1}	e	So I jus' turn' aroun'
		f	an' shoved 'im,
		g	an' told 'im,
		h	I said, "Go away,
		i	I don't even wanna fool with ya."
EV	e_0	j	An' next thing I know I'm layin' on the floor, blood all over me,
		k	An' a guy told me, says, "Don't move your head.
		l	Your throat's cut."

The inexplicable character of the initiating event, the complaint of the Norwegian sailor, justifies Shambaugh's refusal as the only rational course of action, and the choice of the initial matrix excludes any prior events that might have been relevant. But there is an alternative set of possibilities that we can project from other discussions of typical patterns of behavior in this situation. In a later exploratory interview in Liverpool, a working-class man in his early twenties gave me this insight on bar room behavior:

(7) Joe Dignall's explication of a similar matrix in Liverpool.

A lot of fellas, if they're with a gang, they let their birds sit with their mates, while he stands up at the bar with his mates, talkin' about things. And you could go up, start chattin' this bird up, and next thing—y'know, you're none the wiser. An' she's edgin' yer on, on, you're a nice fella, you've got a few bob. Great! And—you're chattin' it up there, you're buyin' her a few shots . . . Next thing, eh, a fella comin' there over there, "Eh ay lads, what are ya doin?" Well

YOU don't know he's goin' with her, so you tell HIM to push off. Next thing he's got his friends—his mates on to you, an' uh . . . you're in lumber! You've either got to run, or fight!
—Joe Dignall, Liverpool

An alternate scenario for the events in Buenos Aires, suggested by (7), is that there was at least one woman nearby, possibly at the next table, and that he or others at his table had bought drinks for them, without realizing that they had previous connections with Norwegian sailors at the bar. The expression *come over* indicates the kind of bar-hopping with separation of the sexes that Dignall described. In this view of the situation, the escalation of violence e_0 is an expected consequence of ignoring a valid complaint. In a number of other cases, a sudden explosion of violence is the result of treating someone in an interaction as a nonperson and the refusal to pursue a complaint by continued verbal interaction has violent consequences (Labov 1985).

In this situation, Shambaugh's choice of initiating event and initial matrix was consistent with the view of his behavior as a reasonable reaction to irrationality, rather than a mistake in judgment. His own view of the incident takes one step further:

(8) It taught me a very valuable lesson. Like now if I'm settin' at some place drinkin' and somebody comes up bothering me an' I shove him, I stand up and hit 'im. I don't like the idea of somebody bein' behind me that's mad at me, even my own brother.

He told me that he still had the knife at his house, which made me think that there was more to the story:

(9) As a matter of fact, one of my shipmates killed him. He didn't mean to, just meant to stop him. . . . He picked up one of the big oak chairs down there, hit him in the head with it.

Jacob Schissel's Story

In the course of my study of the Lower East Side of New York City, I interviewed a retired Jewish postman in a brownstone house. Again, a response to a question on the danger of death elicited a narrative that has proved to have a strong emotional impact on listeners. The abstract has already been cited as (1); the full narrative is given as (10).

(10) Jacob Schissel's narrative of the conflict with his younger brother.
(What happened then?)
a Eh—my brother put a knife in my head.
(How'd that happen?)
b Like kids, you get into a fight
c and I twisted his arm up behind him.
d This was just—uh—a few days after my father died
e and we were sittin' shiva.
f And the reason the fight started,

g He saw a rat out in the yard—
h this was out in Coney Island—
i and he started talk about it.
j And my mother had just sat down to have a cup of coffee,
k and I told him to cut it out.
l 'Course kids, y'know, he don't hafta listen to me.
m So that's when I grabbed his arm
n and twisted it up behind him.
When I let go his arm,
o there was a knife on the table,
p he just picked it up
q and he let me have it.
r And . . . I started bleed—like a pig.
a And naturally first thing to do, run to the doctor,
t and the doctor just says, "Just about this much more," he says,
"and you'd a been dead."

The preconstruction of Schissel's story must plainly have begun with (1) as the most reportable event. The series of causal relations is shown in (11).

(11) Causal preconstruction of Jacob Schissel's story

e_0 My brother stuck a knife in my head
e_{-1} because I twisted his arm up behind him[7]
e_{-2} because he said something
e_{-3} because I told him to stop talking
e_{-4} because he was talking about a rat
e_{-5} because he saw a rat in the yard
i_0 when we were sitting shiva in Coney Island after my father died

The initiating event e_{-5} is again one with no prior cause relevant to the narrative. This disturbance initiated by the rat occurred in the initial matrix of sitting shiva (meaning "seven"), the Jewish custom of honoring the dead for seven days, where the seven principal relatives stay at the home of the deceased and receive visitors.

This story is again marked by an extraordinary escalation of violence, and it requires some searching to understand what caused that violence. Though most stories of conflict show a polarization of participants, exaggerating the difference between protagonists and antagonists, Schissel's story is of another kind. The form of telling tends to integrate the participants, obscuring the sources of conflict.

The result of narrative construction in (12) shows how the narrative is built upon the results of preconstruction. Schissel first creates another abstract, which serves to mitigate the conflict as if it was in fact not reportable—the fight as simply the kind of thing that kids tend to do. He then builds the orientation: the time is just after his father has died; and from the definition of shiva we know that the place is Schissel's home, all other members of the family are participants, and the activity is minimal: sitting quietly in the living room and partaking of the food and drink that friends and neighbors have brought to the house. Three other elements of the orientation are postponed and interspersed with the complicating action.

(12) Narrative construction of Jacob Schissel's story.

(What happened then?)

ABS		a	Eh—my brother put a knife in my head.
	(How'd that happen?)		
ABS		b	Like kids, you get into a fight
		c	and I twisted his arm up behind him.
OR		d	This was just–uh–a few days after my father died
	i_0	e	and we were sittin' shiva.
		f	And the reason the fight started,
CA	e_{-5}	g	He saw a rat out in the yard—
OR		h	this was out in Coney Island—
CA	e_{-4}	i	and he started talk about it.
OR		j	And my mother had just sat down to have a cup of coffee,
CA	e_{-3}	k	and I told him to cut it out.
	e_{-2}	l	'Course kids, y'know, he don't hafta listen to me.
	e_{-1}	m	So that's when I grabbed his arm
		n	and twisted it up behind him.
			When I let go his arm,
OR		o	there was a knife on the table,
CA	e_0	p	he just picked it up
		q	and he let me have it.
	e_1	r	And . . . I started bleed—like a pig.
	e_2	s	And naturally first thing to do, run to the doctor,
EV	e_3	t	and the doctor just says, "Just about this much more," he says, "and you'd a been dead."

The causal connection between actions e_{-5} and e_{-4}—seeing the rat and talking about it—need not be made explicit. This is the kind of thing that kids do. But Schissel's consequent reaction e_{-3} ("Cut it out!") is not so immediately obvious. The narrator assumes that the listener is aware of the conventions of sitting shiva: "Visitors have an obligation to remain silent unless the mourner initiates conversation. The mourner is allowed to remain silent, and if so, this shall be respected by the visitors. Any conversation that does take place shall typically be about the deceased."[8]

In e_{-3} Schissel undertakes to enforce this norm. The action e_{-2} that follows is obscured. Instead of the actual quotation, the narrator substitutes an excuse for his brother's conduct. Whatever was said, it triggered the explosion of violence in clauses m, n, p, and q. Even here, the report of the action is mitigating: the murderous attack with a knife is presented in an idiom that is the obverse of agency: "He let me have it."

What then did Schissel's brother say that had such a profound effect? Several decades of reflecting on this matter led to a suggestion that has met with general consensus. What his brother said was something equivalent to "I don't have to listen to you! You're not my father and you can't tell me what to do!" A story which first seems to resemble the conflict between Cain and Abel then shifts to the paradigm of Jacob and Esau, engaged in a competition for their father's birthright. Though Schissel's manner of telling the story may shift this struggle to the background, it seems likely that this sequence of events was not triggered by something besides the rat in the yard. We must assume a longer history of conflict that dates back some time, perhaps even before their father's death.

It follows that Schissel's decision to begin with the incident of the rat in the yard is not the only possible one. If he had chosen to rehearse a longer history of arguments between him and his brother, the outbreak of violence might have seemed more predictable. As it is, any longer-term conflict is placed out of view, and what we hear is a frightening outburst of uncontrollable anger, all the more compelling because it is unpredictable.

The Falling Out

Over the years, our family has had extensive contacts with another Philadelphia family, headed by a husband and wife. The husband Frank died suddenly of a heart attack, some fifteen years ago. Among their children are twins, now young women in their early thirties with children of their own. Along with various accounts of their family history, I had heard mention of an event that occurred just after their father's death. It concerned the possibility of communication with the dead, a theme of many other stories that had been told to me and my students over time. I pressed one of the twins, Melinda, for a complete account of what happened, and she agreed to have me record her version. Her sister Melanie was present, and made a number of cooperative additions along the way, but here I am giving Melinda's account only.

(13) The Falling Out: Melinda's version.

a Well, I'm gonna give you a small history.
b My father's best friend, he—when we were young
c His name was Ray,
d and uh they had a falling out, the parents,
  because their dog bit my sister
e and they didn't talk after that incident.
f So, you know, my father died unexpectedly
g and Ray was in surgery on his knee in the hospital the same day
  my father died
  When he woke up from his surgery

h he said to his wife Linda
who was also my mother's best friend
he said, "Lin, I had a dream,
that Frank came to me,
and said, "Let bygones be bygones.
Like—forget it. It's over."
i And then she said to him, "Ray, Frank died today."
j The man was like a ghost.
k He came to the hospital—I mean to the funeral, on crutches
because he was so freaked out by it
m He was really quite hysterical.

The location of the most reportable event in this story becomes clear in retelling it to various audiences. The report of the dream in clause h does not tell listeners that something unusual has happened until Linda informs Ray in clause i that Ray has just died. At this point there is a rapid intake of breath from most listeners. The narrative develops that evaluation with clauses j and m; even more than the listener, Ray is affected by the fact that i follows h. Like other narratives of premonition and communion with the dead, "The Falling Out" deals with the flow of information and the coincidence of two sources of information. Two streams of information are delivered in rapid succession through different channels: external source through Linda, internal source through Ray, and crucially with Ray preceding, h preceding i. The commonsense expectation would be that Ray first heard of Frank's death, and then Ray dreamed about Frank. But if Linda's source of information did not reach Ray, what did? In narratives like "The Falling Out," it is the failure of the expected source that is in focus. The narrative does not use a formulation that assumes communication with the dead: "Frank appeared to Ray in a dream and said to him. . . ." Rather, it quotes Ray's report "I had a dream . . ." and challenges listeners to avoid the inference that the figure in the dream was Frank, and not a memory of him.

The preconstruction of "The Falling Out" (14) then establishes Linda's statement as the most reportable event e_0. The cause of this event is a complex combination of preceding events. First, that Linda informed Ray of Frank's death e_0 because e_{-1} Ray had dreamed about Frank and the inference from e_{-2} that he did not know of Frank's death when she learned about it because he was in surgery. She might have delivered the news of Frank's death at some other time, but its relevance was foregrounded by the account of Ray's dream. First, if Ray had already learned that Frank had just died, the dream would have been motivated and would not have required any further explanation. Second, this is coupled with background information from the initial matrix i_0 that Ray had not communicated with Frank for a long time. If Ray had habitually been in communication with Frank, the dream would have been a minor coincidence. It is the combination of the sequence e_{-1}, e_{-2}, and i_0 that leads to the evaluation of the most reportable event e_0 as e_1—"The man was like a ghost":

(14) Preconstruction of "The Falling Out"

e_1 Ray realized
that Frank had come to him after death
e_0 because Linda told Ray that Frank was dead
e_{-1} because { Ray had dreamed that Frank had come to forgive him
and Linda knew that Ray did not know
that Frank had died
e_{-2} because he was in surgery
when Linda learned that Frank had died
e_{-3} because Frank had died when Ray was in surgery
i_0 and Ray had not communicated with Frank for a long time
because they had had a falling out
e_{-4} because their dog had bit Frank's daughter
i_0 though they had been best friends before that.

Given this preconstruction, Melinda's construction of the story follows as (15):

(15) Narrative construction of "The Falling Out," Melinda's version.

ABS a Well, I'm gonna give you a small history.
OR b My father's best friend, he—when we were young
c His name was Ray,
i_0 d and uh they had a falling out, the parents,
e_{-4} because their dog bit my sister
i_0 e and they didn't talk after that incident.
CA e_{-3} f So, you know, my father died unexpectedly
e_{-2} g and Ray was in surgery on his knee in the hospital
the same day my father died
h When he woke up from his surgery
e_{-1} he said to his wife Linda
OR who was also my mother's best friend
CA he said, "Lin, I had a dream,
that Frank came to me,
and said, "Let bygones be bygones.
Like—forget it. It's over."
e_0 i And then she said to him, "Ray, Frank died today."
EV e_0 j The man was like a ghost.
RES e_1 k He came to the hospital—I mean to the funeral, on crutches
because he was so freaked out by it
EV m He was really quite hysterical.

We are not concerned here with all aspects of narrative art: Melinda's dramatic expansion of e_{-1} and the contrasting brevity of e_0 in clause i or the interweaving of temporal information with the succession of events. It is the location of the orientation that is our focus. The state of "falling out," the breach of communication among people who were best friends, does not satisfy the usual definition of orientation as a situation that needs no further accounting. Melinda does embed one piece of causal explanation, e_{-4}, in clause d: "Their dog bit my sister." This still does not satisfy the normal expectation of an explanation for why best friends—husbands and wives—should not have talked for a long time. Further inquiry in the family establishes the time gap as thirty years.

Let us free the preconstruction from the flow of information that is so important in (14) and simply present the facts as in (16):

(16) e_0 Frank came to Ray in a dream and forgave him
e_{-1} because Frank died
e_{-2} and Frank had not forgiven Ray for thirty years
e_{-3} for the fact that Ray's dog bit Frank's daughter

The unforgiving character attributed to Frank in this sequence is not the focus of Melinda's version (15). Instead, the act of forgiveness is highlighted, resting on the initial understanding that the families had not communicated for a long time. When I inquired further into the causes of the breach, I learned that some time after the dog bit Melinda's sister, Frank asked his wife, "Have you heard from Linda?" She said "No." "That's funny," he said, "I haven't heard from Ray either." Shortly after this, Frank instituted suit against Ray for Melinda's hospital bills.

These events give us a better understanding as to why the breach was such a permanent one. But they do not explain why Ray did not call and ask how Melinda was getting on. Given the earliest stage of the initial matrix, the initiating event was the dog's attack on Melinda. Was this an unpredictable event? On further inquiring, I learned from Melinda's mother that the dog was considered vicious and had already attacked and killed a neighbor's dog. Knowing more about Frank's temperament and temper, I think it is possible that hard feelings between him and Ray began with Frank's demand that the dog be put down, and that the distance between the families followed Ray's refusal. Melinda's mother gave some support to this conjecture. In any case, Ray's distancing and Frank's following suit clearly indicates some hostile interaction between him and Ray shortly after the attack.

The orientation as Melinda constructs it is built upon the information she had. The events surrounding the dog bite occurred when she was eight years old, and the story is built upon the family traditions that have survived over the years. The focus of the story is not upon Frank's character or the disagreement that alienated the two families. The spotlight is entirely upon the eerie coincidence of the death and the dream. The image of Melinda's father that emerges from this version is limited to his act of forgiveness. It is just and fitting that the story be told in this way, because all who knew Frank remain saddened by his early death. His friends and his children think of him often, and it is comfortable to hear his words emerging, "Let bygones be bygones. Forget it—it's over." If the orientation had been placed earlier, and the acts to be forgiven were preserved in greater detail, it would have been a different and an angrier Frank who emerged. I like the narrative as it is, even if the falling out is not fully explained to those who would pry further into it.

The Notice in the *New York Times*

In the mid-1970s, Tony Kroch (1996) carried out a series of twenty interviews with upper-class Philadelphians, which became integrated into the study of language change and variation in Philadelphia (Labov 1980, 2001). In the course of his work, he posed questions that we commonly use to elicit accounts of premonitions. The narrative is presented as fully constructed in (17), with the sections, events, and clauses included in a format similar to (6), (12), and (15). Like the preceding narrative, it concerns the experience of the older generation, as passed on in family tradition:

(17) Narrative construction of "The Notice in the *New York Times*"

(Kroch: In some families there's someone famous for being able to tell what was going to happen before it happened; was there anybody in your family like that?)

ABS		a	Yeah, there is an instance.
OR	i_0	b	Dad was being driven out from town—ah—by his chauffeur.
		c	This was a good many years ago.
		d	And he had the *New York Times,*
CA	e_{-8}	e	and he read in the *New York Times*
		f	and noticed that—
			the death of a person whom he knew
			but he knew was a very close friend of George Jensen.
		g	George Jensen lived in Chestnut Hill.
	e_{-7}	h	So Dad said to the chauffeur,
			"Stop at Mr. Jensen's house on the way home
			'cause I want to commiserate with him."
	e_{-6}	i	So they did stop
	e_{-5}	j	and Dad went in
		k	and Dad said,
			"George, I'm so sorry to hear about the death of—"
		l	I don't know his name,
EV	e_{-4}	m	and George Jensen said
			"I don't know
			what you're talking about,
		n	If he had died,
			I would have been one of the first people to know."

CA	e_{-3}	o	And Dad said,
			"Well it's in the newspaper,
		p	I'll go out to the car
		q	and get the newspaper."
	e_{-2}	r	Went out
		s	and got the newspaper,
		t	came back
	e_{-1}	u	and he and George went through the newspaper,
EV		v	No sign of this death notice,
CA	e_0	w	And just as they were finished perusing it,
			the telephone rang from somebody in New York
			telling George Jensen that,
			guess
			he'd died.
EV		x	But there was nothing in the newspaper,
RES	e_1	y	Dad brought the newspaper home.
	e_2	z	My sister—
			guess George was home at the time—
			and I all went through the newspaper, meticulously,
EV		aa	Couldn't find anything.

This construction of an account of a premonition has a considerable impact upon listeners, including those who do believe that communication across the final barrier is possible and those who do not. Many aspects of effective narrative construction are exemplified in (17). The effect of the narrative is heightened by the confident use of an elaborate and precise vocabulary: *commiserate, perusing, meticulously.* Negatives are artfully placed to intensify the evaluation of the events in clauses m, n, v, x, and aa. The narrative syntax is prototypically simple, but complexity is concentrated in the evaluative clauses. This is particularly marked in the delivery of the most reportable event e_0 in clause w, which combines seven predicated propositions into one sentence, as sketched in figure 1.1.

The key temporal clause, "just as they were finished perusing it," is left dislocated to initial position. The temporal relations of sources of information play the same crucial role as in the previous narrative, "The Falling Out." Information from an internal source (perception of the *New York Times*) antecedes the flow of information from an external source (the telephone). The unreliable character of the internal source is comparable to the dreamlike character of Ray's information, but the fact that it precedes and predicts the external source is equally mysterious and challenging. A preconstruction of this story in (19) shows a long chain of causal connections but begins with a temporal conjunction of the telephone call e_0 and the failed search in the newspaper e_{-1}.

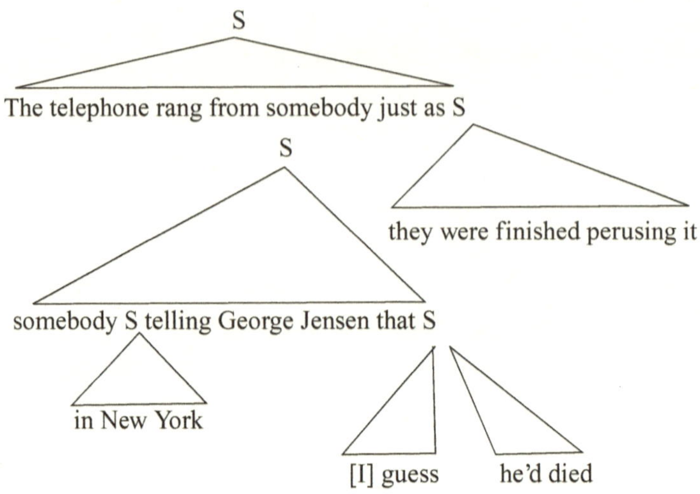

Figure 1.1 Predicated Propositions in Event e_0

(19) Preconstruction of "The Notice in the *New York Times*"

e_{-0}	Someone in New York called with the information that this man had died
e_{-1}	just when my father had searched for a death notice in the newspaper
e_{-2}	because he had brought it in from the car
e_{-3}	because he said the death notice was in the newspaper
e_{-4}	because George Jensen denied that this man had died
e_{-5}	because my father told him he was sorry the man had died
e_{-6}	because they stopped at George Jensen's house
e_{-7}	because my father wanted to commiserate with him
e_{-8}	because my father had read in the *New York Times* that this man had died
i_0	when he was driving home with his chauffeur.

The preconstruction establishes the initial matrix as the ordinary event i_0, the narrator's father being driven home from work; we are not reasonably entitled to ask, "Why did that happen?" The initiating event e_{-8} is the notice in the *Times,* unusual enough to trigger the sequence of following events, and given without any preceding account or explanation. In this construction of the story, it just happens to occur in this ordinary context.

If we were to probe further into this initiating event, we might ask, "How well did your father know this man?" "Did your father know that this man was sick or in danger of death?" George Jensen's denial that the man had died did not preclude the possibility that his death was likely. These skeptical considerations are foreclosed by the selection of the orientation. It seems clear that the narrator's father did not see in the *New York Times* what he thought he saw, but the reasons for this illusion are hidden. This is not to suggest for a moment that there is a false bottom to this construction. Rather, the striking coincidence of illusory perception and hard news is told in a way that maximizes its effect upon the listener through the decision to begin with that particular homeward journey. If the family tradition had included a counter to such skeptical questions, the orientation might have been shifted backward in time.

The Program for Narrative Construction

Assembling the considerations advanced in this study of four narratives, we can begin to put together the outlines of a program for narrative construction:

- A narrative of personal experience is a means of transferring the experience of events, as originally encountered by the narrator, to listeners in a form adapted to the evaluative norms of speaker and listener.
- To accomplish this end, a narrative must move forward in time from some initial point to the resolution without flashbacks.
- Before beginning a narrative, a narrator must construct a chain of events, each the cause of its successor, that links the most reportable event of a narrative to an initiating event set in an initial matrix that needs no further accounting and is not in itself reportable.
- The narrator begins the narrative with an orientation section, which incorporates the initiating event into a static situation with no previous history. Accepting the orientation as needing no prior explanation is equivalent to accepting the narrator's theory of the causes of the reportable events.
- The first narrative event that follows the orientation is presented without prior cause, because the ordinary events of the orientation do not generate reportable events:
- This Norwegian sailor come over . . .
- There was a rat out in the yard . . .
- My father died unexpectedly
- and Ray was in surgery . . .
- He noticed the death of a person who . . .

The manner in which the chain of narrative events is transformed into narrative clauses will of course depend upon the linguistic resources of the speaker's language. In any case, our understanding of this process will be illuminated by a reconstruction of the chain of causal connections between the most reportable event and the orientation selected by the narrator. Our review of other possible orientations pointed toward earlier alternatives rather than later ones. In less dramatic narratives, we may find later alternatives more attractive. Some narrators pursue the chain of relevant events further than necessary into the domain of ordinary occasions. As we move backwards in time, relevance diminishes and the claim to speakership may falter. In the more dramatic narratives that we have considered here, the impact of the most reportable event is intensified by the brevity of the chain that precedes it. Digging further into the past in our preconstruction may make the end result more credible but therefore less surprising. The selection of orientation and initiating event demands good steersmanship in navigating between the menacing Scylla of disbelief and the yawning Charybdis of ho-hum.

NOTES

1. Or as Sacks (1992, vol. 2, 3–5) pointed out, justify the automatic return of speakership to the narrator after the interposition of other turns in the form of back channel or other comment. The concept of reportability is of course relative to the social situation and competing claims for speakership.
2. Excluding of course the special genre of tall tales, where the demand for credibility is canceled.
3. Following the abstract, if there is one. An abstract need not be considered as part of the narrative itself.
4. In this notation, each independent clause (together with its subordinate clauses) is lettered separately.
5. The notion that the behavior of drunken Scandinavian sailors is irrational and unpredictable is widespread in vernacular narrative.
6. The verb phrase of clause e, *turn around,* is frequently used in narratives of personal experience to elaborate the description of activity when no literal motion of the body is necessarily implied.
7. Clause m, "grabbed his arm," is not a separate element in the causal chain, but an instrumental specification which increases the sense of activity. In this respect, it is similar to "turned around" in clause e of "The Norwegian Sailor."
8. See http://en.wikipedia.org/wiki/sitting_shiva#processealthgrades.com/.

REFERENCES

Kroch, Anthony. 1996. Dialect and style in the speech of upper class Philadelphia. In *Towards a social science of language,* vol. 1, ed. G. Guy, C. Feagin, D. Schiffrin, and J. Baugh, 23–46. Philadelphia: John Benjamins.

Labov, William. 1980. The social origins of sound change. In *Locating language in time and space,* ed. W. Labov, 251–66. New York: Academic Press. Reprinted in *Dialect and language variation,* ed. H. B. Allen and M. D. Linn, 524–41. Orlando: Academic Press.

———. 1985. Speech actions and reactions in personal narrative. In *Analyzing discourse: Text and talk,* ed. D. Tannen, 219–47. Georgetown University Round Table 1981. Washington, DC: Georgetown University Press.

———. 1997. Some further steps in narrative analysis. *Journal of Narrative and Life History* 7:395–415.

———. 2001. *Principles of linguistic change, volume 2: Social factors.* Oxford: Blackwell.

———. 2006. Narrative preconstruction. *Narrative Inquiry* 16:37–45.

Labov, William, and Joshua Waletzky. 1967. Narrative analysis. In *Essays on the verbal and visual arts,* ed. J. Helm, 12–44. Seattle: University of Washington Press. Reprinted in *Journal of Narrative and Life History* 7 (1997): 3–38.

Sacks, Harvey. 1992. *Lectures on conversation, vol. I and vol. II,* ed. Gail Jefferson. Oxford: Blackwell.

2

The Remediation of Storytelling: Narrative Performance on Early Commercial Sound Recordings

RICHARD BAUMAN
Indiana University

FROM THE LATE EIGHTEENTH CENTURY and the first scholarly recognition of oral tradition as a cultural process, there has been a concomitant concern among students of language and expressive culture with the transformative effects of new technologies of communication on oral performance. One facet of the problem that has concerned scholars of oral narrative from the Brothers Grimm to the theorists of ethnopoetics and the orality-literacy debates is the process of remediation, specifically, the rendering of face-to-face performance forms through the mediation of another communicative technology.[1] What happens when we render oral stories in writing? What are the epistemological, cognitive, aesthetic, and other implications of transferring storytelling from live performance to the printed page? There is a large and ever-growing scholarly literature on these matters, and I shall not even attempt to summarize it here.[2] Rather, I propose to extend the exploration of remediation in a new, largely unexplored direction by examining the adaptation of storytelling to another technology of communication, namely, sound recording. More specifically, I deal here with the representation of oral storytelling on early commercial sound recordings in the United States, from the late 1890s through the first couple of decades of the twentieth century. This was the formative period in the development of commercial sound recording in the United States, a period of experimentation as the early producers of records for a popular market explored the technological and commercial potential of the new medium. The advent of sound recording was widely hailed as a means of capturing and preserving the living voice for later reproduction, a means of transcending the ephemerality of performance. But how did the process actually work? What aspects of their history did the recorded performances carry with them as they were recontextualized from live events to commercial recordings? What new features did the process of recording call forth? And what was the broader cultural field in which these transformations occurred?

As a point of entry into this broad arena of investigation, I deal in this chapter with a series of recordings made by some of the earliest featured performers of the new medium, performers whose recordings demonstrate significant transformations that reshaped oral storytelling as it was adapted to commercial recording. I intend this chapter to serve as an exploration in the history, culture, and technology of storytelling as a performance form, with special attention to changes that attended the process of remediation from copresent, live performance to sound recording made for a nascent commercial market.

Jim Lawson's Hoss Trade

The first example I consider, "Jim Lawson's Hoss Trade," was recorded in 1903 by one of the earliest stars of the new medium, Cal Stewart. Stewart's recorded performances in his adopted persona of Uncle Josh Weathersby of Pumpkin Center, a fictional small town in rural New England, were immensely popular from the last years of the nineteenth century through his death in 1919 and for some years thereafter.[3] Uncle Josh, as Stewart portrayed him, was an incarnation of a stock figure in nineteenth-century American popular culture, the comic rustic Yankee, a symbolic vehicle for the representation of social contrasts between old-fashioned and modern social types and of the encounter of passing ways of life with the new ways of emergent modernity (Rourke 1959, 3–32; Tandy 1964, 1–19).

The stage Yankee appeared in a number of performance vehicles, including prominently dramatic sketches of rural and small town life, rendered in a distinctive vernacular style that was characterized by stereotypical dialect forms, homely images, colorful exclamations, and an understated but loquacious mode of delivery. One of the popular guises in which the stage Yankee appeared, from the mid-1820s onward, was as a performer of stories and recitations in the form of a comic monologue (Nickels 1993, 76–77), a platform format well suited to that mode of traditional storytelling that involves virtuosic performance by a narrator who holds the floor for an extended period of time. Though Stewart was an experienced actor in Yankee theatrical roles, the comic monologue was the performance form in which he excelled and which he cultivated with enormous success in the persona of Uncle Josh Weathersby. The overwhelming majority of Stewart's recorded performances as Uncle Josh are in narrative form, but for present purposes I focus on one of his popular recordings that illustrates one important presentational mode in the remediation of oral storytelling to phonograph records.

"Jim Lawson's Hoss Trade" is a version of a tale reported to be one of Abraham Lincoln's favorites, part of a large class of narratives in American oral tradition revolving around the horse trader as a trickster figure whose quick wit and glib tongue allow him to manipulate less clever victims to his own advantage (Bauman 1986, 11–32; Dorson 1959, 71).[4] In Stewart's version, the story becomes a local character anecdote featuring Jim Lawson, one of the more colorful citizens of Pumpkin Center and the key figure in a number of Stewart's Uncle Josh routines.[5]

Cal Stewart, "Jim Lawson's Hoss Trade," Monarch 1475, pre-matrix, take 6; April 27, 1903.[6]

Jim Lawson's Hoss Trade, by Mr. Cal Stewart. [Laughs]

Well, sir, Jim Lawson,
he was calculated to be just about the best hoss trader in Punkin Center.

But a gypsy come along one day
an' I guess he took all the conceit outa Jim in the way o' tradin' hosses.
You see, he trade'im a mighty fine lookin' animal
only had one very bad fault:
any time he'd go to ride 'im,
happened to touch 'im on the sides,
then he'd squat right down.

Well, Jim knowed if he didn't get rid o' that hoss,
his reputation as a hoss trader was forever gone.
So he went over to see Deacon Witherspoon.
Deacon was old an' gouty,
kinda hard for 'im to get around,
an' he was mighty fond o' goin' a'huntin.
He had to hunt on hossback.
An' Jim says, "Deacon, I got a hoss you oughta have.
He's a setter."
Deacon says, "Why, Jim, I never heered tell o' such a thing in all o' my life.
Idea of a horse bein' a setter.
Bring 'im over, Jim,
I'd like to see 'im."

Well, Jim took the hoss over, an' they went out a'huntin'.
They was a'ridin' along an' Jim, he saw a rabbit a'sottin' in the bushes
an' he just touched the ol' hoss on the sides,
an' he squatted right down. [Laughs]
Deacon says, "Well, what's the matter with your hoss, Jim?
Look what he be a'doin'."
Jim says, "Keep still, Deacon.
Don't you see that rabbit over thar in the bushes?
Ol' hoss is a'sottin' of 'im."
Deacon says, "Well, well, I wanta know,
most remarkable thing I ever seen in my life.
Well, now, did you ever?
How would you like to trade?"
'N' Jim says, "I'll trade you, Deacon,
hundred 'n' fifty dollars to boot."

Well, they traded hosses,
an' when they was a'comin' home,
they had to ford the creek back o' Punkin' Center.

Well, when the ol' hosses was wadin' along through the water,
Deacon went to pull 'is feet up,
keep 'em from gettin' wet,
'n' he touched the ol' hoss on the sides,
and 'e squatted right down'n the creek. [Laughs]
Deacon says, "Now, lookee here, Jim.
What's the matter with this here hoss?
He ain't a settin' now, be he?"
Jim says, "Yes, he is, Deacon.
He sees fish in the water.
He's trained to set for suckers same as for rabbits, Deacon."
[Laughs]

As featured on the recording, "Jim Lawson's Hoss Trade" is told as if to a copresent interlocutor in a face-to-face, immediate interaction. In the opening line of the narration, Uncle Josh addresses his interlocutor as "sir," the conventional appellative of respect. And in line 6, the second person pronoun in "You see" serves as a phatic gesture that picks out the addressee and signals that the narrative is directed at him. These deictic forms serve as contextualization cues that invite the listener to the recording to assume the participant role of targeted addressee, eliding the temporal gap and technological mediation between the recording event and the listening event.

Uncle Josh delivers the story in his characteristic speech style: informal, vernacular, marked by stereotypically "rural" dialect forms. Stewart, who was born and raised in Virginia, made some effort to sound like a New Englander in his Uncle Josh performances, but even those features that he considered distinctive to that region extend more broadly across the country. Stewart apparently considered the preterit form "sot" for "sat" or "set" to be especially distinctive of Yankee speech and he used it heavily, not only in this performance but in others. Indeed, he overused it, coining grammatical variants ("sottin'") that were not current in actual speech. Yet "sot," as well as "knowed" (for 'knew') and "heared" (for 'heard') had a wide currency in American vernacular speech (Atwood 1953, 21, 17, 16; Wentworth 1944, 580, 344, 283). Perhaps the most distinctive New England usage to mark Uncle Josh's speech is "be" as a progressive aspect auxiliary verb for "am," "are," "is," as in "Look what he be a'doin'" (line 29), yet it too was occasionally documented in other parts of the country (Atwood 1953, 27; Wentworth 1944, 45–46).

In addition to the general dialect features that characterize Uncle Josh's speech, several elements came to define his personal style, including his relatively flat intonation, and his trademark laugh, which punctuated the narration on all his recordings. In all, however, though Uncle Josh's speech displayed a few features that would have been recognizable indicators of New England dialect to those familiar with the region, his overall speech style was an amalgam of lexical and grammatical elements of relatively broad regional distribution in American rural vernacular speech that listeners throughout the United States would have recognized as a generalized "country" dialect—perhaps not precisely like the dialect of their own region, but with enough familiar elements to do the indexical work of establishing Uncle Josh as a quintessentially rustic figure.

The formal structure of the narrative exhibits many of the common features of American oral storytelling, including prominently the following:

1. The use of "well" as an opening and subsequently as an episode marker (lines 11, 24, 39, 42) (cf. Bauman 1986, 23, 25, 42, 56–58, 83–90, 108–11);
2. The division of the narrative into three principal episodes consisting of dyadic interactions between the dramatis personae (here Jim Lawson and Deacon Witherspoon), played out in quoted dialogue (cf. Johnstone 1996, 40);
3. The predominant use of the historical present ("Jim says," "Deacon says") of the verbs of saying employed as quotative frames (cf. Johnstone 1990, 77–88);
4. Uncle Josh's signature laugh, an exuberant cackle that signals the narrator's own amusement at the narrated event and serves as an evaluative marker of the key element on which the plot turns, namely, the squatting of the horse;
5. The clever, reportable final utterance, which has the effect of a capping punch line, a characteristic formal feature of the oral anecdote (cf. Bauman 1986, 54–77); and
6. The polysyndetic, additive chaining of narrative clauses, present here (lines 25–27), but more common in other stories (cf. Johnstone 1990, 50–58; Schiffrin 1981, 131–32).

All these features—the deictic contextualization cues, the vernacular speech styles, the formal organization of the narratives—impart to the recorded performance of "Jim Lawson's Hoss Trade" as it is played back in the listening event some of the immediacy of face-to-face vernacular storytelling. To be sure, the recorded performance is conspicuously fluent and devoid of any signs of audience participation, but the most virtuosic of traditional oral storytellers do approach or even attain this level of fluency, and the organization of participation in such performances does allow the performer to monopolize the floor while limiting the audience essentially to backchannel responses. The listener can still respond at a distance with a smile or a laugh, and Uncle Josh's own trademark laugh provides a functional substitute for other participant responses.

An additional mediating element is the introductory announcement that opens the recording, transcribed in line 1: "'Jim Lawson's Hoss Trade,' by Mr. Cal Stewart (laugh)." Announcements of this kind were common on early recordings and served, among other functions, as orienting frames for the recorded performances (Feaster 2006, 304–46). Here, by giving the recitation an objectifying title, by identifying himself by his own name (not Uncle Josh), and by including his trademark laugh, Stewart frames the narration to follow as a simulation, a reenactment, of a traditional, oral storytelling performance. This framing is entirely consistent with Stewart's public characterization as an "impersonator" or "delineator" of the comic Yankee type. The announcement, and Stewart's identification as the animator of Uncle Josh, serve a mediating function, framing the storytelling performance as a constructed display object, albeit one that is a skillful and persuasive simulation of the real thing.

To be sure, however, the platform performances of the Yankee storyteller on which Stewart modeled his Uncle Josh recordings were already simulations, representations of traditional storytelling.[7] The production framework of oral storytelling performance—extended holding of the floor, phatic gestures to a copresent, gathered audience—lends itself readily to platform performance and allows quite well for the retention of the core features of traditional storytelling we have identified. But the crafted rustic persona, and his stylized, stereotyped dialect, are artifacts of the stage Yankee, a symbolic construction of nineteenth-century American popular culture. "Jim Lawson's Hoss Trade," then, is a mediated representation of a stage representation of oral storytelling.

The Farmer and the Hogs

If we consider "Jim Lawson's Hoss Trade" to represent a second-order transposition of oral narrative performance, insofar as it involves the adaptation to sound recording of a platform performance that is itself a representation of a traditional face-to-face storytelling performance, our second example, "The Farmer and the Hogs," adds still other layers of mediation to the performance. This recording, a rendering of a traditional American tall tale,[8] begins with a bit of metanarrational contextualization by the performer, Edwin Whitney, reporting and evaluating a "mighty good" story that is part of the active repertoire of another raconteur, one Strickland W. Gillilan,[9] identified as a "funnyman." Whitney thus offers a number of warrants for telling the story again: It sustains multiple tellings by Gillilan, Gillilan is known for being funny, and it is "a mighty good story" to boot. In functional terms, these devices both authorize and traditionalize the story, aligning Whitney's performance to follow with antecedent performances:

Edwin Whitney, "The Farmer and the Hogs," Victor 16489B, matrix B8055; June 15, 1909.[10]

A mighty good story is told by Strickland W. Gillilan,
    the *Baltimore American* funnyman,
better known to you possibly as the author of
"Off Agin, On Agin, Gone Agin Finnigan."
He tells the story of a gentleman who was traveling in the state of Arkansas.
He was on horseback,
    going from one village to another,
and while riding past a piece of woods,
he noticed a number of hogs,
all acting very strangely.
He stopped and watched 'em.
The hogs would all stand still,
    tuck up their ears and listen,
and at the same time would all start and run in the same direction

as fast as they could go.
They would run a little ways,
stop,
listen,
run again in a different direction.
Run a little ways,
stop,
listen,
and run some more,
and they kept at it.

The gentleman's curiosity was so much aroused
that he stopped at the first cabin he saw
as he rode on
and greeted the old man who came to the door.

The old man replied,
[hoarse, gravelly voice; slowly] "Howdy, stranger."

"Now, my friend,
have, uh, you lived here all your life?"
"No, sir."

"Well, maybe you've lived here long enough to be able to tell me
something about who owns this piece of woods up the road,
the first piece on my right."

"Yes, sir,
I reckon I can tell you."

"Well, who owns it, please?"

"I do."

"Well, those must be your hogs in the woods, then,
are they?"

"Yes, sir,
I reckon those're my hogs."

"Well, I wish you could tell me what's the matter with them.
I've been up there watching 'em for the last half hour,
and I never saw anything act the way they do.
They all stand and listen,
then start 'n' run

all in the same direction at the same time.
They run a little ways,
stop,
'n' listen,
run again in the opposite direction perhaps.
Run a little ways,
stop,
'n' listen,
'n' run again,
stop,
listen,
and run some more,
always in a different direction,
and they keep at it.
Can you explain to me
why they do that?"

"Yes, sir,
I reckon I kin tell you.
You see, stranger,
this is the season o' the year
when we're fattenin' up the hogs
and gittin' 'em ready for market.
Well, I been a' goin' out 'n'
callin' 'em up to the fence,
throwin' over a little corn to 'em
as fur as it gets 'em
started along.
Here about two weeks ago,
I got this cold,
and it settled right on my vocal cords
so I cain't talk.
I can't holler
and call the hogs no more,
so I had to go out 'n'
sound on a tree with a stick to call 'em up.
Well, they got so they'd answer that all right.
An' now these dumb woodpeckers,
they keep 'em crazy."

Whitney's telling is framed initially as a report of Gillilan's tellings, but Gillilan soon recedes from the scene as Whitney takes over the responsibility for the current performance. This is a common move in traditional storytelling: establishing one's authority for the current performance and claims on the audience's attention by intertextual linkage to antecedent authoritative performances, and then taking over the performance oneself. I will have more to say about the attribution to Gillilan a bit later. For now, however, I would note that like Cal Stewart's "Well, sir" at the opening of "Jim Lawson's Hoss Trade," Whitney's suggestion that Gillilan is "better known to *you*" as the author of a widely circulated poem can plausibly be heard, I think, as an invitation to the hearer of the recording to assume the participant role of targeted addressee.

The narration itself begins by setting up the symbolic tension that will provide the central dynamic of the story, namely, the classic confrontation between the cultivated—often urban, often Eastern—outsider and the frontier rustic (Dorson 1959, 92). One inflection of the dynamic that drives these symbolic encounters is a turning of the social tables, as the sophisticated outsider is baffled by a feature of the rustic environment that is completely beyond his ken but readily explainable by the backwoods farmer, even though the explanation may turn out to be a tall tale. Here, we have a "gentleman" traveling through Arkansas, the quintessential region of backwardness and rusticity, and encountering a herd of pigs behaving in a strange and puzzling manner, the complicating action of the story. All of this narrative setup is accomplished by past-tense description of the narrated event, which continues to the point when the gentleman stops at the cabin and greets the old man who came to the door.

Then, with the old man's return greeting, framed by the quotative frame "The old man replied," the narrative framework shifts to direct discourse, from diegetic to mimetic modes of performance. The entire remainder of the story is rendered as quoted speech, with the attendant deictic shifts in pronouns, tense, demonstratives, and the like. What is especially striking about the dialogic interaction in this performance, however, in marked contrast to "Jim Lawson's Hoss Trade," is that it is accomplished without quotative attribution, but it remains abundantly clear nevertheless who is speaking throughout the remainder of the tale. The overall effect is to foreground the mimetic mode of presentation, drawing the performance closer to theatrical enactment than to narrative exposition. It is crucial to recognize, however, that unlike staged theatrical performance, which combines verbal and visual semiosis, the recorded performance is restricted entirely to the acoustic channel. When dialogic interaction is enacted on stage, the audience can see as well as hear who is speaking at any given time. In the recording of "The Farmer and the Hogs," Whitney must rely on speech alone. He manages the narrative dialogue with three expressive means that build up and sustain the contrast between the dramatis personae.

The two interlocutors are differentiated, to begin with, by contrastive speech varieties: The gentleman speaks standard English, marked by formal syntactic constructions, politeness forms, phonologically standard pronunciation, and carefully marked word boundaries, whereas the farmer speaks a rural dialect, distinguished by stereotypically rustic grammatical constructions and phonology and by honorifics that acknowledge his interlocutor's gentlemanly status.

Second, the two speakers are further distinguished by voice quality and expressive style. The gentleman's voice is well modulated, whereas the farmer speaks with a husky, raspy timbre, a consequence, we discover, of a cold that "settled right on my vocal cords so I cain't talk." In a related vein, the farmer tends toward laconicity of expression, at least in his early turns at talk, as he responds to the relatively voluble solicitations of the gentleman "stranger."

Third, the contrastive ways of speaking that distinguish the two interlocutors are further augmented by the structure of the conversation they play out, with their respective turns both differentiated and tied together with a range of cohesion devices:

- Question-answer adjacency pairs: "Well, who owns it please?" "I do."
- Yes-or-no responses that are tied to antecedent utterances by assuming a positive or negative alignment to them: "Now, my friend, have you lived here all your life?" "No, sir."
- Lexical repetition: "Well, those must be your *hogs* in the woods, then, are they?" "Yes, sir, I reckon those're my *hogs*."
- Syntactic parallelism, as the old man responds with variants of the gentleman's solicitational questions: "Well, I wish you could tell me. . . ." "Yes, sir, I reckon I kin tell you."

All these devices are found in traditional oral storytelling, but I cannot recall a performance, even by the most virtuosic of storytellers, in which quotative frames are so systematically and completely dispensed with and direct discourse managed with such a complex inventory of devices to differentiate the voices of the dramatis personae. As I suggested a bit earlier in the chapter, part of this strong effort at differentiation is attributable to the exclusive reliance in recordings on sound, which must bear all the burden of keeping the characters clear.

Medium alone, however, cannot account fully for the performance style of "The Farmer and the Hogs." To bring the style of the recording more clearly into focus, it is illuminating to consider more specifically what performance forms underlie Whitney's recorded representation. Although he identifies Strickland W. Gillilan, the source of his story, as a journalist and author of popular poetry, Gillilan was also an active performer on the Chautauqua and after-dinner circuits, delivering humorous "entertainment lectures" on a variety of subjects. One of the lectures he offered to prospective clients was "A Sample Case of Humor," in which he essayed a definition of humor and a typology of humorous themes, "illustrated with stories." Among his stock themes was "Humor of Rusticity," for which "The Farmer and the Hogs" might well have been one of the illustrative examples. Gillilan, then, like Cal Stewart, was a platform performer, but whereas Stewart performed in the guise of a stage Yankee, animating a rustic storyteller, Gillilan delivered lectures, using stories for illustrative purposes. Tent Chautauqua was conceived and framed as an educational institution, a means of bringing culture and learning to the rural parts of the country (Canning 2005; Tapia 1997). The Chautauqua lecture was formally marked by smooth and showy fluency, without hesitation phenomena, false starts, or repairs, and by a tendency—passages of quoted speech aside—toward phonologically and grammatically careful standard English.

Like Gillilan, Edwin Whitney was an active performer on the Chautauqua circuit, known, among other things, for his dapper, fastidious dress; he was no Yankee rube dressed in rustic garb like Stewart (Harrison 1958, 103–5; Tapia 1997, 138–39). More important, however, for our purposes, Whitney was a skilled "monactor" or "monodramatist," a specialist in a distinctive mode of Chautauqua dramatic performance in which an individual animated all of the characters in a play or dramatic sketch (Case and Case 1970, 54–55; Rieser 2003, 231–32). Whitney was advertised in a program brochure as being able to voice "a whole play company at once." It is these Chautauqua skills that we hear on "The Farmer and the Hogs." The opening metacommentary, with its intertextual allusion to Gillilan's story, is in lecture register, extending into the early diegetic exposition: smooth, fluent, Standard English, though with a few vernacular touches. The shift into direct discourse marks the transition from diegetic reporting to mimetic enactment, and this latter portion of the performance is in the "monactor" mode of animating all the dramatis personae.

The monactor mode of dramatic performance was largely a concession on the part of Chautauqua promoters to the religious sensibilities of their core constituencies, who had deep moral reservations against full, staged theater. Having one person—not in costume, not a morally suspect actor—voice all the parts of a classic or properly uplifting play could be promoted as modeling skilled elocution and thus warranted as consistent with the intellectual and moral goals of Chautauqua. Adapted to storytelling, the same mode of dramatic performance became a virtuosic, formalized, theatricalized adaptation of the taking on of voices in direct discourse that is a common feature of traditional vernacular storytelling. Moreover, it is readily adaptable, without significant modification, to sound recording. Whitney's performance of "The Farmer and the Hogs," like Cal Stewart's "Jim Lawson's Hoss Trade," is thus a remediated representation of a mode of storytelling characteristic of tent Chautauqua, adapted to more extended lecture presentations and marked by theatricalized voicing of narrative dialogue in a manner drawn from one-person dramatic readings or monactor performances.

Uncle Jim's Racetrack Story

Our final example, "Uncle Jim's Racetrack Story," has presentational affinities with "The Farmer and the Hogs" in certain respects, but represents an entirely new departure in the remediation of storytelling. The recording was made by Len Spencer, one of the first, most versatile, and most successful of the early commercial recording performers (Gracyk 2000, 314–19). Spencer's father operated a business college in Washington, where the son worked as an instructor. The college made use of recording machines as instructional tools, and Spencer had frequent occasion to visit the nearby headquarters of the Columbia Phonograph Company to have the machines serviced and to replenish the school's supply of cylinders. On one of his visits, Spencer expressed his desire to have his own voice recorded, and he turned out to have a strong baritone that was well suited to the recording technology of the day. He began his recording career around 1889 or 1890, making song recordings for commercial coin-operated machines that were placed in train and ferry terminals, arcades, and other public places. That is to say, Spencer was from the beginning a phonograph performer.

Unlike Stewart or Whitney, his entire career was linked to the new technology of sound recording. Thus, though he was clearly familiar with the popular entertainment forms of his day, including the monactor mode of performance in which one performer animates all of the characters in a dramatic enactment, he was more professionally attuned to the performance potential of the new communicative technology.

At the heart of "Uncle Jim's Racetrack Story" is an enacted representation of a storytelling performance in which the narrator relates a story to an audience whose members contribute back-channel responses and evaluative metacommentary. The story itself is an exemplar of another genre like the tall tale that represents a playful, rekeying transformation of a personal experience narrative. Uncle Jim's story is a catch tale, which derives its effect by drawing the audience to a particular interpretive expectation, only to pull the rug out from under them at the end by deflating and discrediting their assumptions. As we will see, audience response is essential to the narrative exchange represented on this recording: without the expression of mistaken understanding, Uncle Jim cannot produce his rekeying response.

Len Spencer, "Uncle Jim's Racetrack Story," Victor 2790, matrix B1246; April 21, 1904.[11]

[Hoofbeats]
Jim: Whoa! whoa! whoa!
Get over there!
Host: Hello, Jim.
Why, uh, here's some friends of mine from New York.
I'm just uh, showing them through the paddock
and I want, uh, you to tell them that story about the Tennessee Derby.

Guest 1: Go ahead, Jim,
we always enjoy a good horse story.

[Bugle call]

Jim: You durn fool!
Whoa, there! Whoa! Whoa!
Durn that horse.
Ol' Marster Dan'l entered Possum in the Tennessee Derby a down in Memphis.
I was only a stable boy, them days.
[Band starts to play]

Guest: Yessir.

Jim: Just before the race,
while the band was a'playin'
just like you hear it out yonder in the grandstand now,
the old master run in and he says, "Jim,
Little Pete just done broke his leg in the last race,

and uh, you'll have to ride Possum.
Now don't stand there lookin', boy,
but get into them colors quick,
and here's, uh, your instructions:
Now, uh, there's only one horse I'm afraid of in the derby,
that's Arizona.
Watch 'im!
Lay close to 'im, boy, till the stretch,
and them climb up and beat 'im up!
If you don't, I'm a ruined man."
Yessir.
[Hoofbeats]
Whoa! whoa there! whoa!
Durn that horse!
I never rid a race in my life,
but I knowed how to watch the flag
and this time up
I seen the yellow flag swish down
and we was off!
[Crowd cheers; rapid, multiple hoofbeats]
You couldn't hear nobody's step [?]
for yellin' in the grandstand
just like they are there now,
At the first pole, Arizona was a length ahead of Possum.
[Crowd cheers; music stops]

Guest: Yes, yes, well?

Jim: Possum was a' goin' easy, pullin' for 'is head.
At the second pole, Possum was right behind Arizona,
still a pullin' for 'is head.

Guest: Yes, yes, well?
[Crowd cheers]

Jim: In the back stretch, Ol' Buck come up on the outside.
and then Possum was in the pocket,
with Arizona five lengths ahead.
[Crowd cheers]

Guest: Gee, whiz!

Jim: So we turned to the three quarters,

Guest: Yes?

Jim: then we piled into the stretch.
I worked Possum up on the outside and let 'im go.
[Crowd cheers]

Guest: Good ploy, Jim!

Jim: Tear up toward the stands,
[Crowd cheers]

Guest: OK.

Jim: all together like mad.
[Crowd cheers]

Guest: Yes? Yes?

Jim: Arizona two lengths ahead,

Guest: Well, go on!

Jim: I give Possum the whip
Go there!

And I'm in!
[Crowd cheers]
Four lengths ahead of Arizona.
[Crowd cheers]

Guest: Then you won the race!

Jim: Heh. Aw, no, sir.
There was, heh!, four-five other horses ahead o' Arizona.
[Laughter; bugle call; hoofbeats stop]

Although "Uncle Jim's Racetrack Story," like "The Farmer and the Hogs," uses the monactor presentational mode, this performance exploits a more extensive range of semiotic means and formal devices for dramatic ends and achieves, by these means, a far more complex sonic representation than any of the other recordings we have examined.

Consider, to begin with, what a wealth of theatrical business is accomplished in the first twenty lines of the transcript, solely by acoustic means. Let us start with the mise-en-scène. The opening sound effect of hoofbeats, the command "Whoa! whoa! whoa! Get over there!," the command plus exclamation "Whoa, there! whoa! whoa! Durn that horse," and the explicit reference to "the paddock" evoke a man on horseback in the paddock area of a racetrack. Voice changes, marked by a dialect shift and pronominal deixis, the greeting, "Hello, Jim," and the reference to "friends of mine from New York" round out the dramatis personae: The rider is Jim, an African American jockey, and his interlocutors are a white racing man hosting two or more white friends from New York. The band music that begins to play around line 16 serves as a further sound effect that allows for additional spatial contextualization; the low volume of the music and the adverbial phrase "out yonder in the grandstand" expand the mise-en-scène to include additional and more spatially distant features of the racetrack complex. These devices set the stage for the storytelling performance, which is elicited by the host in line 7: "I want you to tell them that story about the Tennessee Derby," marking the narratives as a part of Jim's repertoire, a set piece that he had told on other occasions.

The narration itself begins on line 11, as Jim offers some characteristic orientational information concerning the narrative event to follow, an account of his first race as a jockey. Drafted at the last minute to substitute for a rider who has broken his leg in the preceding race, Jim takes on the voice of his master in direct discourse, as his master coaches him in the strategy for his horse, Possum, to beat the rival, Arizona, in the Tennessee Derby. In terms of the recorded performance, this bit of direct discourse represents a double lamination, with Spencer voicing Jim voicing his master. Jim's affirmative response, "Yessir," marks the end of this first episode, followed by a frame break, as Jim steadies the horse on which he is mounted in the ongoing storytelling event. Returning to his account of the Tennessee Derby, Jim offers a bit more orientational information concerning his readiness for the race and then launches into an increasingly suspenseful account of the race itself, from start to finish. The tension is provided by the shifting dynamics of the race and his closing drive to the finish line, four lengths ahead of the rival horse, Arizona.

Jim's narrative performance is punctuated by several effective metanarrational devices. No sooner does the starter's flag drop and the race begin in his account, when other contextualizing sound effects of the mise-en-scène link the narrative event to the narrated event, intensifying both. The crowd in the grandstand, in the background of the narrative event, cheers in the distance (indicated by the low volume of the noise), and Jim draws that noise into his account by linking it to the corresponding cheers of the crowd at the Tennessee Derby when his first big race began (lines 41–44). At the same time, multiple hoofbeats sound in the distance as a race in the background of the narrative event proceeds. As the Tennessee Derby progresses and the narrative suspense intensifies, the back-channel responses of Jim's audience grow more and more excited and come at shorter and shorter intervals, urging him on to the climax as Possum gains on Arizona. The effect is further intensified by the cheering of the crowd in the background of the narrative event, which serves at the same time to punctuate Jim's story. Then the climax: "And I'm in! Four lengths ahead of Arizona." "Then you won the race!" exclaims an excited guest. But no—here's the catch: "There was four-five other horses ahead o' Arizona."

"Uncle Jim's Racetrack Story" thus emerges as a small piece of audio theater (Feaster 2006, 375–89; Fish 2001), a dramatic representation of a narrative event that contains a storytelling performance. All the dramatic effects of this little enactment are acoustically crafted; that is to say, the recorded performance is more than a simple matter of placing a performer in front of a recording apparatus. Rather, the performance is the product of sound design, an essential quality of audio theater (Fish

2001). Let us examine the elements and organization of the sound design that shapes "Uncle Jim's Racetrack Story" a bit more closely.

Clearly, the primary semiotic resource exploited in the sound design of the recording is speech, which serves multiple functions in the crafting of the performance. It contributes, as I have noted earlier in the chapter, to the setting of the scene; recall, for example, the way that Jim's commands allow us imaginatively to picture him on horseback. Or consider how the host's references to the paddock or Jim's to the crowd "out yonder in the grandstand" establish the proximal and distal features of the racetrack complex in which the narrative event takes place.

In addition to the evocation of setting, speech serves in a variety of ways as an instrument of characterization. Absent any visual means of establishing the cast of characters as embodied individuals present before us on a stage, speech has to carry the entire burden: by address ("Hello, Jim"); reference ("some friends of mine from New York"); aural contrast (African American English vs. Standard English as a means of distinguishing Jim from the host and his guests, or lower vs. higher pitched voices as a means of distinguishing the host from a guest); or other means. Likewise, speech alone must serve as the means of establishing and inhabiting participant roles, without gesture, proxemics, gaze, or other visible signs to help us sort out the storytelling performer from his audience. And finally, of course, speech is the means by which Jim performs his story in the narrative event that is the centerpiece of the recorded enactment.

A critically important complement to speech in the sound design that makes up "Uncle Jim's Racetrack Story" as a dramatic enactment is the repertoire of sound effects that figure prominently in the recording. Indeed, sound effects bracket the entire recorded enactment. The first thing we hear, on playing the record, is a clopping sound that is a sonic icon of hoofbeats, which suggest in turn the presence of a horse. That indexical inference is reinforced a moment later by the commands, "Whoa! whoa! whoa! Get over there!" The bugle call, just before Jim begins his story (line 10), the band music that strikes up as he opens his narration (line 16), and the cheers that ring out in the background (indicated by relative volume) as he tells his story of the Tennessee Derby all serve as environmental and spatial indicators, filling out our imaginative understanding of the racing complex, its configuration, and the deictic center and periphery of the focal event within it. The sound effects are supplemented by Jim's explicit references to the band "out yonder in the grandstand" or the crowd "there now." Perhaps the most ingenious aspect of the use of sound effects in the acoustic design of the skit is the way in which the sounds of the narrative event—the band music, the cheers, the multiple hoofbeats in the background—merge with the sonic features of the narrated event, Jim's first race, to enhance the semiotic texture of his suspenseful account. The crowd cheering the riders in the background of his storytelling performance seems also to be cheering him in the race he is recounting, helping to build the excitement as Possum gains length by length on Arizona.

Also impressive is the use of sound effects to punctuate the structure of the dramatic enactment and the story performance within it. The first bugle call and the second set of hoofbeats as Jim steadies his horse once again (lines 10–12) mark the transition from the dramatic setting of the scene to the commencement of his narrative performance. In a similar vein, the point at which the band begins to play marks the transition from the orientation section of his story to the first narrative episode, in which his master drafts him to ride in the Tennessee Derby and schools him in strategy for the big race. The next set of hoofbeats and his third effort to control his horse (lines 34–36) signal the shift to the principal narrated episode, namely, the Tennessee Derby itself, and the cheers of the crowd continue to mark the stages of the race as he ticks off his stage-by-stage gains against Arizona and, ultimately, his climactic finish as Possum comes in four lengths ahead of his rival. The final bugle call, following the responsive laughter of Jim's audience, serves as an acoustic closing curtain, framing the end of the dramatic enactment and of the recording. Sound, then, is an integral structural element of the narrative event, the narrated event, and the narrative itself in the construction of this pioneering piece of audio theater.

Conclusion

The three recordings I have examined in this chapter are mediated representations of oral storytelling performances. As we have seen, however, they are far from direct, transparent transpositions of traditional storytelling by vernacular storytellers in conventional contexts. Rather, our examination has revealed them to be remediations of what were already transpositions of traditional oral storytelling from sociable encounters to the produced and commodified platform events of stage monologues and Chautauqua lectures. Moreover, the recordings were made by professional performers, in carefully fitted-out recording studios. And notwithstanding the association of storytelling with rustic, agrarian milieus that figures in the representations we have examined—the small-town, cracker barrel philosopher; the backwoods farm in Arkansas; the southern racetrack—the recordings were produced in the urban centers of New York and Washington. Still, in the recontextualized and remediated form in which we encounter them on the recordings, the storytelling performances carry at least some of their contextual history with them, that is, elements of both traditional oral storytelling and the platform events from which they were transposed and adapted for the recordings.

At the center of all three recordings is the representation of the familiar act of storytelling, the verbal production of a narrative text. "Jim Lawson's Hoss Trade" and "The Farmer and the Hogs" are documented in oral tradition and display thematic, formal, and metapragmatic features that establish them clearly as exemplars of two of the most popular narrative genres in the American repertoire of oral narrative. "Uncle Jim's Racetrack Story," though not in itself traditional, is cast in a traditional genre, the catch tale, a double-voiced genre that, like the tall tale, builds upon and dislocates the generic expectations surrounding the narrative of personal experience.

Linked closely to the act of storytelling, of course, is the role of narrator and its complement of related participant roles. Each example configures that participant structure in a different way. Cal Stewart animates the persona of the traditional country storyteller: Uncle Josh is a figuration of the classic rural cracker-barrel raconteur, mediated through the long-established stage figure of the comic Yankee. Through the use of various devices—appellatives, pronouns, an informal register—Uncle Josh addresses his narration as if to a copresent interlocutor in a sociable encounter, inviting the listener to assume that participant role. Edwin Whitney likewise appears to be addressing a copresent audience, but whereas Uncle Josh's "sir" picks out an individual addressee, Whitney's "you" is more ambiguous. With no visual cues to setting and participation frameworks, it may be taken as second-person singular, inviting the listener to the recording to imagine himself or herself in a dyadic encounter with the narrator. Conversely, the register and performance style of Whitney's performance evoke the more distanced participant structure of a lecture, still part of the interaction order, in which his "you" of address suggests the second-person plural of the audience as a collective. In this alignment, the listener to Whitney's recording is interpellated as a member of the gathered audience of the Chautauqua. In "Uncle Jim's Racetrack Story," Len Spencer animates Uncle Jim as another stock figure like the comic Yankee: the amiable, avuncular African American storyteller of whom Uncle Remus, of course, is the most familiar exemplar. The participant structure of this recording, though, is a bit more complicated than the other two. The framing of "Uncle Jim's Racetrack Story" is theatrical; the listener to the recording is a bystander/overhearer of a dramatic enactment, and there is no direct, prior experience invoked by the performance—it is like a staged theatrical drama, but yet not like it. It has a plot, with multiple characters, but it is restricted solely to the auditory channel and relies on sound design for critical dramatic effects: mise-en-scène, spatialization, and other contextualizing functions. This performance is most completely the product of the new medium. The recording is a true media text: a commodified utterance addressed to no one and to everyone (Warner 2002). To be sure, the other recordings are media texts as well in this sense. My point is that they do not show it as fully and clearly.

What is at play, then, in these recordings, is the construction and manipulation of a tension in modes of address to an audience, which interpellates the listener in two different orders of public. The framing of "Jim Lawson's Hoss Trade" and "The Farmer and the Hogs" evokes the public of a copresent, gathered audience. In the former, it is primarily the intimate audience of sociable storytelling, though with elements of the more distanced participant structure of platform storytelling; in the latter, platform storytelling comes more strongly to the fore. In "Uncle Jim's Racetrack Story," the listener is more clearly positioned as the overhearer/consumer of a media text: anonymous, distanced, and dispersed. That is, as a member of a distributive public, constituted by the circulation of the recording as commodity. And indeed, so are the listeners to the other two recordings.

In addition to the relationship between gathered and distributive publics called into play by these recordings, I would suggest that they also align the listener to at least one additional public. I have already suggested the dynamic tension implicated in the representation of oral storytelling, that most traditional of communicative practices, on phonograph records, that most modern of communicative technologies—at least in the turn-of-the-twentieth-century United States. Recall that storytelling on the recordings we have examined also indexes the rural, small-town past as well as the encounter between rural folk and urban sophisticates: the gentleman traveler in Arkansas, the visitors from New York at the southern racetrack. The recordings, in essence, render oral, traditional storytelling as a symbolic vehicle of nostalgia, a trope for the sentimental evocation of a folkloric past still familiar to the marketing targets of the phonograph industry: urban dwellers, bourgeoisified small town people, and prosperous farmers for whom mechanized agriculture provided sufficient leisure and income to indulge in commodified forms of home entertainment. Again, this mode of symbolic construction becomes explicit in the metadiscourse of advertising. Taking Cal Stewart as an example once again, as he was the most famous "talking machine storyteller" of them all, the key throughout his career was nostalgic retrospection: notices and advertisements in newspapers and trade journals characterized Stewart as "'right down tew home' among the folks," his manner as "quaint," Pumpkin Center as "romantic," and the scenes depicted in the recorded stories as "old fashioned."[12]

This form of mediatized nostalgia, then, invites consumers/listeners to align themselves to a shared American past, what we might term a historically founded public. But from the first invention of the idea of folklore, in the eighteenth century, it has always served well as a symbolic vehicle for constructing links to a shared, primordial past, as part of a modernizing and nationalizing vision. The remediation of storytelling on early commercial recordings, then, enlisted a new communicative technology in the service of a time-honored mechanism of modernization, the recreation of a nostalgic vision of the past. That is to say, the recorded performances I have discussed in this chapter are the popular, performative, commodified analogues of the more philosophical efforts of social theorists to folklorize vernacular forms of expression. They are perfect instruments of bourgeois nostalgia—buy a simulacrum of the past that will nevertheless allow you to display how very modern you are.

NOTES

1. Bolter and Grusin (1999, 173) define remediation as "the formal logic by which new media refashion prior media forms."
2. See, e.g., Finnegan (1988), Foley (2002), Scheunemann (1996).
3. For biographical information on Cal Stewart, see Feaster (2006), Gracyk (2000, 332–38), McNutt (1981), Petty (1974), and Walsh (1951a, 1951b, 1951c, 1951d).
4. Motifs: K134, Deceptive horse sale or trade (Baughman 1966, 341); K134.6, Selling or trading a balky horse (Baughman 1966, 342).
5. In the transcriptions that follow, I have had two principal concerns in mind: (1) I intend the transcripts to convey that they are representations of spoken language. The chief means I have employed to this end is nonstandard spelling to capture features of pronunciation. I have not, however, resorted to eye-dialect. One of the recurrent problems in transcribing oral speech, especially oral speech in nonstandard, vernacular dialects, is the danger of making the speakers appear to be unsophisticated rubes. I should make explicit, then, what will be even more obvious in my paper, that those stereotypes are precisely what the *performers* are trying to convey, and if my transcriptions evoke them yet again, so much the better.

   (2) I have endeavored to represent by graphological means some of the significant formal patterning principles that organize the performances. Line breaks mark breath units, intonational units, and/or syntactic structures, which are usually—though not always—mutually aligned. Indented lines mark shorter pauses. Double spaces mark episode breaks or changes of represented speaker in direct discourse.
6. The original recording is accessible online, through IU ScholarWorks: "Jim Lawson's Hoss Trade," https://scholarworks.iu.edu/dspace/handle/2022/3173.
7. On the notion of platform performance, see Goffman (1981, 165–66) and Wilson (2006, 59–94).
8. Motif: X1206(ba) Owner, unable to call hogs because of sore throat, calls them by tapping on fence board with stick. The hogs chase through the woods to various spots where // woodpeckers are drilling, hoping for more food (Baughman 1966, 476).

9. For biographical information on Strickland W. Gillilan, see Harrison (1958, 174–79) and Tapia (1997, 68–69). For an excellent source of materials on Gillilan's career as a Chautauqua performer, see the University of Iowa library's web archive, "Traveling Culture: Circuit Chautauqua in the Twentieth Century," http://memory.loc.gov/ammem/collections/chautauqua.
10. The original recording is accessible online through IU ScholarWorks: "The Farmer and the Hogs," https://scholarworks.iu.edu/dspace/handle/2022/3174.
11. The original recording is accessible online, through IU ScholarWorks: "Uncle Jim's Racetrack Story," https://scholarworks.iu.edu/dspace/handle/2022/3175.
12. These quotations are drawn from the following sources: *Coshocton Daily Age,* March 4, 1902, 1; *Edison Phonograph Monthly* 6 (9) (1908): 26; *Edison Phonograph Monthly* 7 (1) (1909): 18.

REFERENCES

Atwood, E. Bagby. 1953. *A survey of verb forms in the Eastern United States.* Ann Arbor: University of Michigan Press.

Baughman, Ernest Warren. 1966. *Type and motif-index of the folktales of England and North America.* The Hague: Mouton.

Bauman, Richard. 1986. *Story, performance, and event: Contextual studies of oral narrative.* Cambridge: Cambridge University Press.

Bolter, David, and Richard Grusin. 1999. *Remediation: Understanding new media.* Cambridge, MA: MIT Press.

Canning, Charlotte M. 2005. *The most American thing in America: Circuit Chautauqua as performance.* Iowa City: University of Iowa Press.

Case, Victoria, and Robert Ormond Case. 1970. *We called it culture: The story of Chautauqua.* Freeport, NY: Books for Libraries Press. Orig. pub. 1948.

Dorson, Richard M. 1959. *American folklore.* Chicago: University of Chicago Press.

Feaster, Patrick. 2006. *The man who made millions laugh.* Unpublished manuscript.

Finnegan, Ruth. 1988. *Literacy and orality: Studies in the technology of communication.* Oxford: Blackwell.

Fish, Richard L. 2001. Genesis and renaissance: A brief history of audio theatre. www.lodestone-media.com.

Foley, John Miles. 2002. *How to read an oral poem.* Urbana: University of Illinois Press.

Goffman, Erving. 1981. *Forms of talk.* Philadelphia: University of Pennsylvania Press.

Gracyk, Tim. 2000. *Popular American recording pioneers, 1895–1925.* Binghamton, NY: Haworth Press.

Harrison, Harry P. 1958. *Culture under canvas: The story of tent Chautauqua.* New York: Hastings House.

Johnstone, Barbara. 1990. *Stories, community, and place: Narratives from middle America.* Bloomington: Indiana University Press.

———. 1996. *The linguistic individual: Self-expression in language and linguistics.* Oxford: Oxford University Press.

McNutt, Randy. 1981. *Cal Stewart, your Uncle Josh.* Fairfield, OH: Weathervane Books.

Nickels, Cameron C. 1993. *New England humor: From the Revolutionary War to the Civil War.* Knoxville: University of Tennessee Press.

Petty, John A. 1974. Cal Stewart: The acoustic king of comedy. *New Amberola Graphic* 11:1–7.

Rieser, Andrew C. 2003. *The Chautauqua moment: Protestants, Progressives, and the culture of modern liberalism.* New York: Columbia University Press.

Rourke, Constance. 1959. *American humor: A study of the national character.* New York: Harcourt Brace. Orig. pub. 1931.

Scheunemann, Dietrich, ed. 1996. *Orality, literacy, and modern media.* Columbia, SC: Camden House.

Schiffrin, Deborah. 1981. Tense variation in narrative. *Language* 57:45–62.

Tandy, Jeanette. 1964. *Crackerbox philosophers in American humor and satire.* Port Washington, NY: Kennikat Press. Orig. pub. 1925.

Tapia, John E. 1997. *Circuit Chautauqua: From rural education to popular entertainment in early twentieth-century America.* Jefferson, NC: McFarland.

Walsh, Jim. 1951a. Favorite pioneer recording artists: Cal Stewart I. *Hobbies* (January): 20–22.

———. 1951b. Favorite pioneer recording artists: Cal Stewart II. *Hobbies* (February): 20–25.
———. 1951c. Favorite pioneer recording artists: Cal Stewart III. *Hobbies* (March): 19–23.
———. 1951d. Favorite pioneer recording artists: Cal Stewart IV. *Hobbies* (April): 20–24.
Warner, Michael. 2002. *Publics and counterpublics.* New York: Zone Books.
Wentworth, Harold. 1944. *American dialect dictionary.* New York: Thomas Crowell.
Wilson, Michael. 2006. *Storytelling and theatre: Contemporary storytellers and their art.* New York: Palgrave Macmillan.

3

Narrative, Culture, and Mind

JEROME BRUNER
New York University

I AM FASCINATED by how narrative, the story form, is able to shape our immediate experience, even to influence deeply our conceptions of what is *real,* what *must* be real. Indeed, we are beginning to understand how cultures rely upon narrative conventions to maintain their coherence and to shape their members to their requirements. Indeed, commonplace stories and narrative genres even provide a powerful means whereby cultures pass on their norms to successive generations. Narrative is serious business.

Let me pursue these matters a step or two further. I want particularly to explore what narrative is, what functions it serves, and how it finds its way into our lives. Indeed, I sometimes find myself asking whether our narrative capacity may not provide a necessary condition for living our lives in a cultural setting. And I have come increasingly to believe that perhaps it does. So let me explore this matter in this chapter—whether it is not just the gift of *language* that makes culturally mediated life possible but also the narrative form in which we employ our linguistic endowment.

I am even becoming convinced, indeed, that like language itself, our narrative endowment has a deeply innate base. For the mastering of the story form seems to depend less upon "learning" in the conventional sense than upon exposure to its instantiations. Has anybody ever found it necessary to teach a young child what a story *is,* how to understand it? This is not to say, of course, that children do not become better storytellers with exposure. The Andre Gides and Thomas Manns of this world may be born, not made, but that does not mean that they have nothing to learn—both in their ways of making sense of the world and in their ways of telling about it.

Narrative Verisimilitude

Narrative is rather an all-purpose vehicle. It not only shapes our ways of communicating with each other and our ways of experiencing the world, but it also gives form to what we imagine, to our sense of what is *possible.* With its aid, we pole vault beyond the presently expectable. And of course it shapes our conceptions of the past.

And it does all these things in a most permissive manner. For stories, unlike propositional accounts, are not exclusively hemmed in by the demands of *verifiability.* The test of a good story is its truth-likeness or *verisimilitude,* a much less demanding measuring stick. And even when we speak of "true stories," we know somewhere down inside that we are using "true" in a metaphorical sense. Even our vaunted legal system admits as much through its stout volume of precautions against narrative verisimilitude—as witness those Federal Rules of Evidence that we drill into our law students as if it were a vaccination against their being done in by "good stories."

Note one further thing about narrative's allure. Stories, again unlike logical propositions, cannot be context free, cannot live in a vacuum. Even when a story is intended only as a fable, it is always located in a cultural setting, however "imagined" it may be. Setting, I shall argue below, is crucial, so I had better say a word or two to explain what I mean.

It is not simply that all of us, as it were, "live" in a culture and live mostly within its limits. There is another crucial matter that needs underlining. All cultures, however presumably "well structured," are fraught with ambiguities and virtually irresoluble possibilities, notably so in the particulars of daily life. Life in culture is perpetually open to improvisation. And storymaking, I shall try to demonstrate, provides us with an exquisite instrument for taking into account (even for justifying) "real" life's ambiguities and multiple demands. For narrative also provides us with the means of going beyond the culturally ordinary—even in the law, where we invoke the offbeat by pleading "mitigating circumstances."

I need hardly add, in this connection, that storytelling and storymaking can, consequently, be either well or ill intended, benign or malevolent. However intended, stories are rarely "just neutral." In their very nature, they inevitably throw their weight in support of or against what is culturally taken for granted, however subtly.

But I see I am getting ahead of myself again. I had better say a few words more about what I mean by *culture* in this connection, for narrative is deeply imbedded in a culture's ways. To borrow Claude Levi-Strauss's apt definition, culture is comprised of the ordinary ways and means by which we routinely and without much quarrel carry out our exchanges with each other, whether the exchange of goods, services, respect, affiliation, whatever. We are greatly aided in all such exchanges, of course, not only by custom and habit but also by our uniquely human gift of *intersubjectivity.* Unlike any other species on the face of the Earth (vide Michael Tomasello's brilliant research), we humans know or believe implicitly that we *can* know each others' minds. We know, however implicitly, *that* we share though it is never quite plain precisely *what* we share. And one of the principal things that underlies this conviction is our sharing of the narrative gift—surely a prerequisite for the emergence of exchange-based human culture.

But because human culture is fraught with ambiguities, how do we manage the divisiveness that comes from our famous intolerance of ambiguity? Again, narrative provides an invaluable aid—for, as has been noted, the stories we tell ourselves and each other are judged on a criterion of verisimilitude rather than upon the more demanding criterion of verifiability. We accept stories on the basis of their truth-likeness—even though we may believe that there is some deeper, more canonical truth that lies beneath them. Indeed, we tolerate and even expect a certain ambiguity in the story form.

And perhaps it is by dint of all this that storytelling is so often a fraught business. I suspect it may be this very fraughtness that makes us somewhat reluctant to look publicly, interpersonally, at narrative's uses and "misuses," save perhaps among close intimates. Even professionally, we prefer instead to concentrate on narrative's aesthetics. Yet, interestingly, that is changing—perhaps because contemporary common sense is increasingly taking the view that "realities" are *made,* not found—the constructivist view. The dichotomy of "truth versus fiction" is becoming less dichotomous. More latterly, indeed, we have even become interested in how narrative creates its realities. A word about this is useful, for it is close to our concerns.

Let me illustrate with two searching issues of a highly regarded literary magazine, *Critical Inquiry* for Autumn 1980 and Summer 1981—both given over to exploring the nature of narrative, with contributions by such notables as Hayden White, Jacques Derrida, Frank Kermode, and Nelson Goodman. The magazine's editor, W. J. T. Mitchell, expressed the new spirit thus: "This collection is intended to carry thinking about the problem of narrative well beyond the province of the 'aesthetic' . . . and to explore the role of narrative in social and psychological formations, particularly in structures of value and cognition."

Indeed, by 1983 this newly awakened interest in the reality-constructive *functions* of narrative had even invaded the well-guarded upper reaches of the legal academy—in a now-famous lead article in the *Harvard Law Review* by Yale's late lamented and gifted Robert Cover (1983), subtitled "Nomos and Narrative." Law, he argued persuasively, is not just the product of legislation and constitutional decree but stems rather from a culture's store of "jurisgenic" *stories,* themselves expressions of a culture's deeper, axiomatic *nomos.*

Yet is all this so new? Had not narrative's constructional functions come under Aristotle's (1997) close scrutiny in his *Poetics,* even four centuries before Christ? Nor was that classic just a flash in the pan; a good half millennium later, Augustine (1998) in the *Confessions* was still speculating about narrative's realities.

However, though interest in narrative goes far back, something new seems to be growing. Take Paul Ricoeur's (1990) masterful *Time and Narrative* as an example. Narrative, for Ricoeur, is not just a way of constructing lifelike literature but also a way of knowing the world, a metaphorical way to be sure, but often our only way. Using the question of how we "know" time as his starter, he remarks: "I see in the plots we invent the privileged means by which we re-configure our confused, unformed, and at the limit mute temporal experience. 'What then is time?' asks Augustine. 'I know well enough what it is, provided that nobody asks me; but if I am asked what it is and try to explain, I am baffled.'" So what *is* narrative that it has the power to create even duration?

How to Define Narrative

How shall we define narrative? Well, a story obviously requires a starter, perhaps some shared, virtually taken-for-granted expectation about the world and what it should be like—as when we start with "I was walking down the street the other day, and. . . ." There then follows what Aristotle cleverly called the *peripaeteia* (Greek for "adventure"): something that upsets or runs counter to the expected—a surprise that should not have happened under the canonical circumstances in being. Then the story's *action:* what is done to set things right again. And finally a *resolution*—how things came out, sometimes accompanied (pace Aesop) by a moral, hammering home the story's point.

But today we look beneath these grand dimensions. Kenneth Burke (1969) provides a good example in *A Grammar of Motives.* Narrative, he says, requires a pentad of features: an agent, an act, a goal, a recipient, and a scene. A story is launched if and only if some of these pentad elements are in conflict. It is such conflict or incompatibility—"trouble," to use Burke's unadorned term—that launches the narrative.

Now, as noted, cultures have their own stock of prototype narratives—characteristic pentads with characteristic troubles. They are given immediacy and particularity by highly local instantiation. So, for example, there is the challenged-authority prototype—whether the tale of a cocky Yale law clerk taken down a bit by his boss who puts him to work on some impossibly boring appeal briefs, or the too-proud star minor leaguer fresh to the big leagues put to fielding at batting practice to take down his arrogance.

Narrative prototypes—Jung long ago might have called them "archetypes"—are intended, of course, to shape or instantiate our expectations about how the culture works and, especially, how others think. In this sense they are necessarily local. So how ever do we "master" our culture in the broader sense?

The Unruly Ordinary

What of Clifford Geertz's insistence that culture is always local—which, interestingly, did not keep him from writing with deep insight about both the larger Indonesian and Moroccan cultures? Let me propose that a larger culture is like *continuing stories,* much like (to borrow from my colleague Ronald Dworkin) common law. For just as the controlling principle in common law is *stare decisis*—roughly, we decide new cases under litigation as we decided ones like it in the past—so with life in culture. Yes, we enunciate doctrinal principles, both before and after the fact, but their practice is in their instantiation, in the particular. Common law, bear in mind, originally took the form of a loosely connected set of writs, specifying particular impermissible violations of what, implicitly, was taken as permissible behavior. We spell out the general case only in an abstract, remote summary—as in preambles to the Constitution, Supreme Court rulings, and the like.

Our told stories, in short, are about particular deviations from the ordinary. But though particular, they find connection with the general through what I shall call narrative prototypes—common, recognized deviations from particular paradigms. And thus we can fall back on something like *stare decisis* in justification: "The mind of man runneth not to the contrary." We even employ this reasoning when things have changed, pleading story continuity, as in the *Brown v. Board of Education* (1954) Supreme Court holding dismissing as insufficient the separate-but-equal story in *Plessy v. Ferguson* (1896). Storytelling in the interest of continuity over time seeks to redefine the canonical starting point of the story, better to include a wider range of deviations to fit its narrative form. So, for example, Lord Mansfield's dictum in the renowned 1792 Somerset's case, that all men are free unless by statute otherwise specified, can be taken as a canonical "precedent" for race discrimination cases argued two centuries later.

Please note, however, that I am not proposing that storytelling is like legal pleading—rather the reverse, that legal pleading is, in effect, adversarial storytelling. What

I am saying, though, is that ordinary, day-to-day storytelling rests upon the same underlying principles of narrative making and narrative using. I am told, indeed, that law's *stare decisis* derives from an old Icelandic folk custom to the effect that once you have told your story, you must stick to it—and others will do so as well.

And it is in this sense that any culture, for all its ambiguities and internal contradictions, is held together. Culture, in this sense, is the maintenance, the legitimization, of the ordinary by rendering the past and present seamlessly continuous. And that is best accomplished implicitly by reference to the local and familiar. A culture only requires a formal system of laws with its explicit methods of dispute resolution when its size, diversity, and inner irreconcilabilities render its narrative paradigms insufficient.

So ought we not, then, be more aware of how fraught are the consequences of storytelling? But our legal system surely is! Would a better sense of narrative improve life-as-local? Would it have calmed the sibling quarrelsomeness of my childhood home? And would that have been worth doing? Even worth trying? I am a bit like Clifford Geertz commenting on the formalized face-off of that famous Balinese cockfight. That was their way of containing their fraughtness of life. Are our narrative habits our way of doing so for our own? Is not that, after all, what culture is about?

REFERENCES

Aristotle. 1997. *Poetics*. New York: Penguin USA.

Augustine. 1998. *Confessions*. Oxford: Oxford University Press.

Brown v. Board of Education of Topeka. 1954. 347 U.S. 483. Findlaw, http://laws.findlaw.com/us/347/483.html.

Burke, Kenneth. 1969. *A grammar of motives*. Berkeley: University of California Press.

Cover, Robert. 1983. The Supreme Court 1982 term foreword: Nomos and narrative. *Harvard Law Review* 97 (4): 4–68.

Plessy v. Ferguson. 1896. 163 U.S. 537. Findlaw, http://laws.findlaw.com/us/163/537.html.

Ricoeur, Paul. 1990. *Time and narrative*, vols. 1–3. Chicago: University of Chicago Press.

4

Positioning as a Metagrammar for Discursive Story Lines

ROM HARRÉ
London School of Economics and Political Science / Georgetown University

POSITIONING THEORY is the most recent in a long-running sequence of efforts to try to make social psychology more scientifically respectable—that is, to make methods of inquiry and theoretical models conform to the nature of the phenomena of interest, namely, *meanings*. In carrying through this program, one of the first and most prominent casualties is the concept of "causation." The explanation of the succession between two social acts, a1 and a2, is not to be looked for in some causal law that a1s cause a2s to occur. Rather, it is to be found in the meaning relations between the acts. If a1 is thought be offensive to someone, then his or her subsequent performance of the act a2 needs to be seen as conforming to some canon of norms of politeness and the respondent's right to make use of it. If someone is confronted with a popular view on some matter that he or she believes to be mistaken, then that person's agreement with the majority is not caused by "peer pressure" but is an act conforming to a local norm of agreeable behavior.

Positioning theory was first developed as part of the psychology of personhood, one of the ways in which people acquire the concepts and practices of selfhood—that is, what a person is or takes himself or herself to be as a singular being, and how they are shaped by the positions available to that person in the collectivities in which that being lives.

Another aspect of positioning theory as an important development of discursive psychology (and perhaps the ill-named "qualitative psychology") is the effort to remedy the "unrealism" of attempts at premature cross-world generalization in social, cognitive, personality, and emotion psychology. By attending to features of the local context, in particular normative constraints and opportunities for action within an unfolding story line, it becomes clear that access to and the availability of certain practices, both conversational and practical, is not determined by competence alone but also by having rights and duties in relation to items in the *local* corpus of sayings and doings. These unfolding story lines are often realized in conversations, but not necessarily exclusively. In conversational form they are more readily available for analysis. For this reason alone, narratology is a close ally of positioning theory. Narratological analysis reveals the normative constraints on the unfolding of a story line, constraints that are expressible in the alternative language of locally valid patterns of rights and duties.

The fundamental insight on which positioning theory and other antimainstream psychologies are based is the principle that psychology must be primarily the study of meanings, not of the material bearer of those meanings. It should scarcely need saying that the same physical object can carry different meanings and that the same meaning can be carried by different physical objects. Physical objects are recruited to the role of meaning bearers in the course of entering into a culture—first of all, one's own. The practices of a religion, in contrast to but not as dependent of its dogma and theology, illustrate the meaning modulation of material things into the symbols. One of the most startling is the meanings given to the materials of the mass or communion, the bread and wine, in traditional Catholic and in Protestant thinking. Accustomed to driving on the right in countries where distances are expressed on road signs in kilometers, one of the authors found himself multiplying American road distances by five-eighths to find the distance in miles. The emphasis on meaning and its management covers the whole of the traditional fields of psychology, laid out under those useful old titles cognition, conation, affection, and perception.

Main Psychological Theses of Positioning Theory as Social Psychology

Positioning theory is concerned with three fundamental interconnected aspects of interpersonal encounters:

1. The changing patterns of distributions of rights and duties to perform certain categories of actions.
2. The story lines of which such actions are meaningful components. Any encounter might develop along more than one story line and support more than one simultaneously evolving story line.
3. The meanings of people's actions as social acts. The illocutionary force of any human action, if it has one as interpreted by the local community, determines its place in a story line and is mutually thereby determined. Any action might carry one or more such meanings.

Positioning theory has been explicitly drawn on in narratology. Thus, if we take the view that life unfolds as a narrative—with multiple, contemporaneous interlinking story lines—the significance of the actions that people carry out, including speech acts, is partly determined by the positions of the actors then and there. What story line is unfolding is mutually determined, pro tem, by the speech acts people are heard to produce, and these in turn are mutually determined by the positions that they are taken to be occupying in the episode—that is, what are their assigned, ascribed, claimed, or taken-on rights and duties to make use of the available and relevant discursive tools (Harré and van Langenhove 1999).

Recent research on the psychological conditions of the coming to be and the maintenance of conflicts and alliances, from internal personal relations and crises to national and cultural tension and agreements, has been more or less focused on only one side of the range of possibilities, namely, on conflict *resolution* at all levels of scale. However, much interesting work remains to be done on how conflicts are exacerbated, how alliances are formed, and what it takes to strengthen or to disrupt them.

Yet what a person *is* is not determined by what he or she can do. Cognitive psychology studies what a person "can do"—the upshot of laboratory experiments in which context is standardized. Behaviorists collected data on what a person "does" under various conditions of stimulations. Positioning theory focuses on bringing to light the normative frames within which people actually carry on their lives, thinking, feeling, acting, and perceiving—against standards of correctness. In short, positioning theory looks at what a person "may do and may not do." "Rights" and "duties" are shorthand terms for clusters of moral (normative) presuppositions that people believe or are told or slip into and to which they are momentarily bound in what they say and do.

Positions are clusters of beliefs about how rights and duties are distributed in the course of an episode of personal interaction and the taken-for-granted practices in which most of these beliefs are concretely realized. Positions are more often than not simply immanent in the everyday practices of some group of people. The positioning analyst displays the positions that seem to have been immanent in an interaction (Harré and Moghaddam 2003).

"Positions" are features of the local moral landscape. People are assigned positions or acquire or even seize positions via a variety of prior implicit and explicit acts, which, in the most overtly "rational" positioning situations, are based on personal characteristics, real or imaginary. The upshot could be positive or negative, as sketched above. This "moral landscape" consists of practices—for example, taking notice of someone or ignoring them, giving them tasks, or praising them. We, as analysts, extract something we call a "position," which someone seems to "occupy" from these practices.

The realization that the content of positions is local and may even be momentary and ephemeral is the deep insight of positioning theory. As such, any positioning act can be challenged. Challenges to positions, implicit or explicit, are possible only within an established context of metapositionings, which may in their turn be challenged. Change in positionings can change the meanings of the actions people are performing, because beliefs about positions partly determine the illocutionary force of members' actions. Changes in the meanings of actions can consequently modify, sometimes drastically, the story lines that are taken to be unfolding in an encounter. Given that, generally, things do not fall apart, members must have a repertoire of narrative conventions.

Positioning as Process

Positioning is something that happens; as such, it is a discursive process. It can be ceremonial (electing the pope), characterological (appointing a chief executive or assigning tasks at a picnic), biographical (choosing a presidential candidate by reference to voting records), or historical (family recriminations over who let the cat out). People undertake positioning, and as such they are or claim to be positioned in certain ways. There are higher and higher order positionings. "Prepositioning" discourse involves listing and sometimes justifying attributions of skills, character traits, and biographical "facts" that are deemed relevant to whatever positioning is going forward. Prepositioning might be positive or might be negative—it is just as much a positioning act to delete someone's rights and duties as to assign them—"You don't have the right to, . . ." or "You don't have the duty to, . . ." and so on.

The most powerful attributive schemata are based on a range of presuppositions usually embedded in implicit or explicit practices—to local and even idiographic practices implying powers, abilities, or status levels that support ascriptions duties; and vulnerabilities, incapacitations, social deficits, and so on that support rights ascriptions and claims.

"Well-being" is a catch-all default consideration parallel to duties. Though vulnerabilities call forth specific duties of care, remedy, and the like, a "lack of well-being" can be imported to support a rather vaguely specified atmosphere of duties of charity.

The link between positioning theory and social psychology has appeared in the recent emphasis among the countermainstream (e.g., Bruner) on psychology as the study of the management of meanings, their sequential flow in complex braided patterns of lived stories. It follows that cognition, affection, conation, and perception all occur at the level of meanings, not at the level of the physical or material bearers of meanings; that is, they are features of discursive fluxes of various sorts and make use of various modes of presentation—words, signs, gestures, architectural conventions, and so on.

Actual positions include groups of rights and duties. Sometimes, when there is internal conflict in a position, this can bring on a phase of second-order positioning: "You do not have the right to claim that right." Also, cultural differences may emerge between rights and duties, for example, fundamentalists in a secular society.

Positioning Theory and Narratology

The dominant story line of a narrative can be determined by the local assignment of rights and duties. As positioned, the act-force of a person's speaking and acting are given this or that meaning and consequently play this or that role in a story—perhaps even disambiguating a fuzzy story line.

What you *are* is partly constituted by what roles you have—in conversations, both personal (ruminating) and social. And this depends in part on how one is positioned—that is, what rights and duties you are effectively able to exploit.

The useful concept of "footing" sits well with positioning theory. However, in the terms of the analysis sketched above, it is a third-order status that a person can occupy. The first-order status—as one might say, candidate status for a position—is that to which prepositioning is germane. The second-order status is to have an acknowledged position, implicit or explicit. Finally, the third-order status of "having a footing" is immanent in the way one can enter into a conversation, a game, a trial, or someone else's private affairs—unchallenged, as of right. Someone with footing is listened to, and thus the illocutionary force of their speech acts is taken notice of and the intended illocutionary force of their speech acts is "taken up" by the members.

It seems to me that "frame" is used to refer to story line genera—for example, the medical frame, which can be realized in a wide variety of specific story lines.

Frame is important because it allows one to consider the coherence or incoherence of contemporaneous story lines and the kind of challenges that can emerge. For example, one might challenge a story line in the medical frame by shifting to a legal frame—that is, by breaking the frame. Or one may shift from one medical story line to another, without breaking the frame.

Scale

In recent studies using positioning concepts, scale has now been extended to interactions among groups, nations, cultures, representatives, and so on. It has also shrunk to the micro level of the analysis of certain kinds of interactions between aspects of the inner life of a single person. In the most recent collection of positioning theory research reports (Moghaddam, Harré, and Lee 2008), the scale of encounters that have been topics of positioning analysis has been extended in two directions. Nations can and do position one another through television and radio, newspaper articles, and so on—so do religious groups, corporations, and even universities. Turning to the opposite end of the spectrum, it also makes sense to approach the study of the flux of thoughts and self-directed actions of a single individual in terms of positioning theory. For example, as a self-positioning act, a devout person could take on the duty of a careful examination of conscience reflecting on his or her own actions.

REFERENCES

Harré, Rom, and Luk van Langenhove. 1999. *Positioning theory.* Oxford: Blackwell.

Harré, Rom, and Fathali M. Moghaddam. 2003. *The self and others.* Westport, CT: Praeger.

Moghaddam, Fathali M., Rom Harré, and Naomi Lee. 2008. *Global conflict resolution through positioning analysis.* New York: Springer.

5

"Ay Ay Vienen Estos Juareños": On the Positioning of Selves through Code Switching by Second-Generation Immigrant College Students

ALAN D. HANSEN
Carroll College

LUKE MOISSINAC
Pacific University

CRISTAL RENTERIA AND ELIANA RAZO
Texas A&M University–Corpus Christi

IN THIS CHAPTER we examine what appears to be a perfect storm related to identity work in social interaction: the use of language alternation in quoting others' speech in the course of telling conversational, or "small," stories. Central to language alternation is laying claim to, putting off, or otherwise constructing and negotiating social identities (Torras and Gafaranga 2002). Similarly, identity formation and construction are based in narrative forms and functions (Georgakopoulou 2006; Taylor 2006). Last, identity work is at the core of reported speech (Clift 2006; Stokoe and Edwards 2007). Here we analyze two conversational stories from group interview sessions with college students who are first- and second-generation immigrants from Mexico. In these stories participants switch from English to Spanish in the course of quoting others' speech. Not only do participants quote others, but they also perform or enact (even "channel") nonpresent persons and personas. In these stories language alternation permits participants to accomplish delicate identity work and also to engage societal/dominant discourses related to issues such as racial intolerance, border politics, and assimilation.

Discourse Materials and Analytic Methods

The discourse materials analyzed in this chapter were collected in February and March 2006.[1] We conducted five group interviews with students attending a university in South Texas. All students were first-generation college students, and first- or second-generation immigrants from Mexico. Each group interview consisted of two student facilitators and between four and six students. Four of the group interviews lasted more than two hours, with a fifth lasting about eighty minutes. The data were transcribed, and extracts containing Spanish-language alternation in conversational stories were identified and analyzed over a period of several months.

Language alternation occurred mostly in two of the group interviews; here, we analyze extracts from the two interviews. The primary facilitator for both group interviews (female; F in the data extracts) was an undergraduate research assistant—also a second-generation immigrant from Mexico—who was trained in facilitation. In analyzing these data, we employed positioning analysis (PA) and membership categorization (MC).

PA in social interaction is rooted in the notion that selfhood is formed in relation to preexisting cultural, institutional, and societal/dominant discourses while also interactively formulated and accomplished in social interaction (Bamberg 2004; Harré and van Langenhove 1991). PA facilitates the analysis of conversational (small) stories (Moissinac 2007) by attending to three identity positioning levels faced by interactants. Level 1, story positioning, involves how the storyteller positions characters in a story realm; level 2, interactional positioning, involves how the participants position themselves in relation to one another in social interaction; and level 3, discursive positioning, involves participants' positioning relative to cultural, institutional, and societal/dominant discourses, which participants talk into being in the course of doing identity work in social interaction.

Just as PA is ultimately concerned with how the multiplicity and complexity of the self (Davies and Harré 1990) play out in social interaction, MC is concerned with how people are categorized amid potentially salient descriptors (see Sacks 1995). Collections of categories are *inference rich,* meaning that a great deal of what "ordinary people" (Schegloff 2007, 469) know about society is stored up in reference to collections (Sacks 1995). Also, category-bound features ("actions and activities and forms of conduct"; Schegloff 2007, 470) are tied to collections of membership categories (Sacks 1995). Consequently, "one can allude to the category membership of a person by mentioning that person's doing of an action that is category bound" and vice versa (Schegloff 2007, 470). Just as category membership (e.g., Mexican/Hispanic ethnicity) forms a basis for members from which to infer certain features associated with it (e.g., speaking Spanish), features bound to categories also form a basis from which members might infer category membership (Hansen 2005).

Language Alternation and Reported Speech

Although a comprehensive review of language alternation literature is outside of the scope of this chapter, a large of body of literature (Auer 1998, 2005; Wei 2005) has been amassed that connects language alternation—which includes switching to Spanish as well as borrowing Spanish-language terms (Marian and Kaushanskaya 2007)—to the achievement and negotiation of identities in social interaction. Traditional, reason-based models of language alternation (e.g., Myers-Scotton 2000) have more recently been supplemented with models of language alternation more closely attuned to analysis designed to reveal the underlying apparatus through which participants themselves arrive at the interpretation of language choice (Wei 2005). Such analyses emphasize how participants utilize language alternation as an interactional resource (Maryns and Blommaert 2001). This functional turn is relevant insofar as people use language alternation to assert, claim, and put off social identities (Torras and Gafaranga 2002; Williams 2005) and to index connections among language, ethnic identity, and community membership (Cashman 2005; Lo 1999). In this sense, language preference and alternation itself is a device for positioning oneself vis-à-vis others and categorizing *oneself* or *self* and others in social interaction (Auer 1984).

In our group interviews, participants alternated between English and Spanish, with alternation occurring mostly when they shaped their discourse as constituting the words of others. Recent analysis of talk-in-interaction has paid detailed attention to reported speech as a discursive phenomenon and resource (for a review, see Holt and Clift 2006) that is consequential in both function and form. The functions of reported speech include giving veracity or authenticity to claims or descriptive accounts (Stokoe and Edwards 2007), giving others so-called direct access to nonpresent events and circumstances (Holt 2000), embedding other contexts (Goodwin 2003), indirectly evaluating others (Günther 1999), and positioning oneself vis-à-vis others (Sacks 1995). The forms of reported speech identified are direct and indirect or summaries (Stokoe and Edwards 2007); the speech of individuals, aggregates, and typical group members (Buttny and Williams 2000); real and hypothetical reported speech (Irvine 1996); and attributed and unattributed reported speech (Goodwin 2003). Also included under the rubric of reported speech are reported thoughts (Barnes and Moss 2007) as well as subtexts or implications of speech or behavior that are articulated as reported speech (Buttny and Williams 2000). Reported speech thus includes not only citations of what an actual person *did* say in a particular circumstance but also citations of what any *kind* of person or group *could have* said or thought, in a real, typical, or hypothetical circumstance.

Reported speech often takes on a performance quality (Bauman and Briggs 1990), which serves as a resource for speakers to "show" and not just tell listeners what was said (Holt 2000) by means of prosody (i.e., the auditory aspects of speech, including loudness and pitch) and voice quality (production of whispery, breathy, falsetto voices) (Günther 1999). The layering of voices (Bakhtin 1981) permits speakers, in the staging of characters in stories, to embed evaluations of reported utterances as "appropriate, hysterical, unjustified, too aggressive, etc." (Günther 1999, 691–92). Reported speech makes the narrator also the "animator," who enacts multiple identities at once to produce an utterance that functions simultaneously as a quotation and something else, such as mockery (Bucholtz 1999). Performance is commonly utilized to mimic and parody others (Basso 1979). The layering or "evocation" (Bell 1999) of voices is a form of stylization or "styling" (Georgakopoulou 2005), in which speakers make present, or procedurally consequential, certain aspects of others' identities and re-present or constitute story characters in some way (Deppermann 2007).

Data Analysis

Here we analyze extracts from group interviews in which participants utilize language alternation and reported speech as resources in positioning themselves and others in telling small stories.

Positioning the Self and Others in a Cluster of Oppositional Stories

In this subsection we analyze a small story that is the fourth of four small stories clustered together, as conversational stories commonly are (Ryave 1978), during a span of about six minutes of a group interview. The stories occur in an extended segment, in which R builds contrasts between El Cruce (a Texan city along the Mexican border, home town to R and another participant) and South Town (the city where all the participants now live). The participants then engage in a point-and-counterpoint discussion in what may be termed an extended "action-opposition sequence" (Hutchby 1996). Each of the four stories features quoted speech in Spanish; moreover, in each instance the quoted speech is performed with animated voice qualities.

To review, leading up to the talk shown in extract 1, R compares El Cruce and South Town, stating that she (as a Mexican) is not "talked down" to in South Town as she consistently was in El Cruce. R tells a story designed as a typical encounter with a saleswoman in a department store in which the woman offended R by speaking to her in Spanish (the first of four stories). R's interpretation is contested by other participants, including by D, who tells a story in which elderly women innocently speak to her in Spanish (second story). In response, R tells a story designed to function as a model for how one *should* approach someone who looks like they might speak Spanish (third story). This leads to a brief sequence in which R and M align on one side of a disagreement about differences between El Cruce and South Town in how Mexicans are treated. The fourth story in the cluster of stories ensues following this disagreement. Consider:

Extract 1 (DG 3, at 1:55:03–1:57:22)

```
      M:   .hh I don— it's— it's really hard to explai:n, (.)
           [li:ke
      A:   [But I know— I get what you saying, but
             [(thes-)
      O:   [Yeah I think it's different there   [(but) (.)       ] it's— [(0.2) yeah
      R:                                        [It's different.]        [
      M:                                                                 [Yeah it's
→          [<very very> different.      ]
→     R:   [It's different and you know ] what I've hea::rd, I've heard
           comments, (0.2) °Ay: ay vienen estos juareños. Ay:°
           >blah blah blah
           [blala<
      (M): [he: he ha ha ha ha ha ha [ha .hhh  ]
      R:                             [I've     ] heard it. =
      F:   =hmmhm
      R:   I've heard it and (0.5) .hh and I pretend like I don't know English,
```

I- I mean Sp- Spanish sometimes and they're talking in- in,
Spanish .hhh we::ll it's becau:se
she's saying in Spanish (0.7)
(>blahblahwawawawa:<) like she's ^ talking about me.
F: hmhm=
R: =You know that's why I'm sayi:ng, (0.5) it's a different story over
there.
F: hmhm.
R: It's like- (0.2) °we're° not like- we don't love each other over there
and it's like (0.7)
populated by just like a hundred percent Hispanics(h).

As this extract begins, M states that the difference between El Cruce and South Town, in how Mexicans are treated, is hard to explain (line 1). This conversational move projects the closing down of an argument (Hutchby 1996). At this point, A appears to effect a softened oppositional move ("I get what you're saying, but," line 3). O takes up a third-party role in ending the dispute (Vuchinich 1990) by stating that "it's different there" (line 5). The referent to "there" could be Mexico (aligning with A's recent example) or El Cruce (aligning with the contrast drawn by R and M). Both R (lines 6, 9) and M (lines 7–8) take up O's construction of contrast. R appears to interpret "there" as El Cruce, as she reports having heard comments, representing them in the form of reported speech: "Ay ay vienen estos juareños" ["oh no, here come those Juareños"] (lines 9–10). R's quoted Spanish indexes a recognizable "invasion" discourse associated with fear and prejudice related to border politics (positioning level 3). R's quoted speech is performed in a way that the written transcript does not fully capture. By quoting the speech in a volume lower than her talk before this, it is as if she is relaying a secret. In this manner, R goes into character to re-present discourse in the voice of the unidentified person who uttered it. The switch to Spanish is consequential here, insofar as speaking Spanish is an activity bound to membership in a Mexican or Hispanic category. By giving a Spanish-language voice to the prejudiced discourse she reports, R implies that *Hispanics* living in El Cruce are prejudiced against "juareños" (residents of the Mexican border city Juarez).

This quoted speech follows R's claim that, unlike in South Town, Hispanics in El Cruce act in prejudiced ways against Mexicans from Juarez, which places Hispanics in El Cruce in the path of prejudice from fellow Hispanics. Following the reported speech, R elaborates by telling of typical instances in which she has pretended not to be able to speak Spanish in order to hear what is said about her, in Spanish, apparently by El Cruce Hispanics (lines 16–19). R opens a slot for reporting this speech in Spanish, and then fills that slot with ceremonial gibberish ("blahblahwawawawa:," line 16), through which she enacts a dismissive stance toward her antagonists. R's assessment—that "we don't love each other over there" (line 25)—coupled with a formulation (Pomerantz 1986), which treats El Cruce as populated by only Hispanics (line 27), implies that El Cruce Hispanics are the perpetrators of prejudice against Juareños.

Quoted Speech and Language Alternation in Animating the "Other"

Whereas the analysis presented above illustrates positioning through language alternation in a small story that is part of a cluster of stories, extract 2 leads to two small stories in which B positions herself vis-à-vis her own community and family. In extract 2, from a different group interview, B (a first-generation immigrant and returning student with grown children) animates typical "others" from her community and her mother-in-law. In the talk leading to the discourse presented in extract 2, S says that she has encountered difficulties in reentering her community once she has gone to college (not shown here). F asks other participants whether or not they agree with S's observation; B's complex response appears to both agree and disagree with S's observation (which is not shown). Consider:

Extract 2 (DG 4, at 55:42–57:20)

→ B: But- I hear what you're saying. .h I— I ge:t a lot of fingers pointed
a:t me and say pues ^ mira:. She thinks she's it cuz she's going to
college. (h) hehe I don't fee:l that I act any different. .hh=
S: =Exactly.=
B: =But, I- I see (0.7) jealousy
o [:r (.) a:nger: ah, pointed toward me because .hh ah (h:) she
P: [hmhm
B: ≈thinks she's ^ it.
P: Right
[and it— it's— it's perception of other people [thinking] that
[(ni: denih) [uh huh]
P: ^ you think you're better than— and you do:n't you're just-
B: And I— [righ:t
P: [^ that's j(h)ust the way you ^ we:nt.
(0.5)
(P): Yeah
B: Righ:t, [and— and— I tol— because my mother in la:w is my
(?): [well-
B: biggest enemy.
(0.2)
B: She'll stand on the porch and I don't know if ya'll understand
Spanish.=
B: [Me:nd] iga mala madre.
B:2 [*]

F: =[^ yeah::]
(.)
B: Ya te [vas:. Quedate a [qui::. Co [cina lava:] (.) cuida tus
[hijos. ^
B: [# [* * * * [* * **]
[*
B: That's what you should be doing. .hh
F: W [o:w
B: [And I tell her grandma, cuz she's my mother in law but I
ca(h)ll her(h) gr(h)-
gra(h)ndma .hhh I'm gone a go
bring money grandma.=I'm
gone a make- .pt .h no
no no no what
[choo need to do you need to cook, wash clean and]]
[* * * * * * * * * * * * * *]
iron. That's what women are supposed to do
so .hh she's my
bi:gge:st e:nemy: and eh,
well I was going to Palo Alto every morning she'd lock
the door behind me and
ahehehehe .hh tah get
[ba(h)ck i:n(h)] .ghhh She wouldn't let me i:n.
[* * * *]
B: And even no:w, (.) she's- pissed at me because (0.2) °I'm going to
^ college.° Course that's not going stop me.
B(h)(h)(h)ut [.hhh
F: [Wo:w
P: And that's the men— eh right and I agree— you're right that
is the ment— and that wa:s, and-
[is the mentality] in so [:me,] (0.2) in our s- in our society in
B: [(it's- hell)] [hm^hm]
P: some, ^ ages like you [said-
B: [Or our culture I [don't know what]
P: [our culture]
B: it i:s but (.) .hh and I still can't tu- turn her arou:nd.
(0.2)

In this extract, B engages prior talk by way of telling of an experience—which she constructs as typical—in which she is the object of derision on the part of others, first by recounting: "I ge:t a lot of fingers pointed a:t me and say pues ^ mira" ["well ^ look"] (lines 1–2). This vivid recounting is intricate, in that it appears to be metaphorical in part ("fingers pointed at me"), and it is unclear whether the quoted speech ("pues ^ mira. She thinks she's it cuz she's going to college," line 2) is a report of direct speech or interpretation of the subtext (Buttny and Williams 2000) of these common episodes. In any event, B reports here what the unspecified set of actions she glosses as "fingers pointed at me" *means* to her; moreover, insofar as language is tied to ethnic categories, quoting Spanish is a resource for delineating just who is doing the proverbial finger-pointing: members of her own community, fellow Spanish speakers (Hispanics) who resent her because by enrolling as a college student "she thinks she's it" (lines 6, 8). This vivid recounting of behavior constructed as typical allows B to suggest that she is experiencing resentment from members of her own ethnic/cultural community.

Similarly to the quoted Spanish in the cluster of stories in excerpt 1, B enacts "pues ^ mira:" and, to a lesser extent, the quoted speech following it. As partly apparent from the transcript, this quoted speech is animated through elongated prosody and a falsetto-like voice quality. The speech is performed; it is a performance that exists independently of whether or not B is quoting *actual* speech or its subtext.

P's affiliative uptake following B's story recasts the finger-pointing as others' perception ("thinking that you think you're better," lines 10, 12) and, supportively of B, counters this perception (lines 12, 14). B apparently confirms P's alignment move by agreeing (line 17). B then launches into dramatic narrative about her mother-in-law (lines 21–48). B displays speakership incipiency (Zimmerman 1993) both during (line 13) and following (line 17) P's aligning move. Laying claim to the speaking floor, B appears to begin to report something she said before ("and— and— I tol—," line 17), before self-correcting to label her mother-in-law as her "biggest enemy" (line 19). The use of "because" (line 17) marks what comes next as logically prior to whatever report she apparently abandoned, and it implicates the mother-in-law as the would-be object of the abandoned report. It is apparent that B wraps up the provision of background information (which began with her mother-in-law being her biggest enemy) when she reports what she tells her mother-in-law (line 33). In this sense, discourse in lines 13 ("And I—"), 16 ("and— and— I tol—") and 33 ("And I tell . . .") appear to be attempts at the same report. Insofar as the report B started to give (in lines 13, 17) is actually what she gives after providing background and orienting information (in line 33), then the part of the story leading up to this report is consequential not only for how B positions her mother-in-law in the story world (positioning level 1), but also for how she positions herself in this group interview (level 2).

B sets up her mother-in-law as an antagonist (line 17) before telling about her in narrative form. B then presents as "typical" (note the future tense in "she'll," line 21) the scene of her mother-in-law standing on the porch. Then, after projecting a switch to Spanish, which includes a disclaimer (line 21), B switches, and in so doing, she enacts her mother-in-law with (simplified): "Mendiga mala madre. Ya te vas. Quedate aqui. Cocina lava cuida tus hijos [Fucking stupid bad mother. You're leaving now. Stay here. Cook, clean, take care of your children]."[3] That's what you should be doing." B accentuates the enactment by pounding her hand and fist on the table (marked in the transcript). With this graphic enactment, B symbolically constructs a domestic antagonist in her mother-in-law, and she shows (not just tells) the others why her mother-in-law is her "biggest enemy." Acknowledgment from the facilitator (in lines 32, 53) displays support of this apparent design.

By constructing her mother-in-law as antagonist, B positions herself as justified in pursuing a college degree while having children in the home (level 2). In fact, B reports that she has justified herself to her mother-in-law—that she will bring money into the family (line 36). In response, the mother-in-law reiterates her demand (unreasonable, by implication), that she should stay in the home (lines 37–41). This second enactment of the mother-in-law's quoted speech in "That's what women are supposed to do" (line 41) gives one to understand that B's mother-in-law holds antiquated, traditional, and oppressive views of the woman's role in the family. Thus not only is taking care of the home and family what B should be doing, according to (B's construction of) the mother-in-law, it is also what *women* should be doing. In this manner, this second pass at quoting the mother-in-law indexes societal/dominant discourses related to the rights, roles, and obligations of women in society (level 3). This leads B and P to collaborate on a construction of the mother-in-law's "mentality" as a feature bound up in a category constituting elderly Hispanic/Mexican people (lines 54–61).

Excerpt 2 illustrates identity work at the nexus of language alternation, reported speech, and narrative. Here, B constructs a persona of her mother-in-law as her biggest enemy (lines 19, 43), extremely disrespectful (line 23), sexist (line 41), inflexible (lines 37–40), petty (lines 43–48), and vindictive (line 50). Furthermore, similarly to B's first story ("pues ^ mira:"), insofar as speaking Spanish is an activity bound to being Mexican/Hispanic, B's quoting Spanish categorizes her mother-in-law as Mexican/Hispanic and implies that this membership is consequential. Thus, insofar as language alternation makes salient the indexical link between language, ethnic identity, and community membership (Lo 1999), this connection (though unstated) constructs the "other" as ethnically Mexican/Hispanic. This is evident particularly in the second story, where performance of the Spanish-language enactment plays a central part in permitting B (and P, and arguably F as well) to style the mother-in-law as a Mexican/Hispanic character who is ridiculous, dangerous, and incorrigible.

Discussion

In analyzing language alternation in reporting speech in the course of telling stories, we have utilized positioning analysis and membership categorization. We have utilized PA to show that participants in the group interviews positioned themselves, and were positioned, not only in relation to story characters and other participants but also vis-à-vis societal/dominant discourses. We have utilized MC to show that interactants utilized the category-bound nature of speaking Spanish to stylize "others" in the stories they told. These claims parallel in many respects well-documented clashes between procedural analysis (e.g., conversation analysis) and poststructural analysis (e.g., critical discourse analysis).[4] Although "a complete and scholarly analysis (as opposed to a technical analysis) must range further than the limits" set in procedural analysis (Wetherell 1998, 388), there is also analytic danger in taking "as given and as inescapably relevant" such things as "categories of race, class, and gender; the bearing of hierarchy, power, oppression, macro-structural oppression; etc." (Schegloff 1999, 577).

The views above are largely treated as incommensurate, and they perhaps are. Nonetheless, in combining MC and PA, as we have here, we propose an integration (of sorts), in that MC contributes to grounding *in the discourse data* claims that participants are indexing (certain) societal/dominant discourses at (certain) moments in social interaction. This empirical grounding, facilitated by MC, makes PA more defensible; MC and PA thus can complement one another as analytic tools.

In this chapter we have analyzed discourse where language alternation, reported speech, and narrative meet. In the discourse analyzed here, emergent narratives (small stories) are a site for participants' identity work. Accordingly, just as narrative connects otherwise disparate disciplines of scholarship (Smith 2007), in these data the narrative context itself—the act of telling—connects language alternation and reported speech. As the complex interdisciplinary field of narrative scholarship continues to turn toward analyzing the accomplishment of "fleeting, contingent, fragmented and multiple selves" in conversational storytelling (Georgakopoulou 2006, 128), narrative itself continues to facilitate connections between the field's most enduring and useful concepts.

NOTES

For questions and discussion, please contact Alan D. Hansen, Carroll College, 1601 North Benton, Helena, MT 59602. The authors are grateful to numerous students in the Discourse Analysis Laboratory at Texas A&M University–Corpus Christi who participated in the collection, transcription, and/or analysis of data: Adam Cobb, James Devlin, Florence Garcia, Ashlee Garrett, Andrew Garza, Stephen Jack, Liz Lackey, Cody McDonald, Tammy Metteer-Otani, Kevin Pengelly, and Brooke Seyffert. The authors are responsible—the first author in particular—for errors and conceptual or analytic shortcomings in this chapter.

1. The data were collected as part of a study titled "Development of Resilient Identities by Mexican Immigrant First-Year College Students," funded by the Texas Research Development Fund, coprincipal investigators, Luke Moissinac and Alan D. Hansen. Some transcription was done with a development grant from the Clearinghouse for Mexican American Research at Texas A&M University–Corpus Christi, Alan D. Hansen and Luke Moissinac, coprincipal investigators.
2. In excerpts the numeral symbol (#) represents B slapping the conference table at which the participants are sitting; the asterisk (*) represents B pounding the table with her fist.
3. "Mendiga" translates literally to English as "beggar." In this context, "mendiga" serves as an intense and highly aggravated modifier to "mala madre" ("bad mother"), roughly equivalent to employment of "fucking stupid" as an intense and highly aggravated modifier in English—this is according to an informal translation from a native Spanish speaker who listened to the discourse in context.
4. Ideological disagreements of this sort, which surface in conferences and journals from time to time, are highly interesting and instructive. Prominent interchanges are found in Schegloff (1997, 1998, 1999), Wetherell (1998), and Billig (1999).

REFERENCES

Auer, Peter. 1984. *Bilingual conversation.* Amsterdam: John Benjamins.

———. 2005. A postscript: Code-switching and social identity. *Journal of Pragmatics* 37:403–10.

Auer, Peter, ed. 1998. *Code-switching in conversation: Language, interaction and identity.* London: Routledge.

Bakhtin, Mikhail. 1981. *The dialogic imagination.* Trans. Michael Holquist. Austin: University of Texas Press. Orig. pub. 1935.

Bamberg, Michael. 2004. Form and function of "slut bashing" in male identity constructions in 15-year-olds. *Human Development* 47:331–53.

Barnes, Rebecca, and Duncan Moss. 2007. Communicating a feeling: The social organization of "private thoughts." *Discourse Studies* 9:123–48.

Basso, Keith. 1979. *Portraits of the "Whiteman": Linguistic play and cultural symbols among the Western Apache.* New York: Cambridge University Press.

Bauman, Richard, and Charles L. Briggs. 1990. Language and social life. *Annual Review of Anthropology* 19:59–88.

Bell, Allan. 1999. Styling the other to define the self: A study in New Zealand identity making. *Journal of Sociolinguistics* 3:523–41.

Billig, Michael. 1999. Whose terms? Whose ordinariness? Rhetoric and ideology in conversation analysis. *Discourse & Society* 10:543–82.

Bucholtz, Mary. 1999. You da man: Narrating the racial other in the production of white masculinity. *Journal of Sociolinguistics* 3:443–60.

Buttny, Richard, and Princess L. Williams. 2000. Demanding respect: The uses of reported speech in discursive constructions of interracial contract. *Discourse & Society* 11:109–33.

Cashman, Holly R. 2005. Identities at play: Language preference and group membership in bilingual talk in interaction. *Journal of Pragmatics* 37:301–15.

Clift, Rebecca. 2006. Indexing stance: Reported speech as an interactional evidential. *Journal of Sociolinguistics* 10:569–95.

Davies, Bronwyn, and Rom Harré. 1990. Positioning: The discursive production of selves. *Journal for the Theory of Social Behavior* 20:43–63.

Deppermann, Arnulf. 2007. Using the other for oneself: Conversational practices of representing out group members among adolescents. In *Selves and identities in narrative and discourse.*, ed. Michael Bamberg, Anna DeFina, and Deborah Schiffrin, 273–301. Amsterdam: John Benjamins.

Georgakopoulou, Alexandra. 2005. Styling men and masculinities: Interactional and identity aspects at work. *Language in Society* 34:163–84.

———. 2006. Thinking big with small stories in narrative and identity analysis. *Narrative Inquiry* 16:122–30.

Goodwin, Charles. 2003. Embedded context. *Research on Language and Social Interaction* 36:323–50.

Günther, Susanne. 1999. Polyphony and the "laying of voice" in reported dialogues: An analysis of the use of prosodic devices in everyday reported speech. *Journal of Pragmatics* 31:685–708.

Hansen, Alan. 2005. A practical task: Ethnicity as a resource in social interaction. *Research on Language and Social Interaction* 38:63–104.

Harré, Rom, and Luk van Langenhove. 1991. Varieties of positioning. *Journal for the Theory of Social Behaviour* 21:393–407.

Holt, Elizabeth. 2000. Reporting and reacting: Concurrent responses to reported speech. *Research on Language and Social Interaction* 33:425–54.

Holt, Elizabeth, and Rebecca Clift, eds. 2006. *Reporting talk: Reported speech in interaction.* Cambridge: Cambridge University Press.

Hutchby, Ian. 1996. *Confrontation talk: Arguments, asymmetries, and power on talk radio.* Everyday Communication: Case Studies of Behavior in Context. Mahwah, NJ: Erlbaum.

Irvine, Judith T. 1996. Shadow conversations: The indeterminacy of participants' role. In *Natural histories of discourse,* ed. Michael Silverstein and Greg Urban, 131–59. Chicago: University of Chicago Press.

Lo, Adrienne. 1999. Codeswitching, speech community membership, and the construction of ethnic identity. *Journal of Sociolinguistics* 3:461–79.

Marian, Viorica, and Margarita Kaushanskaya. 2007. Cross-linguistic transfer and borrowing in bilinguals. *Applied Psycholinguistics* 28:369–90.

Maryns, Katrijn, and Jan Blommaert. 2001. Stylistic and thematic shifting as a narrative resource: Assessing asylum seekers' repertoires. *Multilingua* 20:61–84.

Moissinac, Luke. 2007. "Mr. Lanoe hit on my mom": Re-establishment of believability in sequential narratives by adolescent boys. In *Selves and identities in narrative and discourse,* ed. Michael Bamberg, Anna DeFina, and Deborah Schiffrin, 229–52. Amsterdam: John Benjamins.

Myers-Scotton, Carol. 2000. Explaining the role of norms and rationality in codeswitching. *Journal of Pragmatics* 32:1259–71.

Pomerantz, Anita. 1986. Extreme case formulations: A way of legitimizing claims. *Human Studies* 9:219–29.

Ryave, Alan L. 1978. On the achievement of a series of stories. In *Studies in the organization of conversational interaction,* ed. Jim Schenkein, 113–32. New York: Academic Press.

Sacks, Harvey. 1995. *Lectures on conversation,* ed. Gail Jefferson. 2 vols. Oxford: Basil Blackwell.

Schegloff, Emanuel A. 1997. Whose text? Whose context? *Discourse & Society* 8:165–87.

———. 1998. Reply to Wetherell. *Discourse & Society* 9:413–16.

———. 1999. "Schegloff's texts" as "Billig's data": A critical reply. *Discourse & Society* 10:558–72.

———. 2007. A tutorial on membership categorization. *Journal of Pragmatics* 39:462–82.

Smith, Brett. 2007. The state of the art in narrative inquiry: Some reflections. *Narrative Inquiry* 17: 391–98.

Stokoe, Elizabeth, and Derek Edwards. 2007. "Black this, black that": Racial insults and reported speech in neighbour complaints and police interrogations. *Discourse & Society* 18:337–72.

Taylor, Stephanie. 2006. Narrative as construction and discursive resource. *Narrative Inquiry* 16:94–102.

Torras, Marie-Carme, and Joseph Gafaranga. 2002. Social identities and language alternation in non-formal institutional bilingual talk: Trilingual service encounters in Barcelona. *Language in Society* 31:527–48.

Vuchinich, Samuel. 1990. The sequential organization of closing in verbal family conflict. In *Conflict talk: Sociolinguistic investigations of arguments in conversations,* ed. Allen D. Grimshaw, 118–38. New York: Cambridge University Press.

Wei, Li. 2005. "How can you tell?" Towards a common sense explanation of conversational code-switching. *Journal of Pragmatics* 37:375–89.

Wetherell, Margaret. 1998. Positioning and interpretative repertoires: Conversation analysis and post-stucturalism in dialogue. *Discourse & Society* 9:387–412.

Williams, Ashley. 2005. Fighting words and challenging expectations: Language alternation and social roles in a family dispute. *Journal of Pragmatics* 37:317–28.

Zimmerman, Don H. 1993. Acknowledgement tokens and speakership incipiency revisited. *Research on Language and Social Interaction* 26:179–94.

6

A Tripartite Self-Construction Model of Identity

LEOR COHEN
Bar-Ilan University

THE PURPOSE of this study is to explore how people negotiate their place in the world through the discursive manipulations of identity. A social constructionist perspective is assumed, where identity is constructed online through discourse in social interaction. Constructionism views identity as a dynamic, fluid, multiplicitous construct able to adjust to the demands of the almost infinite array of contexts. Interactional sociolinguistics emerged out of a constructionist framework (De Fina, Schiffrin, and Bamberg 2006, 1–6), where the microanalysis of discourse affords diverse opportunities to uncover that which would otherwise be rationally invisible (Garfinkel 1967, vii; Shotter 1993, 102). This chapter explores the dynamics among social identities and between identities and discourses by analyzing those locations within a narrative where identity constructions are evident. The problem posed by the emergent quality of identity is addressed here. In particular, I discuss the question of how good interactional analysis can maintain a dynamic view of identity and yet account for the more stable "brought along" features (Auer 1992; Williams 2008). As described by Bucholtz and Hall (2005), Rauniomaa (2003) develops Du Bois's (2002) notion of stance accretion, in which patterns of local positioning in discourse build up and contribute to more global and durable social identities.

This chapter argues for the incorporation of the social psychological tripartite model of identity (Brewer and Gardner 1996; Sedikides and Brewer 2001) into an interactional sociolinguistic framework for the purposes of discourse analysis. The tripartite model of identity, originally conceived as a cognitive structure of self-knowledge, is composed of three layers of identity: personal, relational, and collective. In the present study, these three layers are adapted into an interactionist approach as three social orientations or ways of being. This will allow for a more emergent view of identity than the original model allowed. These orientations allow for a comprehensive account of a wide variety of identities and relationships in which people engage on a day-to-day basis.

The particular sociopolitical context studied in this chapter is that of immigrants to Israel. In particular, I analyze two texts from the narrative of an Ethiopian Israeli female college student (whose pseudonym here is MA), discussing the strategies she implements to manipulate her identity constructions in order to manage impressions

(Goffman 1959) and gain social capital. The desire for social capital is not viewed here as duplicitous but as natural for all social interaction. MA can already be said to be successful in that she is a first-generation college student in a prestigious program. Her successes are her community's successes, and the research here analyzes the interactional effectiveness of her self-presentation. The excerpts provided below construct an immigrant experience, an ethnic minority experience, a friendship experience, and a personal experience of changing schools. Thus, the model aids in viewing the construction of different types of social processes as they unfold and intertwine in discursive interaction. The contextual and identity processes intertwine as they emerge simultaneously.

To support these claims, two pieces of discourse taken out of a semi-spontaneous (solicited yet not elicited) narrative are analyzed. The definition of narrative follows Labov and Waletzky (1997; originally published 1967), who proposed the following components: abstract, orientation, complication, resolution, coda. Before the analysis, advantages of the social constructionist/interactional approach for discourse analysis are outlined. Next, the tripartite model as it was originally conceived is described. Finally, the tripartite model is revised to fit an interactional approach to discourse analysis.

Social Constructionism, Interactionalism, and Discourse Analysis

Shotter (1993) develops a rhetorical/responsive version of social constructionism, where smaller, everyday discourses borrow from and influence the larger discourses circulating throughout societies. For this reason, a method of analysis based on indexicality (Silverstein 1976; Ochs 1992; Auer 1992) is useful to help explain the relationship between specific discourses and the larger social framework. Ochs (1992) expands on Silverstein's method to include indexical relationships where language is constitutive of a social structure (i.e., gender, ethnicity) and temporally transcends the time of the discourse event to recontextualize events in the past and the future. It is this view of discourse that seems most appropriate for discourse analysis, because it is through discourse and its indexical nature that the world, identities, and relationships are constructed.

Central to Shotter's account is what Wittgenstein terms the "hurly-burly," what Bakhtin (1981) calls "the background of language," and what Shotter labels background conversation. The hurly-burly is polyphonic and organizes the world in all its diversity (Shotter 1993). There are constant discourses in the background of our lives, which we draw from in our everyday discourses and relationships. It is against this background that all our utterances are judged (Shotter 1993, following Wittgenstein 1980), which is why it is necessary to analyze discourse within the larger social/historical framework in which it occurs.

Interactional sociolinguistics was born and raised in the context of Goffman's (1959) dramaturgical sociology. Dramaturgy is an approach accounting for how interactants seek to manage impressions, thereby gaining in social capital. This idea is essential for understanding how and why the manipulations of identity construction operate in discourse. A further contribution of Goffman (1974) is the idea that there are multiple embeddings of the self in one's narrative. These different embeddings (principal, emitter, animator, figure) create further possibilities for the manipulation of identity construction. Essential here are the distinctions between the narrator and herself as a figure in her own story (see Schiffrin 2006 for a fuller description).

The rhetorical/responsive social construction is the approach that yields the richest data in discourse analysis because of its two central claims: (1) Discourse constructs our worlds, and (2) the dialectical relationship between small discursive events and larger hurly-burly discourses creates an infinite potential for the analysis of social relationships and identity construction. The next section reviews the tripartite model of identity as it was originally conceived in mainstream social psychology.

The Tripartite Model of Identity in Social Psychology

Brewer and Gardner (1996) propose a theory that integrates three types of self-representation: personal, relational, and collective. The major body of research based on this model is concerned with self-worth, social motivation, and cross-cultural understanding. The approach has been applied in cross-cultural studies, contrasting collective/relational perspectives of the East to the more individualistic/personal perspectives of the West (Matsumoto 1999; Kitayama et al. 1997). More recently, research in this framework has been presented in Sedikides and Brewer (2001). Their main purpose is to explore the relationship among the three fundamental categories of self-knowledge: personal, relational, and collective. The theoretical assumptions in these studies treat identity as a relatively stable and quantifiable entity.

The cognitive structures that make up each of the three branches of the model can be traced to Linville's (1987) "Self-Complexity as a Cognitive Buffer against Stress-Related Illness and Depression." Self-aspects are defined as multiple cognitive structures that represent knowledge of self. Self-aspects activate based on a number of factors, such as context, thoughts, and other activated self-aspects. A limited number of self-aspects are active at any given time. Thus, Linville's (1987, 674) model allows for variability of self-representations across contexts. The tripartite model groups these self-aspects into "distinct forms of self-representation with different origins, sources of self worth, and social motivations" (Brewer and Gardner 1996, 83).

Using the tripartite model has led some (e.g., Deaux 1992, 1993, as interpreted by Brewer and Gardner 1996) to claim that collective identities are integrated into personal identities. Others (Onorato and Turner 2004) claim that, when salient, collective identities suppress personal identities. This follows from earlier work by Haslam and Turner (1992), wherein self-categorizations at different levels can be antagonistic and even incompatible.

Two common assumptions are maintained throughout all these research efforts in quantitative social psychology. First, the self is stored in memory as a cognitive structure and is part of a "mental" system. Second, the cognitive structures are formative, and language has primarily a referential/representational role. Both these assumptions contrast with those of social constructionist approaches, which understand social linguistic processes as primary in worldmaking, thereby allowing for a more fluid and dynamic account of the self. The following section shows how the tripartite model is incorporated into a social constructionist approach.

Incorporating the Tripartite Model into an Interactional Sociolinguistics

Some renovations to the tripartite model are necessary in order to incorporate it into an interactional sociolinguistics. The first major change must be from conceiving the self as a product of the mind (cognitive structure) to regarding it as a social interactional/relation. According to a revised tripartite model of identity, people interact and construct themselves through discourse in one of three orientations: personal, relational, or collective. In contrast to an account of identity as a product of the mind, here identity is constructed in conversation intersubjectively (between interlocutors) and intertextually (with various larger and smaller discourses influencing local conversations). The reconstruction of the self is an indexical process, both constitutive and recontextualizing (Ochs 1992).

Linville's (1987) self-aspects become identity actualization, whereby indexing a particular identity in conversation creates that identity anew. Identity actualizations are an adaptation of Chafe's (1994) active, semiactive, and inactive foci of consciousness. In the present study, identity orientations are actualized, semiactualized, or not actualized in the discourse through the use of self-oriented speech. Actualization is a process of creation and recreation. This is the major theoretical shift that the construct must undergo in order to participate in this type of constructionist program.

The content of the utterances of interest in this study is self-oriented and thus also reconstructs the self anew. Methodologically, one of the changes that needs to take place to conform to social constructionism is a shift from the use of questionnaires to discourse analysis. Questionnaires are designed by researchers, and the formulations of identity categories therein are not necessarily those of the people whose identities are being studied. Discourse analysis affords the researcher the opportunity to study the nuances of how people depict themselves. The remainder of this section defines each social orientation using the relevant elements of the original definition (Brewer and Gardner 1996) and its reconceptualization in this approach.

Personal orientation. Brewer and Gardner (1996) state that all the layers of identity are social, even the personal one. They explain that the personal frame of reference is based on interpersonal comparison. Knowledge of this kind differentiates the self from others, for example, when a person is described as intelligent, athletic, or talented. In this project, the personal orientation is actualized when one's way of being in the world actualizes one's own uniqueness.

Relational orientation. This orientation deals with one's way-of-being in a particular relationship with a significant other. For example, social roles such as employer and employee, father and son, or student and teacher are included in this construct. Actualizing one's identity in this way is not possible without a significant other. People are constantly engaged in a multiplicity of relationships, and the actualizations of oneself (as well as one's experience of self) can be qualitatively different in each person, as are one's ways of speaking.

Collective orientation. Identity at this level is a further social option for the actualization of oneself in the world. Here, identity is characterized by an impersonal relationship with a group and the ways of being upon actualizing oneself as a group member. Relevant here are the customs and cultures of different groups, as well as their language practices and interactional norms.

The tripartite model affords an opportunity to investigate the levels of identity constructed by discursive interactions. The discourse is constitutive of the three social orientations. In this way, a dialectic relationship between discourse and social relationships is studied. The remainder of this chapter presents a fine-grained discourse analysis of the narrative of an Ethiopian Israeli female college student in order to explain how she manipulates identity constructions so that she can negotiate her place in the world.

Data Analysis

The following excerpts were taken from a narrative of an Ethiopian Israeli female first-year college student during a focus group session in an extracurricular English oral proficiency program. The story is part of a larger corpus of narratives from Ethiopian Israeli college students. The story was told to a group of six students and the researcher. This one was selected because all the three orientations are actualized, and it explicitly exemplifies the negotiation of a minority position to one of strength. MA tells a story of an event that occurred in the fourth grade. Two excerpts from her story are provided here.

Excerpt 1: Creating an Alliance

The first excerpt comes out of the orientation section, even though it precedes the abstract and a second orientation of the larger narrative. It takes place in the same speaking turn and in the same context as the rest of the narrative. These utterances are important to the main storyline of the narrative because the storyteller positions herself in opposition to the Other. The segment is divided into three major sections. Lines c–k are included to give context to the small story (Georgakopoulou 2006) and to show topic transition into the story. The focus of analysis is on lines l–p, within which the small story is contained. Lines q and r are included to show the transition out of the story. The character "Tanya" (a pseudonym) introduced here is not mentioned again, which is evidence that this segment is less central. Code switching from English into Hebrew is indicated with italics:

31/c in the other school everybody liked me
d so here its going to be the same.
e I go there
f everybody's white of course
g just me black.
h and suddenly I was like become very very quiet child
i from (P) child that all the time you can hear and and eh *in the band* and and *school play*
j y'know, its all the time I I be there
k suddenly I was very very quiet and eh
l I remember one eh one girl she was eh:

m her name was Tanya
n she was Russian
o and she was also *new immigrant*
p so me and her y'know become eh best friend
q and then when eh:
r I don't know if you know about it but in elementary school there is eh like eh eh like king of the: of the: eh of the class

MA engages in the three social identity orientations in the telling of the short aside above. Lines c–d are the orientation, lines e–k are the complication, and lines l–p are the resolution. Lines c–k provide the transition in the story of transferring from a religious school (where boys and girls study and play separately) to a public coeducational secular school. According to MA, a major difference between the two social settings runs along ethnic lines, as can be seen by the white/black contrast in lines f and g, implying perhaps that there were more "blacks" in her previous school. The transfer to an environment that positions her minority status as more salient creates a vulnerability which MA must negotiate, and this influences her subsequent utterances. This is a story of forming a friendship in the face of a threatening majority.

The vulnerability is embodied in lines h–k, where MA constructs a shift from actualizing a personal orientation (i.e., "I became quiet") to a relational one, with Tanya being the significant other. The contrast between the selves underscores the rhetorical contour given to the utterance in line h "and suddenly," which introduces the shift in personal way of being, and is also repeated in line k. The repetition increases the strength of the drama developing in the story. Of great importance here is the shift in social setting coinciding with a shift in identity orientation.

The collective orientation is made salient here by making use of color as a way to talk about ethnicity: white and black. The tension between the two ethnicities is built upon in the main story line in excerpt 2 below. According to De Fina (2006, 364), color is often a defining property of category membership, and in many cases "the assumption is that there is a scale of color/ethnicity in which colored people are closer to each other than they are to white people." Color is indexically constitutive of ethnicity in this segment. White and black are understood as opposite ends of a social spectrum (assuming the color scheme of ethnicity is scalar).

If color is chosen as a way for MA to construct herself, does this choice not also operate within a personal orientation, because her color is her own? Skin color differences among Ethiopians is a topic that is part of the hurly-burly of their community, as it is in other communities of color (Salamon 2003, 7). This is reminiscent of Deaux (1992, 1993), who claims that collective identities are integrated into personal identities. How much of the collective (and relational for that matter) is also personal? The question will remain unanswered; this excerpt does not provide a sufficient basis for addressing it. An issue this chapter deals with is: How do the different orientations work together to satisfy interactional concerns?

The next part of the text to be analyzed begins with line l, where the resolution begins with "I remember" and shifts from personal to relational orientations. "As Billig (1997) reminds us, Wittgenstein argued against the view that psychological expressions such as *I remember, I think, I feel* stand for internal processes which provide their criteria of use. Rather the criteria for use emerge from the communicative practices in which these words are embedded" (Wetherell 2007, 664). Even though "I remember" appears to be self-oriented speech, it is not a construct to be analyzed as part of the approach developed in this chapter. The phrase functions more as a discourse marker than as a feature of identity.

In lines l and m, the word "girl" is followed immediately by two feminine pronouns, which actualize a (collective) gender orientation. The subsequent utterances construct a relationship with Tanya, which is partly based on the shared collective orientation of gender. Out of the commonly shared collective attribute, the relational orientation becomes salient and a friendship is constructed. The girls share another orientation of a collective kind, which aids in the construction of their alliance, namely: "new immigrant." Israel, a country with a very high proportion of immigrants, encourages this collective identity. This status affords certain monetary and social benefits at the beginning of the adaptation process, and in the last twenty years immigrant political parties have been born. Immigrant category membership represents an inherent foreignness with respect to the dominant culture, and even across ethnic groups of new immigrants a commonality can be found in opposition to the hegemonic identities. MA deals with her initial vulnerability by forming an alliance with an individual who shares the same vulnerability. Operating relationally helps deal with problems she presented along personal and collective lines, especially those related to "color."

To conclude, a few social relationships are constructed and negotiated in the telling of this story. They operate within all three orientations of the tripartite model of identity. The friendship between MA and Tanya is a relational one, where Tanya becomes a significant other for MA. However, their relationship is born out of social processes operating in the collective orientation, through an emphasis on gender and immigrant status. These orientations are able to bridge national and ethnic lines. Finally, the relationship between lines c–k (the orientation and complication) and lines l–p (the resolution) constructs the opposing position MA takes toward the dominant culture in her new setting, and so she creates an alliance in facing this conflict. The micropositioning of resistance toward hegemonic identities is indexically constitutive of her identity as an Ethiopian by imbuing it with a resistant character. This is evidence of the relationship between the relational and collective orientations. Interactionally, by telling this story to a group of her peers who have recently entered a program in a college with a huge majority of white students, this story may serve as a tool to create new alliances in order to negotiate a social context much like the one negotiated by MA in her story.

Excerpt 2: Fighting an Adversary

The second excerpt is a continuation of the same discursive event from which excerpt 1 was taken. Here MA has already launched into the resolution of the larger narrative. The excerpt begins with an attempt to break up a lunchtime fight between the two kings of her fourth-grade class:

35/x I I I come in the middle and I try to: separate them
y and the other king of the class took me
z and I was very small at that time I was small and thin and and y'know (laughing)
aa *I was very, its hard to imagine me like this, I was was very thin so skinny*
bb and he took me
cc push me away and say nigger (P)
dd and this period of time I never will forget it
ee rea really I I become like like a monster
ff like a monster
gg and I was *so* small *so* thin
hh like a wonder women
ii I don't know from where I got the (????) power
jj I really don't know
kk I I stand up and I *I kicked his ass* (everybody breaks out laughing)
ll *I kicked his ass*
mm and everybody stand like that was in shock because they never heard me nothing
nn I was so quiet
oo and so small
pp and so not known
qq I think that most of them didn't know my name also (P) really
rr so (P) I kick him
ss *I killed him with punches*
tt and from that day MAZ (background coughing)
uu that was my name (P) MAZ.
vv The the MAZ.
ww MAZ was like *god* in class

A fine-grained analysis of the text can begin with the evaluation of the way in which this excerpt operates within the personal orientation. What self-constructions create a unique self? In line z, there is the first occurrence of a physical description of the body as meek. MA, as a figure (in the sense of Goffman 1974) in her own story, casts herself in a weak position, which is reaffirmed in line gg, where the adjectives *small* and *thin* are both buttressed by the discourse marker *so.* In lines ee and ff, she self-constructs as a "monster," which stands in direct contrast with the previously mentioned self-construction (weak). The term "monster" is ambiguous as to its evaluative nature (positive or negative), but it certainly conveys power. This is supported by the subsequent utterance in line hh, "wonder woman," which conveys power but does so positively. Operating in a personal orientation, MA has manipulated different ways-of-being in her story to produce contrasting selves to serve the rhetorical purposes of her narrative. As rhetorical mechanisms, they serve to increase the reportability of the critical event (Labov 1997; Polanyi 1981). On the one hand she is meek, and on the other hand she is powerful, and it is her powerful self that wins the day, as can be seen in line kk, which contains the critical event of the narrative.

Relationally, MA positions herself here in the role of adversary. She is a fighter, a combatant in opposition to the king of the class, who represents the dominant culture, which is both ethnically white and religiously secular. (Excerpts from the text in which MA explicitly constructs these aspects are available upon request.) Note the opposition in the relational orientation here with that presented in the analysis of excerpt 1, where she formed an alliance to negotiate her vulnerability rather than engage in head-on combat. The conflict being negotiated in the story is essentially an opportunity for MA to actualize herself, and with no adversary this would not be possible. This is the debt the self owes to the other, for without the relation between the two (even if antagonistic), she would not have had the opportunity to actualize herself in this way. Her toughness is born out of her relationship with her adversary. In the later lines (tt–ww) of her narrative, she describes this attribute as salient in other relationships as well.

In the collective orientation, MA has her group association thrust upon her in a most antagonistic way. The term used to describe her as a member of a group is "derogatory." It is important to note that the actual event was in Hebrew, and the actual word MA heard (*kushi*) was different from the one she reported (nigger). The two terms have different connotations in their respective languages. Not every translator would have made this same decision in choosing from a wide range of English words that can replace the original word (e.g., black, Ethiopian). But in making her choice, MA encodes her attitude toward the word and the event by choosing the most derogatory English word among those available. And so here another contrast is constructed to serve the rhetorical purposes of the narrative—to tell a good story: the minority group member versus the dominant culture member. Moreover, as a representative of her minority group, MA wins a victory for her people in besting her adversary in this narrative, and in each retelling of the story another victory is acquired. In this way, she indexically amasses power for herself and her group.

The three orientations operate here in concert. Within the personal orientation MA is strong and victorious, within the relational orientation she is combative and adversary, and within the collective orientation she is a minority member successfully resisting antagonism from the dominant group. Operations in each orientation interact to support each other, the overall point of the story, and her self-construction. The personal (thin, weak) and collective (Ethiopian) orientations position her in direct contrast to the relational (adversary) and personal (tough) orientations that win the day in her story. Here local positioning builds resistance toward the hegemony, indexing the more collective Ethiopian orientation. In this light, the story is one of a struggle of the self, where the particular constructions in MA's discourse are crucial.

Until reading the words "wonder woman," one reviewer assumed that the speaker was male, because it narrates like a boy's story. This reading reveals another collective representation operating in this text: The gender category is being deconstructed, negotiated, and reconstructed. In this story, MA enters the world of masculinity, fights on boys' terms, and comes out on top. She relocates the line that would distinguish between the genders. She enters the boys' world as a lady and plays out the role of "wonder woman" (as opposed to superman). She implicitly claims that being strong in this way can no longer be relegated to the masculine but now is also part of the feminine. The act of praising here recontextualizes the gender category, thereby reconstituting it (Ochs 1992). She indexically redefines what it is to be a woman, and in her own way she has creatively reconstructed the female gender category.

The tripartite model is also useful in understanding the interaction between storyteller and listeners. In telling the story, MA recreates herself as a hero in front of her new peers (audience), who were not present at the actual event, but they can now associate the type of person in the story with the storyteller. MA creates an impression and manages the way they view her (cf. "impression management," Goffman 1959). Both of MA's stories can be used a resource by the Ethiopian student audience members to negotiate their new academic context in a white majority college. In this way, MA positions herself as a source of strength for and among her peers.

Discussion

The analysis here affords new opportunities for conceiving and researching the self. What was developed in the original model as a cognitive structure is here adapted as a more interactional construct. Rather than assume causes and motivations of the speaker, the approach here views the speaker in the agentive role (Harré 1999) negotiating a social context through the manipulations of identity construction, which then indexically constitute more global and durable identity constructs. The three orientations help discourse analysts track the actions of interlocutors as they present themselves in situated contexts in three kinds of orientations that are socially constrained. The model is comprehensive in that the three orientations cover interaction in a wide range of contexts.

The analyses expose the manipulations of the speaker in her self-constructions. Within the constraints represented by the tripartite model, she is afforded a great many choices regarding how to construct herself, choices she can base on her judgment of their interactional efficacy. In every case one orientation is chosen, when another could have been implemented. For example, in excerpt 1, MA constructs herself and the story within the personal orientation, focusing on her experience of personal struggle, which rhetorically and interactionally allows her audience to identify with her. Thus, she emphasizes the personal orientation at the expense of other orientations.

This choice allows MA to construct her vulnerability, which serves the rhetorical goal of constructing a weak self and creating narrative tension, eventually overcome at the end of the narrative. In the narrative as well as in her college life, she is faced with a social problem, and by constructing this past victory, she is able to construct a strong self in the present. It becomes evident how the model allows for a sense of self-continuity by discursively building a connection between *animator* and *figure* (Goffman 1974). She was strong in the past, and she is strong in the present. The micropositionings throughout the narrative function at both the textual level and the interactional level, bridging past and present selves. She engages in the same type of positioning across time, evidence of "stance accretion" (Rauniomaa 2003 and Du Bois 2002, as reported by Bucholtz and Hall 2005). In a Bakhtinian sense, the constructions are dialogically related one to the other (Bakhtin 1981, 275–300). The previous construction, being judged as successful, sets a precedent for the next one, and that construction is used as a lens through which the previous one is viewed and reconstructed. From this we can see the dialectic nature of the self-constructions across time and discourses.

What of the relationship between the orientations? We have already seen evidence for the intentional manipulations of the speaker (agent) in choosing one orientation over another for interactional efficiency, but is there any other relationship between them? The analysis reveals a range of relationships manipulated for the purposes of creating a positive impression of self for an audience or as rhetorical devices increasing tellability (Labov and Waletzky 1997; Polanyi 1981) of the narrative. The personal orientation depicts a struggle between selves, and the triumph of the desirous self ("I am tough"). The relational social orientation negotiates between the self and allies or foes and reveals the processes of identification that MA claims for herself and those she resists. In the texts above, the collective social orientation pits the speaker in the minority position of a religious Ethiopian against a white secular hegemony. The identities at each level penetrate each other, in that the relational orientation constructs foes and allies along collective lines, and the personal orientation affords the speaker the ability to overcome her social struggle against an antagonistic dominant culture. The analyses present evidence for the collaborative nature of the orientations, as they rhetorically aid the storyteller in constructing her narrative so that it can be used purposefully in interaction.

The choice to actualize one orientation over another depends on the context within which the interaction takes place. Furthermore, what purposes do each of the orientations serve so that speakers will choose one over the other in order to manage impressions and fulfill other interactional ends? From the analysis of excerpt 2, the personal orientation is seen as preferred for creating a positive impression of strength, because of the pattern of micropositionings that have formed in the narrative. Further, perhaps because of the historical moment within which the discourse takes place, individualistic values (personal orientation) seem to be the most impressive (Stolorow and Atwood 1992; Harré 1989).

The relational orientation helps the storyteller to cast herself either with or against a significant other and to actualize herself in the relationship. Absent the relationship with friend or foe, the particular self-construction actualized in a relational orientation would not be possible. The construction of a relationship with a foe or friend is a discursive manipulation making full use of the processes of identification for the purposes of taking a more socially advantageous position.

The collective orientation casts one into the narrative of a community, and as a figure in that narrative, one is judged against the conversational background of that community. This strategy can be implemented by speakers when they manipulate the accessible information in the hurly-burly (which is also available to listeners), and thus construct themselves as figures in an already ongoing story. This explanation is particularly salient in the case above, because all the members of the audience are

Ethiopian Israelis (except the relatively silent facilitator) and thus can easily access narratives that pit the Ethiopian immigrant against hegemonic Israeli society.

The analysis here has shown how the various self-actualizations indexically reconstitute and recontextualize (Ochs 1992) larger social structures, in particular gender and ethnicity. In excerpt 2, the storyteller's negotiation of a masculine world in a traditionally masculine way is explicit. In fact, a "girl" can be "king of the class" in school, a position often reserved for "boys." Furthermore, not only is gender recast here but so is ethnicity. Ethnicity is reconstituted here to allow for an Israeli Ethiopian identity that is powerful and resistant in minority contexts. MA's story takes place at a historical moment when Ethiopian Israelis are struggling to better their position in Israeli society. The accretion (Rauniomaa 2003 and Du Bois 2002, as reported by Bucholtz and Hall 2005) of resistance local positionings in discourse by MA may index more durable features of Ethiopian identity. By reconstructing identities in new ways, MA redefines larger social structures, for example, gender and ethnicity. If MA is not alone in her pattern of construction, then these discourses may lead to social change.

So, how does MA manipulate her identity constructions to negotiate her social context? She constructs a story, where she initially presents herself as disadvantaged sociopolitically, relationally, and even physically, so that she can later reconstruct herself as the heroine triumphant against all odds. This is a rhetorical device designed to increase tellability (Labov and Waletzky 1997; Polanyi 1981), which enables her to better manage the impressions of her audience. In her narrative, MA presents herself as a potential leader for her peers. She has negotiated the same challenging situation facing them today in the past (negotiating the social context of a white, hegemonic school), and she has done so successfully.

Conclusion

This chapter is an attempt to change the way in which we talk about the self (Shotter 1993; Billig 1987; Shotter and Billig 1998). Rather than labeling an utterance that presents self-orientation as a reference to the self, we should label it as a self-construction, in line with the theoretical assumptions guiding this chapter. A fine-grained analysis of identity actualizations aids in resituating the self as a dynamic, fluid process that can adapt to a continually changing world while maintaining those identities that are "brought along." Those identities that are "brought along" are reconstructed at every actualization in discourse for interactional purposes, and thus are dynamic in character.

The tripartite model of identity has proven adaptable to a constructionist program and useful in an interactional discourse analysis framework. The contribution that the model makes to discourse analysis of this kind is provided by the distinct layers of identity and the composite self-constructions (self-aspects), in which various combinations are manipulated to serve interactional ends.

ACKNOWLEDGMENTS

I thank Joel Walters and an anonymous reviewer for comments on the chapter. I would also like to express my appreciation for the Interdisciplinary Center, Herzliya, for being so conducive to this research project. And most lovingly to my wife and family for being so supportive, I give thanks.

REFERENCES

Auer, P. 1992. Introduction: John Gumperz' approach to contextualization. In *The contextualization of language,* ed. Peter Auer and Aldo di Luzio, 1–38. Philadelphia: John Benjamins.

Bakhtin, M. 1981. *The dialogic imagination.* Trans. M. Holquist. Austin: University of Texas Press. Orig. pub. 1935.

Billig, Michael. 1987. *Arguing and thinking: A rhetorical approach to social psychology.* Cambridge. Cambridge University Press.

———. 1997. Discursive, rhetorical and ideological messages. In *The message of social psychology,* ed. Craig McGarty and Alex Haslam, 55–70. Oxford: Blackwell..

Brewer, Marilynn B., and Wendi L. Gardner. 1996. Who is this we? Levels of collective identity and self-representations. *Journal of Personality and Social Psychology* 71 (1): 83–93.

Bucholtz, Mary, and Kira Hall. 2005. Identity and interaction: A sociocultural linguistic approach. *Discourse Studies* 7 (4–5): 585–614.

Chafe, Wallace L. 1994. *Discourse, consciousness, and time: The flow and displacement of conscious experience in speaking and writing.* Chicago: University of Chicago Press.

Deaux, Kay. 1992. Personalizing identity and socializing self. In *Social psychology of identity and the self-concept,* ed. Glynis M. Breakwell, 9–33. London: Academic Press.

———. 1993. Reconstructing social identity. *Personality and Social Psychology Bulletin* 19:4–12.

De Fina, Anna. 2003. *Identity in narrative: A study of immigrant discourse.* Philadelphia: John Benjamins.

De Fina, Anna, Deborah Schiffrin, and Michael Bamberg, eds. 2006. *Discourse and identity.* Studies in Interactional Sociolinguistics 23. Cambridge: Cambridge University Press.

Du Bois, John W. 2002. Stance and consequence. Paper presented at the annual meeting of the American Anthropological Association, New Orleans.

Garfinkel, Harold. 1967. *Studies in ethnomethodology.* Englewood Cliffs, NJ: Prentice Hall.

Georgakopoulou, Alexandra. 2006. Thinking big with small stories in narrative and identity analysis. *Narrative Inquiry* 16 (1): 122–30.

Goffman, Erving. 1959. *The presentation of self in everyday life.* New York: Doubleday.

———. 1974. *Frame analysis.* New York: Harper & Row.

Harré, Rom. 1989. Language games and the texts of identity. In *Texts of identity,* ed. J. Shotter and K. J. Gergen. London: Sage.

———. 1999. The rediscovery of the human mind: The discursive approach. *Asian Journal of Social Psychology.* 2:43–62.

Haslam, Alex, and John C. Turner. 1992. Context-dependent variation in social stereotyping 2: The relationship between frame of reference, self categorization and accentuation. *European Journal of Social Psychology* 22:251–77.

Kitayama, S., H. R. Markus, H. Matsumoto, and V. Norasakkunkit. 1997. Individual and collective processes in the construction of the self: Self-enhancement in the United States and self-criticism in Japan. *Journal of Personality and Social Psychology* 72 (6): 1245–67.

Labov, William, and Joshua Waletzky. 1997. Narrative analysis: oral versions of personal experience. In Oral versions of personal experience: Three decades of narrative analysis, ed. M. Bamberg. Special Issue of *Journal of Narrative and Life History* 7 (1–4): 3–38. Orig. pub. 1967.

Linville, P. W. 1987. Self-complexity as a cognitive buffer against stress-related illness and depression. *Journal of Personality and Social Psychology* 52 (4): 663–76.

Matsumoto, David. 1999. Culture and self: An empirical assessment of Markus and Kitayama's theory of independent and interdependent self-construals. *Asian Journal of Social Psychology* 2:289–310.

Ochs, Elinor. 1992. Indexing gender. In *Rethinking contexts: Language as an interactive phenomenon*, ed. A. Duranti and C. Goodwin. Cambridge: Cambridge University Press.

Onorato, Rina, and John Turner. 2004. Fluidity in the self-concept: The shift from personal to social identity. *European Journal of Social Psychology* 34:257–78.

Polanyi, Livia. 1981. What stories can tell us about their teller's world. *Poetics Today* 2 (2): 97–112.

Rauniomaa, Mirka. 2003. Stance accretion. Paper presented to the Language, Interaction, and Social Organization Research Focus Group, University of California, Santa Barbara, February.

Salamon, Hagar. 2003. Blackness in transition: Decoding racial constructs through stories of Ethiopian Jews. *Journal of Folklore Research* 40 (1): 3–32.

Schiffrin, Deborah. 2006. From linguistic reference to social identity. In *Discourse and identity,* ed. Anna De Fina, Deborah Schiffrin, and Michael Bamberg, 103–31. Studies in Interactional Sociolinguistics 23. Cambridge: Cambridge University Press.

Sedikides, Constantine, and Marilynn B. Brewer, eds. 2001. *Individual self, relational self, collective self.* Philadelphia: Psychology Press.

Shotter, John. 1993. *Conversational Realities.* London. Sage.

Shotter, John, and Michael Billig. 1998. A Bakhtinian psychology: From out of the heads of individuals and into the dialogues between them. In *Bakhtin and the human sciences,* ed. Michael M. Bell and Michael Gardiner, 13–29. London: Sage.

Silverstein, Michael. 1976. Shifters, linguistic categories, and cultural description. In *Meaning in anthropology,* ed. Keith H. Basso and Henry A. Selby. Albuquerque. University of New Mexico Press.

Stolorow, Robert D., and George E. Atwood. 1992. *Contexts of being: The intersubjective foundations of psychological life.* Mahwah, NJ: Analytic Press.

Wetherell, Margaret. 2007. A step too far: Discursive psychology, linguistic ethnography and questions of identity. *Journal of Sociolinguistics* 11 (5): 661–81.

Williams, Ashley M. 2008. Brought-along identities and the dynamics of ideology: Accomplishing bivalent stances in a multilingual interaction. *Multilingua* 27:37–56.

Wittgenstein, Ludwig. 1980. *Remarks on the philosophy of psychology,* vols. 1 and 2. Oxford: Basil Blackwell.

7

Narratives of Reputation: Layerings of Social and Spatial Identities

GABRIELLA MODAN AND AMY SHUMAN
The Ohio State University

PLACES, LIKE PEOPLE, have reputations, and these reputations are created through relations in narrative—relations among places, the kinds of people who inhabit them, and the kinds of things that are said to occur there. Narratives are oriented not just temporally, but spatiotemporally; many narratives use places strategically, not only as a backdrop for events but also as a means for asserting some connections and negating others. As De Fina (2003) and others have noted, we need to understand orientation as a process ongoing throughout a narrative. And as we argue here, the strategic use of orientation can be crucial for asserting the larger meaning of a story. Places are key to narrative; as Baynham (2003) and Herman (2001) point out, narrative action is constituted in, motivated by, and understood with reference to the particularities of place.

In this chapter we ask what happens when a speaker invokes other, distant, seemingly disconnected places to establish a claim to a more immediate place. What are the structural means for creating the reputations of these places, what is the textual interplay of these place characterizations, and how do place reputations afford certain subject positions for the narrator and others? To answer these questions, we analyze a set of narratives collected as part of a larger project on ethnicity and local identity in the Washington neighborhood of Mount Pleasant. Mount Pleasant is a multiethnic, gentrifying neighborhood with residents who express strong local affiliations. The teller of these narratives is a man in his late forties who we call Boaz, an Israeli immigrant of Iraqi descent; he leads us from a present-day walk through Mount Pleasant, to a bar fight in Germany in 1975, then to Jews facing pogroms in Baghdad in the 1920s, and finally back to a hypothetical confrontation in Mount Pleasant or elsewhere. We trace three narrative features through these accounts—invocation of place, deixis, and negation. An analysis of these features will lead us to some insights about how these narratives of distant times and places—chronotopes, in Bakhtin's (1981) terms—layer upon each other to ultimately create Mount Pleasant as a certain kind of place, and Boaz as a certain kind of Jew.

Invocations of Place

Research on discourse and place has shown that narrators invoke places in order to do cultural work, from delineating moral or appropriate behavior (cf. Basso 1996; Hill 1995; Modan 2007), to reinforcing community history (Toren 1995) and community identity (Johnstone 1990), to creating cosmopolitan personas (Gaudio 1997).

In narratives, places can be evoked both explicitly, through narrative orientation, and implicitly, through presupposition, allusion, or even silence where one might expect a place to be invoked. We make a distinction here between formal orientation, in the Labovian sense, and more implicit invocations of place; these strategies set up different relations among narrators, listeners, and place knowledge. In the case of implicit invocations, place knowledge is constructed as shared, whereas in orientation, it is constructed as not shared.

De Fina (2003, 372) states that orientations are "occasions for narrators and audience to negotiate and build shared understandings of experiences." Thus, orientation does more than merely setting the scene; it is an interactional resource. We argue that orientation is not simply about *creating* shared knowledge, however, and that it is not necessarily related to a narrator's assumptions about what a listener knows. Rather, the presence, absence, or level of detail of orientation serves as a strategy to include or exclude the listener as an in-group member. The strategic use of orientation can *frame* knowledge as shared in order to achieve an ideological goal. As we shall see, Boaz provides orientation for places that it is clear the listener knows, and he does not provide orientation at points in which place reference is textually ambiguous and he might assume that the listener does not know. This lack of orientation goes hand in hand with the total lack of reference to one particular place, Israel. The complete lack of reference to Israel constructs this place as maximally shared information that is maximally relevant for the story.

Georgakopoulou (2003) considers time and place as interactional resources, and Boaz's manipulations of orientation certainly function in that way, because they construct the listener as an in-group or out-group member. But such interactional moves serve the larger goal of establishing his reputation, as well as the reputations of the places he discusses. Through his delineation of place knowledge as shared or unshared, he creates a scale of positionality from the personal to the familial to the ethnic. The subject position that he claims depends on a series of locations in which he demonstrates how events at different points on this scale necessitate his becoming a particular kind of Jew. Indeed, as an ideological move, his narrative choices necessitate the emergence of this kind of Jew in general.

Georgakopoulou (2003)—having been influenced by Ochs and Capps's (2001) work on affordances—argues that time and place references enable certain storylines and inhibit others; they invoke semiotic meanings, and in so doing create affordances for stories about other places, and linkages between multiple places across storyworlds.

As we will see in Boaz's stories, the spatial deictic shifts both within and across storyworlds create or disallow certain subject positions for Boaz and the people he talks about. And what happens within each storyworld is as important as what happens across storyworlds: Stories about Germany and Baghdad at key historical moments serve as orientation to Mount Pleasant in the present. What happens in those stories affords both the subject position and the spatial position that Boaz takes up in the last Mount Pleasant story that concludes the narrative set.

Deictic Centers

Much early narrative work privileged time over place (Labov 1972; Propp 1968; Ricoeur 1984) in understanding narrative structures, but more recently many scholars have shown that the internal organization of a narrative can be accomplished primarily through references to place. Likewise, the relationships *among* narratives can be structured through the relationships between the social meanings of the places where the narratives are located. As Georgakopoulou (2003, 415) notes, "The relationships between time and place transcend the boundaries of one taleworld and involve the interplay between different narratives." Such relationships come about through deictic shifts. As Maryns and Blommaert (2001, 75) explain, deictic shifts in narrative "reveal . . . the speaker's positioning towards . . . events." More specific to spatial concerns, scholars such as Hill (1995) have shown that speakers use spatial shifts between deictic centers to set up *moral geographies* in which alignments between people and places set up reputations for both. In our analysis, we look at the shifts in deictic centers from story to story, as well as investigate various characters' relationships to each story's deictic center—whether they are in it, how they move around it, and the like.

Negation

Negation is an example of what Greimas (1983) described in terms of a fundamental opposition in narrative, in which making meaning depends on differences, opposites, and contrary positions. As Labov (1972) and others have noted, negation sets up a contrast to expectations. In so doing, negation brings those expectations into the discourse, making them part of the larger story. Labov considers negation to be an evaluative device, for it casts something as narratable because it violates our assumptions of how the world is or should be.

In *Coming Out Jewish,* Stratton (2000, 85) discusses what he calls *ghetto thinking,* "a way of being in the world in which the world is considered to be, in and of itself, dangerous and threatening, and to which, culturally speaking, the only appropriate response is considered to be fear." He writes that, while such thinking is indicative of the experience of the diaspora Jew, Zionism turns this model on its head; for the Zionist, the proper response to the danger of various places is to show fearlessness and even aggression. Stratton, along with Berkowitz (1993) and Oz (1962), propose that the "new Jew" that Zionism theorizes is not actually something new; instead, it is an inversion—a mirror image—of the anti-Semitic portrait of the weak, submissive diaspora Jew.

In Boaz's narratives, negation is the linguistic resource by means of which such inversion occurs. Through negation, he sets up a mirror-image storyworld of strong and weak people—specifically, strong and weak Jews. Through negation, his position as a tough urbanite contrasts with a mirror-image pre-Zionist world.

The Data

Boaz's narratives were told during a sociolinguistic interview conducted by one co-author (Modan, hereafter GM), as a response to her question about how he thinks his ethnicity influences his take on the neighborhood. Boaz was one of a number of Jews participating in this study, but the only Israeli, and his narrative was quite different from those of the American Jews. The narratives that the American Jews told in answer to this question centered on two themes, both having to do with living in an ethnically heterogeneous neighborhood. The first was feeling at home in a mixed community that did not have a majority ethnicity, and the second was civil rights as a Jewish value that made them want to live in a mixed neighborhood.

Boaz's response creates a very different kind of subject position—a very different kind of Jew. Through his narratives of danger and toughness in the Mount Pleasant neighborhood of Washington, Germany, and Baghdad, he stakes an aggressive claim to the places he discusses, and he creates an orientation of fearlessness as a personal, familial, and ethnic characteristic. Specifically, he creates what we can call a Zionist Jewish subject—a subject that is strong and tough, not vulnerable and afraid.

In addition to the three narrated places, there is a fourth place that plays a role in this story, namely, Israel. As we will see, Israel is only obliquely referenced, but it was also discussed in an earlier section of the larger talk of which this narrative is part. Because the narrator and the listener share a connection to Israel (because GM is part Israeli), and because Israel has already been discussed, Israel and particular symbolic values of it become maximally shared knowledge, such that Israel can serve as the unnamed pivot point around which the other storyworlds revolve. It is exactly through its not being named that its pivot power is created.

Mount Pleasant: Vulnerability and Aggressiveness

The first storyworld in the set of accounts starts with Boaz's report of how his wife views Mount Pleasant:

GM: So how do you think that your, ethnicity, influences, how you see what goes on, around here. Or how you see what kind of neighborhood this is.

Boaz: U:m, well, to put it like my wife says, you walk around like, you know, like you're in the middle of uh, attacking a, some guerrilla stronghold somewhere. I have- doesn't scare me one bit. I mean I walk through the worst, parts here. And uh, maybe because I project, you know the, sort of– you know I've learned to to project an image of, don't mess with me?

GM: mm hmm

Boaz: I don't know. Cause I'm not very powerful physically. But um, I know how to handle myself. . . . The way what they project towards you if somebody project intimidation, it will be clear within the first 60 seconds that the person to be intimidated here is, you. Not me. Okay because, ^Oh, you can do this and you can do that and you can do this but you won't get away with much. Um. Cause it can get pretty scary around here.

GM: Yeah?

Boaz: You know.

GM: Have you had any bad experiences?

Boaz: Well I've had some pretty bad experiences of course you know I've had, I've had- you know. I've had people, um, . . . My windows were shattered on the night of the Million Man March. . . . Okay? Um, what do I attribute it to? I don't know. Nothing was stolen. It was just damage for damage sake. Um, . . . Cause it can get pretty scary around here. Um, I think this neighborhood you you, I don't care where you're from, you have to show that– you know where you're going, and that you're not– *you're not vulnerable.* You know? 'Cause if you show a little bit of vulnerability you're done. Whether you're Black White Hispanic. And um, my background is such that *this word does not exist.* I'm *not vulnerable to anything.* Yeah, to some– some, vices that I have! But uh, but as far as uh, be– *being somebody's lamb. It's just not in the lexicon.* You know. We draw blood where we come from.

By attributing to his wife the characterization of Mount Pleasant as dangerous, Boaz is able to simultaneously present the idea that some people walk around the area afraid and others, like him, project a "don't mess with me" image. His embedded account of the Million Man March (a march organized by Louis Farrakhan) alludes to ethnic tensions (specifically, Black-Jewish tensions) and anti-Semitic violence—a theme that is developed in the subsequent discourse—and it sets up a potentially ethnic framework with which to interpret his discourse. However, he negates this ethnic lens with his comments "I don't care where you're from" and "Whether you're Black, White, Hispanic." Not only is the ethnic lens negated, but following this story, Boaz returns to his earlier topic; thus the Million Man March account remains contained within the Mount Pleasant context. Although it does foreshadow the ethnic valence to come, structurally it does not bleed into the other storyworlds. Therefore, for the purposes of this chapter, we do not discuss it at length.

In the general Mount Pleasant storyworld–the guerilla stronghold–negation sets up Boaz as a fearless person, in contrast to the mirror-image Boaz who exists in a parallel universe in which he might be scared, vulnerable, and intimidated, where people mess with him, and so on. Negation asserts a universe, then, in which his emotions, actions, and the general state of affairs are characterized by invulnerability. Negation sets up the dynamic that continues through the other storyworlds, which are also scary places in which he cannot be messed with.

The utterance "it can get pretty scary around here" and the description of having to show where you are going and that you are not vulnerable, work as place orientation: They characterize the neighborhood and claim a reputation for it. In terms of creating shared knowledge, however, this orientation is not necessary; Boaz knows that GM has lived in the neighborhood for seven years—some of that time just one block away from where the discussion is taking place—so he has reason to assume that she knows what the neighborhood is like. What the orientation *does* is construct Boaz's knowledge as insider knowledge, and this helps to shore up his legitimacy as a community member. It also individualizes his perspective as a personal one based on his experience in this particular place.

At the same time, though, Boaz generalizes his experience to that of others in the neighborhood. With the presupposition "I don't care where you come from," he casts the neighborhood as being comprised of people who come from other places and who are not anchored in this place—the characters move in and out of this setting. Just as Boaz's relation to this deictic center is one of "walking through," the generalized others "come from" somewhere, and they are "going somewhere," as in the utterance, "You have to show you know where you're going." Boaz and these other characters are all on the same footing as outsiders coming in, but what differentiates them is whether they know where they are going or whether they know how to act as if they know where they are going. Boaz differentiates himself from other, potentially scared, people in this setting. His stance negates the association between the place and a character's vulnerability. Thus, narrative orientations do not merely locate events in places; they can also morally differentiate among different characters in those places, and they set up a range of possible morally imbued alignments among characters and between characters and places.

In narrating his own personal orientation to this place and putting that orientation in conversation with other people of various backgrounds—Black, White, Hispanic—Boaz has not really answered the question about how his take on the place relates to his ethnicity. However, he ends the section with an utterance that opens the potential for his stance to be contextualized as an ethnic stance. The utterance "We draw blood where we come from" simultaneously indexes Israel and constructs it as a place that instills in its people a needed aggressive orientation to the world. It is ambiguous whether the "we" in this utterance is inclusive or exclusive—whether or not it includes GM, an Israeli-American—but in any case, this image and its indexing of Israel begins to show Boaz's stance as a Jewish stance, and—in linking it with Israel—a Zionist Jewish one.

It is worth pointing out that "We draw blood where we come from" is an alignment with a particular aspect of a Zionist orientation to the world and not an alignment with Israeli government policy or military actions. In the larger speech activity, this set of narratives follows 45 minutes of Boaz's critique of the Israeli government's policies and praise of the Oslo accords, and discussion of his own participation in the Peace Now movement. (Also, the data were collected in 1998, before the second intifada.)

The lack of orientation to explain "where we come from" and the vagueness of the utterance overall set up narrative tension. How is this utterance a response to GM's question about ethnicity? This question starts to be answered with the two following stories that Boaz narrates, one in Germany and one in Baghdad. These two stories serve as retrospective and prospective orientation to the Mount Pleasant scenes between which they are sandwiched. The utterance "We draw blood where we come from" is both the coda of the first Mount Pleasant story and an abstract that enables Boaz to spontaneously launch into the Germany story. "Where we come from" is the transition point between Mount Pleasant and Germany, but "where we come from" is neither of those places. In the Germany story "where we come from" is not technically a part of the orientation to that place, but it is an orientation to the kind of person Boaz claims to be.

Germany: "We're a New Breed"

After the "we draw blood" utterance, Boaz begins his narrative about a German bar fight in 1975 with an extensive localized orientation that casts the scene as nonshared knowledge:

> We draw blood where we come from. I gotta tell you a funny story I was in Germany in 1976. I had a German girlfriend. And I was staying in her apartment. She was a student. And it was her birthday and we went to the cafeteria in the university one night. No, it was a bar—we went to a bar.

The beginning of the narrative has two deictic centers—Anna's apartment and the bar. In contrast to Mount Pleasant, where Boaz was walking *through* the space, here he locates himself *within* these various deictic centers. First, he is staying in the apartment. Then they go to the bar, but when the narrative action happens, Boaz is already in the bar, and it is the antagonist who comes from elsewhere:

> In comes this German guy and this big fat guy and he goes, he yells in German, Oh look what Anna got for her birthday, a Jew. This was end of it man this guy got bottles on his head and everything we went outside and, as it was going on i- j- when I, was done with him, I told him, see we're a different breed. You made a big mistake. We're not the kind that you put on the table and you start doing experiments and then when you end up you *burn* them so there'll be nothing left. You said the wrong thing, that's why I had to beat you. I got arrested for it, and all that but. Some explaining and all that, got me off of this but. That's how I am. You know I was brought up to be this way. You know you don't turn the other cheek.

In this narrative, we follow Boaz as he remembers the particular location of this event in the bar, and he further distinguishes between what takes place inside the bar and what occurs outside. But when we get to the punchline of the story—what Boaz told the German—there is no orientation whatsoever to "the kind you put on the table and you start doing experiments." This table is not located in the bar but rather in a past that is not occupied by either Boaz or, most likely, the fat German. Because there is no orientation to this table and the events that occurred there, exactly where the table was in time and space and what happened on it is constructed as shared knowledge. What happened was the Holocaust. As was the case with Boaz's off-record invocation of Israel, the off-record invocation of the Holocaust here casts the importance of the event as shared Jewish knowledge. It is this move that casts Boaz's stance here as an ethnic stance. The shared ethnic-group nature of Boaz's stance, as well as the German's stance, is heightened by the pronoun use in the constructed dialogue: The German becomes a generalized "you" who performs experiments on a generalized "we." When he then switches back to the specific German guy and Boaz, in "You said the wrong thing and that's why I had to beat you," this individual German is the representative of a past group, but Boaz is a representative of a past group that has been reconfigured—"a new breed."

It is negation in this narrative that sets up the characterization of this new breed, and that reconfigures the agentive relations between Germans and Jews: In the mirror image world that arises through negation, Germans acted upon Jews, and Jews were not in control of their own movement—Germans put Jews on tables, started doing experiments on them, and burned them, and the only thing that Jews did was "turn the other cheek." This is in stark contrast to the new storyworld, where Boaz violently acts on the German—although the violence is mitigated through the use of passive voice (this guy got bottles on his head). Another interesting use of the passive voice is the utterance "I got arrested": The German guy shows agency at the beginning of the story by confronting Boaz, but after Boaz beats him and explains the new order of things, the agency of the police officer is obscured. So Germans are no longer portrayed as acting upon Jews.

Now we begin to have a sense of how the particular present of Mount Pleasant is related to the generalized past of Boaz's ethnic group. Although the generalized past of the Holocaust is indirectly connected to Boaz as a member of a persecuted group, however, he has no direct connection because his family is from Iraq, not Europe. The coda of the narrative—"That's how I am. I was brought up to be this way. You know you don't turn the other cheek"—reinforces the narrative's start, "We draw blood where we come from," as an orientation to the kind of person that Boaz is. The coda also gives a hint as to how he came to be that way. With the utterance "I was brought up to be that way," he affords the telling of a story about his own family. Structurally, "I was brought up to be that way. You know you don't turn the other cheek" functions like "We draw blood where we come from," in that it serves both as a coda to one of his stories and an abstract to a subsequent story. It occasions a deictic shift to Baghdad, where we finally learn why he does not turn the other cheek, and where the mirror-image world where Jews *did* turn the other cheek becomes explicit.

Baghdad: The Uniting of Storyworlds

In his story about Baghdad, Boaz describes the city's pogroms in the 1920s and his father's refusal to suffer silently, but instead to join the Zionist movement:

> That's how I am. You know I was brought up to be this way. You know you don't turn the other cheek. And it's totally against my father's uh, you know my father lived, all his life until he was like seventeen, in an Arab country. And, they have much dislike to, the Muslim Arabs, because of all the discriminations, and the persecutions, and all that. But much of their life was—my father, being the first one, to join the Zionist movement, was the first one that said well there's no more second cheek. They can't come in here and pogrom us. But uh— . . . They just went there and killed them so the thing was okay, don't upset them too much. Well, you see—this, to me it doesn't exist.

In the Baghdad section, an ethnic position is accomplished through presupposing descriptions of things that happened in Baghdad as shared knowledge ("all the discriminations, and the persecutions, and all that"). Conversely, Boaz uses orientation clauses to explain his father's roots in an Arab country ("my father lived . . . in an Arab country") and to describe the Pogroms and the status of Jews in the city in the 1920s and later. These orientation clauses frame knowledge of Baghdad as particular rather than general, relating specifically to Boaz's family history. By creating this as a familial connection and not an ethnic one (not one shared with the listener), Boaz broadens the ideological base that he uses to solidify his stance.

The Baghdad (or Arab country) account becomes, retrospectively, an orientation to the Germany story. It is a prequel that sets up the conditions for Boaz's actions in the Germany story. As we learn, the Germany story is an example of Boaz not turning the other cheek, but it is not the original occasion for this behavior. Germany is a particular instance of a more general stance or alignment, and that stance is occasioned not just by ethnic affiliation but also by family history.

In terms of negation, what distinguishes the Baghdad storyworld from the other storyworlds is that here there is much more explicit contrast between the actually narrated storyworld and its mirror image. In the Baghdad case, the mirror-image storyworld emerges out of the shadow of negation and gets narrated in its own right, merging the two halves of the Baghdad storyworld into one, where the "old breed" vulnerable Jews exist in the same space as the "new breed" tough Jews. In this space, there *was* a pogrom, the Arab Baghdadis "went there and killed" the Jews, the Jews responded with the attitude, "Don't upset them too much." The confrontation of the mirror-image world with its own negation discursively enables the turning point in which a new Jewish subjectivity can be established, and it is here that that subjectivity gets linked with Zionism. Boaz explains that, in the face of the narrated pogrom, "My father, being the first one to join the Zionist movement, was the first one that said well there's no more second cheek. They can't come in here and pogrom us."

Along with this negation comes a placement of Jews in the deictic center—*they* can't *come in here* and pogrom *us*. This serves to anchor the Jews' position in that deictic center. Ironically, however, what enabled this steadfast stance was the father's turn to Zionism and subsequent immigration to Israel. The relationship between Baghdad and the other narrated places is critical for understanding Boaz's orientation toward staying put; the various places in Boaz's stories are used themselves as orientations to a particular stance. It is a *stance* of staying put, but it is not about *actually* staying put. It is about being able to be in control of your actions and comfortable in various places, deciding to stay or leave on your own terms. This is made clear in Boaz's discursive return to Mount Pleasant. He narrates the old vulnerable Baghdad position, and then, with the utterance "Well, you see, to me this doesn't exist," he abruptly shifts back to Mount Pleasant to contrast the Baghdad pre-Zionist Jews with his own contemporary position in Mount Pleasant. Like "We draw blood where we come from" and "I was brought up to be this way . . . you don't turn the other cheek," the utterance "To me this doesn't exist" serves both as a coda to the Baghdad story and an abstract to the closing Mount Pleasant story.

Back to Mount Pleasant: An Aggressively Anchored Stance

> Well, you see—this, to me, doesn't exist. My being here. What I am. Upsets you? You turn around and go. And if you want to make an issue out of it, you'll have to push me out of the way. And because of this, there is the Israeli Defense Forces, who gave me all the training and instilled in me the confidence that, push and shove, I can push as– well as you can, without any, any any uh,

qualms about it, all my— I don't think my grandfather– had that– in him. You see? That's the big difference.

In this conclusion to the set of narratives, Boaz is not an untethered individual walking through the space of Mount Pleasant. Instead, now with the discursive support of his family and his ethnic group, he is firmly anchored "here." It is notable that this is the first place reference to use a proform with no prior direct referent. Using the term "here" allows for flexibility; "here" is any place he is, and any place he may be in the future.

The multiple places and times Boaz has taken us through afford a singular, coherent subject position for him as a person who does not turn the other cheek. This position is discursively enabled by the narration of his father's alignment with Zionism and subsequent move to Israel. And again we see Israel as the unspoken super-deictic center—indexed obliquely by "the Israeli Defense Forces"—that enables him not only to lodge himself in the deictic center of Mount Pleasant but also to resist any attempts to dislodge him. Negation drives home the difference that a Zionist sensibility makes in this regard, in the closing utterances "I can push and shove as well as you can, *without any qualms* about it. I *don't think my grandfather had that in him.* You see? That's the big difference."

Throughout his account, Boaz uses negation to establish his alignment as someone who does not turn the other cheek. As in the Mount Pleasant story, the alignment is both personal and part of membership in a larger "we" group. He accomplishes this by establishing coherence in his actions across time and place.

Conclusion

Orientation in Boaz's account occurs on a continuum of scale, from the localized individual experience to the experience of an ethnic group in several time periods and places to the subject position of the post-Zionist actor who cannot be pushed out of the way. These multiple positions on the continuum accumulate and layer, to strengthen the reputation that Boaz claims. In this continuum, the largest, most overdetermining deictic center, Israel, gets the least invocation. Orientation works at two levels. First, orientation is not placed up front but rather is used strategically, both to shift the deictic center and to provide information more and less precisely and about some things and not others. Orientation is not simply an interactional move to establish shared knowledge. Rather, it is an ideological move that positions the events and the characters at various points along a continuum of historical consequentiality.

Second, each story serves as an orientation for the others. In these narratives, the strategic, embedded use of orientation establishes Boaz as a coherent character, as someone who does not turn the other cheek, across time and place. Coherence contributes to his credibility. It is not the coherence, however, but the negation of an alternative reputation (weak Jews), linked with multiple places, that serves to consolidate his position. He is one kind of person and not another kind, in a dangerous neighborhood in Washington, and this is tied to a larger historical opposition between Jews who turned the other cheek and Jews who did not.

We argue that the juxtaposition of many places, one orienting another, affords the creation of a larger-than-individual overdetermined subject who is who he is because of who he was elsewhere and because of who his father was elsewhere. Boaz is not only a coherent subject who is the same across time and place; he *has to be* who he is now. Each dangerous place presented choices for action; he conflates these into the same kind of danger and the same kind of choice. Because his father made particular choices (to be a Zionist and to emigrate to Israel), there is no other choice but to be a person who does not turn the other cheek.

Finally, this overdetermined subject position is afforded through orientation, negation, and deixis. The strategic use of orientation determines the choices available for action, one negated and one chosen. What happens in Mount Pleasant is conditioned by what happened in Baghdad, which is made possible through Zionism. The implicit allusion to the decision by Boaz's father to move from Baghdad to Israel is critical in that it creates an overarching deictic center for the whole set of narratives, and layers one place and time into another. The creation of a super-deictic center is thus reliant upon its off-recordness, silently created through its omission from orientation and consequent invocation as shared knowledge.

The Zionist subject who does not turn the other cheek conditions not only the events in the past, in Germany and in Baghdad, but also, hypothetically, anything that might happen in the future in Mount Pleasant or anywhere else. The Baghdad story resolves the narrative tension set up in the beginning of the whole discourse—how Boaz's ethnicity is related to his view of Mount Pleasant. The utterance "We draw blood where we come from" only hints at the super-deictic center, and the hinting becomes more pronounced by the mention of Zionism in the Baghdad story. But its power is only revealed in the final segment, with the negation "I don't think my grandfather had that in him." Here, Boaz, unlike his grandfather, "can push as well as you can, without any . . . qualms about it." The choice between pushing and being pushed is, by this point, overdetermined. It is not Boaz, the individual, making this choice but his history and the history of Israel. Anyone in this position would make this choice. By the end, the contradiction—Boaz staying put (in Mount Pleasant) by virtue of having left (Baghdad)—makes perfect sense.

REFERENCES

Bakhtin, Michael. 1981. *The dialogic imagination: Four essays by M. M. Bakhtin.* Trans. Caryl Emerson and Michael Holquist. Austin: University of Texas Press.

Basso, Keith. 1996. *Wisdom sits in places: Landscape and language among the Western Apache.* Albuquerque: University of New Mexico Press.

Baynham, Michael. 2003. Narratives in space and time: Beyond "backdrop" accounts of narrative orientation. *Narrative Inquiry* 13 (2): 347–66.

Berkowitz, Michael. 1993. *Zionist culture and West European Jewry before the First World War.* New York: Cambridge University Press.

De Fina, Anna. 2003. Crossing borders: Time, space, and disorientation in narrative. *Narrative Inquiry* 13 (2): 367–91.

Gaudio, Rudolf P. 1997. Gender in motion through Hausa Muslim discourse and space. Paper presented at the 96th Annual Meeting of the American Anthropological Association, Washington, November.

Georgakopoulou, Alexandra. 2003. Plotting the "right place" and the "right time": Place and time as interactional resources in narrative. *Narrative Inquiry* 13 (2): 413–32.

Greimas, A. J. 1983. *Structural semantics: An attempt at a method.* Lincoln: University of Nebraska Press.
Herman, David. 2001. Spatial reference in narrative domains. *Text* 21 (4): 515–41.
Hill, Jane. 1995. Voices of Don Gabriel. In *The Dialogic Emergence of Culture,* ed. Dennis Tedlock and Bruce Mannheim. Urbana: University of Illinois Press.
Johnstone, Barbara. 1990. *Stories, community and place.* Bloomington: Indiana University Press.
Labov, William. 1972. *Language in the inner city.* Philadelphia: University of Pennsylvania Press.
Maryns, Katrijn, and Jan Blommaert. 2001. Stylistic and thematic shifting as a narrative resource: Assessing asylum seekers' repertoires. *Multilingua* 20 (1): 61–84.
Modan, Gabriella Gahlia. 2007. *Turf wars: Discourse, diversity, and the politics of place.* Malden, MA: Blackwell.
Ochs, Elinor, and Lisa Capps. 2001. *Living narrative: Creating lives in everyday storytelling.* Cambridge, MA: Harvard University Press.
Oz, Amos. 1962. *Under this blazing light.* Cambridge: Cambridge University Press.
Propp, Vladimir. 1968. *Morphology of the folktale, 2nd ed.* Trans. Laurence Scott. Austin: University of Texas Press.
Ricoeur, Paul. 1984. *Narrative and time, volume 1.* Chicago: University of Chicago Press.
Stratton, Jon. 2000. *Coming out Jewish: Constructing ambivalent identities.* London: Routledge.
Toren, Christina. 1995. Seeing the ancestral sites: Transformations in Fijian notions of the land. In *The anthropology of landscape: Perspectives on space and place,* ed. Eric Hirsch and Michael O'Hanlon, 163–83. Oxford: Oxford University Press.

8

Identity Building through Narratives on a Tulu Call-in TV Show

MALAVIKA SHETTY
University of Texas at Austin

IN INDIA, the speakers of Tulu, a Dravidian language with 1.7 million speakers concentrated in the South Kannara region of the state of Karnataka, have largely been linguistically subsumed by the greater number of Kannada speakers (38 million nationwide) around them.[1] In February 2005, Namma TV ("Our TV"), a new television channel, started broadcasting local programs, largely in Tulu, for the first time in the region. Based on recorded episodes from a Tulu call-in TV show, *Pattanga,* on the channel, this chapter looks at how the moderators of and callers to the show use narratives on the show to construct and negotiate a linguistic and cultural identity.[2]

I begin by providing some background on the Tulu language, on the sociolinguistic situation in the South Kannara region, and on the Tulu call-in show *Pattanga.* Next, I look at research on language and identity that informs this study. Finally, I present selected interactions and narratives from recorded episodes of the show that I believe are representative of the process of identity construction that I am discussing in this study and look at how the format of the call-in show is used by viewers and the moderators not only to tell stories but also to construct a Tulu identity and to reconstitute social roles and statuses within the community. The social world is created through talk, along with other forms of action (Johnstone 1990). Thus, narratives do not merely mirror social reality; they create it and perpetuate it.

The Tulu Language

Though Tulu is spoken widely in the South Kannara region, the language does not have a script in current usage. The lack of formal instruction in Tulu and the economic and social predominance of Kannada in the region have, over the centuries, led to the loss of the Tulu script (Kekunnaya 2000). The government of India currently recognizes twenty-two "official languages" in the Eighth Schedule of the Indian Constitution, and Tulu is not one of them. Speakers of the "nonofficial" languages of India constantly vie to be part of the group of the country's recognized languages, because the central government provides funds for the educational and cultural development of these languages. Also, the government-run radio and television stations

(All-India Radio and Doordarshan, respectively) encourage programs in these recognized languages (Krishnamurti 1995). Claiming a Tulu identity is thus an act with, potentially, important political and social ramifications. Claims to a "Tulu identity" could be appropriated by groups whose goal is the projection of the community as a viable group, which could lead to the recognition of Tulu as an official language by the Indian government.

The Sociolinguistic Situation

The South Kannara region is often referred to as Tulunadu ("the place where Tulu is spoken"). Tulu speakers in South Kannara are generally bilingual in Tulu and Kannada, and Tulu is usually the first language they are exposed to in the region. Kannada is often learned later, formally, in school. There are no Tulu schools, nor is Tulu taught as a subject in schools. Kannada, Hindi, Urdu, and English are some of the other languages taught in schools in the region. Tulu speakers there are constantly exposed to Kannada, Hindi, and English on television, in films, and over the radio.

Tulu speakers come from distinct caste-based communities such as the Brahmins (the priestly class—the highest caste), the Billavas (a group that used to be largely engaged in martial arts [*garadi*] and toddy tapping[3]), the Bunts (the farmers and the landowning community), and the Adivasis (the so-called indigenous communities like the Koragas, who live largely outside the mainstream). Though caste lines in urban India have become relatively diffused, in rural India, the hierarchy between the various castes is still very salient. Intermarriage between the various Tulu-speaking communities is rare (Shetty 2003). The lack of social interaction between the castes has led to each caste developing its own social dialect, such as the Brahmin dialect, the Adivasi dialects, and the common dialect (a group of community-based dialects spoken by the Bunts and Billavas, as well as the Mogaveeras, the fishing community) (Kekunnaya 1994, 5). Besides caste dialects, Tulu speakers also speak various regional dialects. Within the social dialects, there are variations depending on which part of the region a Tulu speaker is from. Speakers also come from different class backgrounds, ranging from landowners to day-wage agricultural workers.

The Tulu Call-in Show *Pattanga*

The Tulu call-in show *Pattanga* airs once a week live on cable television and is moderated by two male moderators, Dr. Ganesh Amin Sankamar (GS) and Kadri Navaneet Shetty (NS). The moderators decide on the topic of each episode of the show and field calls from viewers. The common dialect is the variety used by the moderators on the call-in show *Pattanga.* The callers to the show also, largely, speak in the common dialect, with certain regional and social variations. The social, caste, and geographical backgrounds of the various callers to the talk show can be identified from the lexical, phonological, and syntactic variations in the Tulu language they speak. Callers come from different caste and class backgrounds. In a social situation where there is little, if no, intermingling between the various castes, the TV show enables people from different backgrounds to have a dialogue with each other. Tulu women—who do not, as a general practice, speak up before older male members, to male members whom they do not know, or in public forums—call in frequently. An important aspect of the show is that female viewers feel emboldened and empowered enough to call in through a non–face-to-face medium and share their views, knowledge, and experiences. Such interactional data provide an ideal corpus for examining how identity is constructed in discourse and how social constructs like gender, caste, and social class can be constituted as well as reconstituted through language.

Narratives on the Call-in Show

Apart from personal narratives, the narratives on the call-in show are largely based on the *paddanas,* or ritual narratives, that are performed during the rituals for the spirit deities who are worshipped by Tulu speakers in the region. These narratives are legends about the origin of the spirit, its supernatural powers, and its heroic deeds. Tulu speakers consider these spirits their guardian angels and conscience keepers. Claus (1989, 56) refers to the *paddana* as an example of a "multistory" tradition that contains the stories of perhaps dozens of heroes who are often linked with one another by participation in one another's stories. These *paddanas* are orally transmitted from generation to generation and exist in different versions in the various parts of the region. They are performed in the context of a village ritual known as the *bhuta kola,* where men from specific castes narrate the stories of the *bhutas* or spirit deities. They are also told in the rice fields by teams of women transplanting rice. The three main stories that are discussed in the following interactions from the talk show *Pattanga* are those relating to the spirit deities Babbuswami, Jumadi, and Guliga.

The Narrative Construction of Tulu Identity

In this chapter I take the view that identity emerges during interactions, and therefore I look at its situational and contextual emergence during interactional exchanges and through the telling of narratives. I follow a social constructionist approach (Davies and Harré 1990) to language and identity that conceptualizes identity as an interactional accomplishment, produced and negotiated in discourse. Identities, in this approach, are thus not stable and independent of language but are constantly negotiated in the course of interactions. This approach differs from traditional sociolinguistic approaches that link already established social categories with language variables and gives more agency to the individual who is seen as choosing from a variety of acts in a given social situation. For example, in a study of African American drag queens, Barrett (1999, 318) uses the term "polyphonous identity" to convey the idea that linguistic displays of identity are often multivoiced and that speakers may index a multilayered identity by using linguistic variables with indexical associations to more than one social category.[4]

Sacks (1992) showed that identities are interactional achievements rather than a priori categories that exist apart from particular interactions. Identities, according to De Fina, Schiffrin, and Bamberg (2006, 3), are seen not as merely represented in discourse but also as performed, enacted, and embodied through a variety of linguistic and nonlinguistic means. In the context of the call-in show, for example, speakers attempt to establish group identity through the performance of certain linguistic acts, such as the act of praising and the act of evoking common cultural practices. For instance, in the following excerpt from an episode of the show, the moderator GS constructs a common identity for the "people of Tulunadu" by referring to their faith in Babbuswami (also known as Kori Babbu) and encourages viewers to call in and write to the show about the stories surrounding this spirit deity:

"The People of Tulunadu":[5]

1. GS: → Kori Babbune ee namma Tulunadudu wah rithidu nambwere
Kori Babbu.of this our Tulunadu.in what way.of faith
in what way do people in Tulunadu have faith in Kori Babbu?
2. wah rithidu awene mechondu baidere
what way.of of.that show come
in what way do they demonstrate that belief?
3. panpinene aah wole baredu kadaple
saying that letter writing send
that way, write and send us letters.[6]

The fact that Babbuswami is the deity of a small portion of Hindu Tulu speakers who usually belong to lower-caste communities (Upadhyaya and Upadhyaya 2002, 115), though his worshippers come from various Hindu castes, is neither acknowledged nor mentioned. The umbrella term "the people of Tulunadu" (line 1) is used to label an otherwise disparate group of people. They are projected as a cohesive group, and differences between group members are ignored. Group identity is built through referencing commonalities, and differences that may be prejudicial to identity building are consciously overlooked.

Identity is often seen as emerging from the twin concepts of similarity and difference (Woodward 1997). However, in the context of the call-in show, where the moderators make a conscious attempt to portray Tulu speakers as belonging to common social and cultural worlds, the more accurate term to use would be "adequation," as proposed by Bucholtz and Hall (2005, 599). The term "adequation" emphasizes the fact that in order for groups or individuals to be positioned as alike, they need not, and in any case cannot, be identical but must merely be understood as sufficiently similar for current interactional purposes. Differences irrelevant or damaging to ongoing efforts to adequate two people or groups will be downplayed, and similarities viewed as salient to and supportive of the immediate project of identity work will be foregrounded. Thus, on the talk show *Pattanga,* no references are made to the different castes or social classes from which people come or to the different dialects that they speak (I did, however, see one episode featuring a guest who spoke the high-caste Shivalli Brahmin dialect of the language.) The moderators and the callers to the show speak, largely, in the common dialect, and the common dialect is presented as the unmarked language variety. The commonalities between the various communities that make up the group of Tulu speakers are emphasized and the differences between them are either glossed over or ignored.

Irvine and Gal (2000, 38) describe the process of selectively ignoring variation as relying on a semiotic process called "erasure," whereby differences, which are regarded by the dominant ideology of a group to be inconsequential, are either discounted or ignored. The dominant ideology renders some persons or activities invisible; for example, a social group or a language may be imagined as homogeneous, disregarding its internal variation. Thus, on the talk-show *Pattanga,* audience members are portrayed as a cohesive casteless, classless group whose members all largely speak the same dialect. As Bucholtz and Hall (2004, 371) write, social grouping is a process not merely of discovering or acknowledging a similarity that precedes and establishes identity but, more fundamentally, of inventing similarity by downplaying difference.

On the basis of the assumption that narratives are useful units for the study of the emergence of identity in discourse, I now look at how they are used on the TV show, to politically and culturally define a Tulu identity. Baquedano-Lopez (2001) describes how the telling of the narrative of Nuestra Senora de Guadalupe (Our Lady of Guadalupe) in *doctrina* classes composed of Mexican immigrants at a Catholic parish in Los Angeles serves as a locus of Mexican identity construction. Comparing these *doctrina* narratives with the narratives told in catechism classes at the same parish that illustrate a different ideology about Our Lady of Guadalupe and about ethnicity, Baquedano-Lopez points out how narratives can be used to collaboratively redefine the setting of a story in relation to the present participants. Like the narrative of Nuestra Senora de Guadalupe, the narratives on the television show *Pattanga* are collaboratively told and socially managed. The following interaction, for example, is from an episode where the moderator, GS, while talking about the historical reasons behind the name of a local pond, tells a story associated with Agolimanjanna, a legendary local strongman who was reputed to eat a lot:

Using Dominant Narratives

1. GS: Agolimanjanne appene
   Agolimanjanna mother.of
   Agolimanjanna of his mother
2. nenepadu banaga
   while.thinking while.coming
   when he is coming along thinking
3. Karlada bakeru
   Karla.of big.field
   the big field of Karla
4. kangana athodu
   courtyard should.have.become
   should have become the courtyard
5. Kodinjada kalludu
   Kodinja.of stone.with
   with the stone of Kodinja
6. udigere athodu
   curry should.have.been.made
   the curry should have been made

7. Gujara kere per athodu
Gujara pond milk should.have.become
Gujara pond should have become full of milk
8. yena appe Doggu balasodu
my mother Doggu should.have.served.the.meal
my mother Doggu should have served the meal
9. GS:→ [yaan magge Manjannay tinthodu
NS: [yaan magge Manjannay tinodu
I son Manjanna should.have.eaten
(NS: should.eat)
I, son Manjanna, should have eaten
(NS: *should eat)*
10. GS: panthe ge
he.said it.is.said
it is said that he said that
11. NS: *aah*
12. GS: paanda aathu malla kere
that.means that big pond
that means a big pond
13. addu upodu
happened must have been
must have been there
14. Agolimanjanne adde poddu awu keretu
Agolimanjanna there going that pond.in
Agolimanjanna went and in that pond
15. meeyondu ithina anchina
bathing was that.way
used to bathe
16. awu onji kathela aadh upereye yawo
that one story happened was perhaps
that story took place perhaps

In the above excerpt, the moderator GS says that the pond could be one where Agolimanjanna used to take a bath, so it had to be a big one (lines 12–14). In lines 3–8, GS recites the popular verse about Agolimanjanna, and NS and GS both say the last line of the verse together with a small variation in tense (line 9), thereby demonstrating a shared knowledge of the narrative. By referencing the story of Agolimanjanna, GS uses the shared knowledge by Tulu speakers of a certain narrative to create connections between a current local place name and a legendary tale of which most viewers of the show have knowledge.

Ochs and Capps (1996) write that adherence to a dominant narrative is community building, in that it presumes that each member relates to a common story and that narrative constitutes a crucial resource for socializing identities and constituting membership in a community. The shared knowledge of a certain narrative is thus used to draw common ground between disparate groups of people. By evoking the well-known story of Agolimanjanna, GS, the moderator, seeks to connect with the viewers of the show, who also share knowledge of the story by virtue of living in the region. As Johnstone (1990) writes, shared knowledge of a community's stories is part of what creates a sense of community in a group. In this particular instance, the stories serve to highlight what people in the community have in common and to take attention away from their differences, in terms of social class and caste.

Narratives are not only used to mobilize a disparate set of people into a loosely cohesive group. They are also used to highlight community achievements, as can be seen in the following excerpt from the show. The following conversation is taken from an episode in which NS, the moderator, is joined on the show by a guest, PK. C1 is a caller to the show who has been asking PK about the significance of using certain oils for lighting lamps placed before deities. In the following excerpt, NS, the moderator, interjects with a seemingly unrelated story of how a man tried to climb a lamp pole the wrong way:

Highlighting Community Achievements

1. NS: tirthudu mith
   bottom.from top
   from bottom to top
2. wori pothavondu poyye
   one.man lighting went
   one man started lighting (the lamp pole)
3. NS: aa?
4. C1: hmm
5. NS: awe baari aa yethorada deepastamba awe
   that very aa high.of lamp pole that
   that is a very high lamp pole
6. PK: ithinetu
   among (lamp poles)
   among lamp poles
7. NS: ithinetu saadarna namma jilledu
   among.in estimate our region.in
   among (the other lamp poles) I
   estimate in our region
8. PK: andh, andh
   yes yes
9. NS: baari yethora da
   very high of

a very high

10. onji kanchi da deepastamba awe
one bronze of lamp pole that
lamp pole made of bronze that is

11. C1: saari
correct

12. NS: tirthudu mithu ponaga
bottom.from top while.going
while going from bottom to top

13. bokka tirthu japyere aayeji
then bottom climb could.not
then (he) could not climb down

14. athu urri ithindu
that much heat was.there
there was that much heat

15. daada malpuni indh
what to.do like.this
what to do

16. gothu aayeji
knowledge did.not.happen
(he) didn't know

17. deveregu kai mugiye
god.to hand folded
he prayed to god

18. apaga devere kuntu pathyere
then god cloth held.out
god held out a cloth

19. ee laagi pandidh
you jump said
(god) *said, you jump*

20. koontu patheyere panpina onji kathe
cloth held.out saying one story
the story goes that god held out a cloth

21. aanda aayegu laagyere
but he.to jump
but to jump

22. daira bathiji
courage did.not.come
he did not have the courage

23. C1: hmm

24. aaye kere ku laagye
he pond in jumped
he jumped in the pond
25. awul kallu aaye
there stone became.he
there he became a stone
26. panpina anchina onji kathe la oondu
like that one story also is.there
it is said, in a story it is there
27. NS: baari shresthavai ithina ehtora da..
very best is height of
(it) is the highest...
28. C1: *hello hello* (trying to call attention to himself and to his question)
29. NS: kanchi da deepa
bronze of lamp
bronze lamp

In the above excerpt, NS, while narrating the story, talks about how the lamp pole the man is climbing and lighting is the tallest one in the region (lines 5, 7, 9, 10, 27, 29). PK, the guest on the show, agrees with him (lines 6, 8). The caller C1 tries to ask his question (line 28), but NS continues with his narrative. NS's eagerness to tell the story despite the caller's interest in asking a specific question, demonstrates his awareness that the interaction and his narrative are not just being heard by the caller he is addressing but also by other Tulu speakers who are watching the show. The talk that surrounds the main core of the narrative stresses those parts of the narrative that talk about how the lamp pole is the highest one, thereby indexing salient accomplishments and achievements by the community in general. In the above excerpt, NS's main purpose in telling his narrative seems to be to draw attention to the height of the lamp pole and to point out how high it is as compared to other lamp poles. The narrative form is used as a framework by NS to emphasize certain discourse elements, in this case, the unusual height of the lamp pole and, thereby, showcase the achievements of the community. A shared sense of place and the achievements of those who live in that place are thus used to create and build cultural identity.

Creating New Social Roles through Narrative

Narratives reflect social hierarchies, but they also create them. They can be used to perpetuate the social status quo, but they can also be used to bring about social change. The TV show provides a forum for people in the community to call in and narrate their version of a certain folktale or song or myth. The talk show format also gives people from the community the opportunity to call in and contest versions of a shared narrative, narratives that would not be normally contested in ritual settings. Women also feel emboldened enough to challenge versions of the narratives, as can be seen in the following interaction from an episode where the stories related to the spirit deity Babbuswami are being discussed. NS and GS, the moderators, are joined on the show by a guest, MK, who is an "expert" on the spirit deity Babbuswami and has written a book on the deity. MK has just finished narrating his version of the story describing the meeting between the two spirit deities Babbuswami and Jumadi, during which Babbuswami gives a tender coconut to Jumadi to quench his thirst. However, a caller, a woman, C4, who calls in, disagrees with what MK has been saying. She says that the main character in the story with Babbuswami is a different spirit deity, Guliga, and not Jumadi:

"Jumadi or Guliga?"

1. C4: anda yechina kade tu uppuni Jumadi bokka
but most stories in exist Jumadi
then
but in most stories, Jumadi then
2. inde Kori Babbu Gulige
this Kori Babbu Gulige
Kori Babbu and Guliga
3. NS: aah
4. GS: aah
5. C4: wotigu banaga Gulige
together while.coming Guliga
when they were coming together, Guliga
6. bajolodu aaye gu
thirsty.with him.to
he was so thirsty
7. yelu samudra da neer parondula
seven seas of water even.if.he.drank
that even if he drank the waters of seven seas
8. aaye gu bajol tadeji ge
him to thirst did.not.get.over it.is.said
it is said that his thirst was not quenched
9. aah portu gu Gulige ge
that time in Guliga it.is.said
at that time, to Guliga, it is said
10. dada malpwe umbe soojidu wote maltude
what did he needle.with hole made
what does he (Babbuswami) do? He made a hole in the coconut with a needle
11. Babbu bonda korpe ge
Babbu tender.coconut gave it.is.said

and Babbu gave the tender coconut (to Guliga), it is said

12. NS: aah aah

13. C4: aah bondude
that tender.coconut.with
with that tender coconut

14. aayena badao bajol telidini
his hunger thirst quenched
his thirst was quenched

15. panpina matha ithe mulpa matha
they.say everyone now here everyone
now everyone says here

16. kelao mastu kadetu ondu mulpa
many a.lot.of places.in is.there here
in a lot of places the (story) is there

17. NS/GS: andh andh
yes, yes

18. C4: Juma . . . Babbu na kola
Juma . . . Babbu of ritual
Juma . . . Babbu ritual

19. yelanji la nette oondu
day.after.tomorrow even here is.there
is going to be held even day after tomorrow

20. yenkul yepala tupa
we always watch
we always watch (the rituals)

In the above excerpt, the woman caller, C4, points out that in most of the stories she has heard, the characters in the story are Guliga and Babbuswami (also known as Kori Babbu) (lines 1, 2, 5). She says that it was not Jumadi but Guliga to whom Babbuswami offers the tender coconut (lines 9, 10, 11). She disagrees with the expert MK and points out that it is Guliga and not Jumadi who drinks the tender coconut in the actual rituals, which she claims to see very often (line 20). The caller here seems to want to communicate that the knowledge that she has, either by watching the rituals or by sharing stories with other people in the community, has more authenticity than that of a so-called expert who has written a book (lines 15, 16). In other words, the caller seems to claim her knowledge as being more rooted in the sociocultural traditions of the region. As Bauman writes (1992, 131), here the narrator contextualizes the narrative itself, weaving a complex web of verbal anchorings for her discourse that link it to a range of other situations and other discourses, endowing it with traditional authority in the process. The narratives produced on the TV show thus give an opportunity to persons, like the women from the community, whose cultural knowledge has hitherto not been acknowledged or appreciated, to put forward their views and engage in conversations with individuals with whom having a conversation would otherwise be socially unacceptable. The narratives that are produced on the show thus seem to be paving the way for changing attitudes towards how certain types of knowledge are valued or devalued. The people who call in to the show do not, generally speaking, have formal knowledge of the topics they are discussing. The show provides a platform where these kinds of traditional knowledge can be given an outlet and could, potentially, change the way different kinds of knowledge are valorized in the community. Because one's caste and gender has traditionally being linked to the amount of education one could have received (the higher-caste Brahmins are the most educated, and female Tulu speakers, largely, do not have the benefit of a formal education, for example), the show, through the narratives produced on it, is also challenging the traditional views of who can or who cannot possess knowledge. The narratives on the show are also used to potentially change the way the language is perceived by its speakers. This conscious attempt to change the way Tulu is perceived can be seen in the way the caller who has been narrating a story is praised for her Tulu in the following interaction. NS and GS are the two moderators of the show; C4 refers to the caller, a woman:

Valorizing Tulu

1. NS: aah Gulabiakka
   aah Gulabi (name) elder sister
2. C4: aah
3. NS: baari porludu
   very beautifully.in
   very beautifully
4. Tanimanige na kathenu pandaru
   Tanimanige of story you said
   you narrated the story of Tanimaniga[7]
5. C4: aah
6. NS: Sasural da tamane wonasu
   Sasural of felicitation meal
   the meal at Sasural restaurant
7. malpyere eeru eerna illadakul
   to.do you your home.members
   to have, you and your family members
8. pura barodu
   all should.come
   all should come
9. C4: aawe (laughs)
   okay (laughs)
10. NS: aah

11. NS:→ baari porlu da Tulu
very beautiful of Tulu
your Tulu is very beautiful

In line 11, NS, the moderator, tells the caller that her "Tulu is beautiful," and that she has narrated the story very beautifully (lines 3, 4). In actual fact, there was nothing remarkable about the way in which the caller had used language in her narrative, so NS's remark about the beauty of her Tulu indicates a conscious attempt to promote the idea of Tulu as a language that is capable of being beautiful. There seems to be, thus, through the use of narratives and through the comments on the narratives produced on the show, a conscious effort to stress the beauty of the language and also what seems to be a move to change the way Tulu is viewed by its speakers.

Conclusions

The analysis of narratives in this study reveals how narratives can be used as significant tools in the construction and negotiation of identity and to build the cultural identity of a disparate group of people. The study demonstrates that narratives cannot only be used to index a traditional past as a way to bring together a group of people who are, currently, only loosely united by the fact of living in a certain place. Narratives can also be used to authenticate, valorize, and glorify the present. They are thus important interactional resources in the creation and building of group identity. They can be used to highlight community achievements, to create new social roles, and to change the ways in which certain types of knowledge and experience are acknowledged and valued. Narratives can also be employed to change how a language is viewed by its speakers and nonspeakers. Finally, this study demonstrates how, through the medium of a call-in TV show, narratives can become instrumental in overcoming social and gender barriers and are, therefore, potential tools for social change.

NOTES

1. The South Kannara region was divided into the Dakshina Kannada district and the Udupi district in 1997. For the purposes of this study, I refer to the region as the South Kannara region.
2. Episodes were recorded over a two-year period from 2005 to 2007 during fieldwork in the South Kannara region. Ten episodes of the hour-long weekly show were recorded.
3. A popular alcoholic beverage produced by fermenting the sap of the palm tree.
4. Indexicality, according to Ochs (1992), is the property of speech through which social identities and social activities are constituted by certain stances and acts. Besides indexing attitudes and dispositions, indexicality can also communicate certain statuses and gender identities.
5. Transcription conventions (adapted from Keating 1998): The first line shows the Tulu words; the second line, an interlinear gloss, shows a literal translation of the Tulu utterance; the third line, in italics, provides a free translation in English. Also:

[ ]	overlapped speech (two or more speakers speaking at the same time).
NS, GS etc.	capitalized initials indicate the names of the participants.
( )	author's comments.
→	highlights a portion of the transcript for the reader.
she.said	the period between the English words in the interlinear gloss indicates that the Tulu word is made up of a number of concepts that in English would have to be rendered separately.

6. Tulu speakers use Kannada to write.
7. Tanimaniga was a lower-caste woman, regarded to be the spirit deity Babbuswami's sister.

REFERENCES

Baquedano-Lopez, Patricia. 2001. Creating social identities through *doctrina* narratives. In *Linguistic anthropology: A reader,* ed. Alessandro Duranti, 343–58. Malden, MA: Blackwell.

Barrett, Rusty. 1999. Indexing polyphonous identity in the speech of African American drag queens. In *Re-inventing identities: The gendered self in discourse,* ed. Mary Bucholtz, A. C. Liang, and Laurel A. Sutton, 313–31. New York: Oxford University Press.

Bauman, Richard. 1992. Contextualization, tradition, and the dialogue of genres: Icelandic legends of the *Kraftaskald.* In *Rethinking context: Language as an Interactive phenomenon,* eds. Alessandro Duranti and Charles Goodwin, 125–45. Cambridge: Cambridge University Press.

Bucholtz, Mary, and Kira Hall. 2004. Language and identity. In *A companion to linguistic anthropology,* ed. Alessandro Duranti, 369–94. Malden, MA: Blackwell.

———. 2005. Identity and interaction: A sociocultural linguistic approach. *Discourse Studies* 7: 585–614.

Claus, Peter J. 1989. Behind the text: Performance and ideology in a Tulu oral tradition. In *Oral epics of India,* ed. Stuart H. Blackburn, Peter J. Claus, Joyce B. Flueckiger, and Susan S. Wadley, 55–74. Berkeley: University of California Press.

Davies, Bronwyn, and Rom Harré. 1990. Positioning: The social construction of selves. *Journal for the Theory of Social Behavior* 20:43–63.

De Fina, Anna, Deborah Schiffrin, and Michael G. W. Bamberg. 2006. *Discourse and identity: Studies in interactional sociolinguistics.* Cambridge: Cambridge University Press.

Irvine, Judith T., and Susan Gal. 2000. Language, ideology, and linguistic differentiation. In *Regimes of language: Ideologies, polities, and identities,* ed. Paul V. Kroskrity, 35–84. Santa Fe: School of American Research Press.

Johnstone, Barbara. 1990. *Stories, community, and place: Narratives from middle America.* Bloomington: Indiana University Press.

Keating, Elizabeth L. 1998. *Power sharing: Language, rank, gender, and social space in Pohnpei, Micronesia.* New York: Oxford University Press.

Kekunnaya, Padmanabha. 1994. *A comparative study of Tulu dialects.* Udupi, India: Rashtrakavi Govind Pai Research Center.

———. 2000. *The Tulu language.* www.yakshagana.com/Tulu.htm.

Krishnamurti, Bh. 1995. Official language policies with special reference to the Eighth Schedule of the Constitution of India. In *Language and the state: Perspectives on the Eighth Schedule,* ed. Anvita Abbi, R. S. Gupta, and Kailash S. Aggarwal, 8–23. New Delhi: Creative Books.

Ochs, Elinor. 1992. Indexing Gender. In *Rethinking context: Language as an interactive phenomenon,* ed. Alessandro Duranti and Charles Goodwin, 335–58. Cambridge: Cambridge University Press.

Ochs, Elinor, and Lisa Capps. 1996. Narrating the self. *Annual Review of Anthropology* 25:19–43.

Sacks, Harvey, and Gail Jefferson. 1992. *Lectures on conversation, volume I.* 2 vols. Oxford: Blackwell.

Shetty, Malavika. 2003. Language contact and the maintenance of the Tulu language in South India. In *Proceedings of the Eleventh Annual Symposium about Language and Society Austin (SALSA XI),* ed. Wai Fong Chiang, Elaine Chun, Laura Mahalingappa, and Siri Mehus. Texas Linguistic Forum 47.

Upadhyaya, U. Padmanabha, and Susheela P. Upadhyaya. 2002. *Folk rituals (of the Tuluva region of coastal Karnataka).* Udupi: Regional Resources Centre for Folk Performing Arts.

Woodward, Kathryn, ed. 1997. Identity and difference: Culture, media, and identities. London: Sage.

9

Blank Check for Biography?: Openness and Ingenuity in the Management of the "Who-Am-I Question" and What Life Stories Actually May Not Be Good For

MICHAEL BAMBERG
Clark University

IN RECENT PUBLICATIONS, Alexandra Georgakopoulou and I (Bamberg 2007; Bamberg and Georgakopoulou 2008; Georgakopoulou 2007a, 2007b) have put forth the argument that life stories—that is, stories in which tellers cover their personal past from early on, leading up to the "here and now" of the telling situation—are extremely rare. People never really tell the true details of their lives, unless for very particular circumstance—as, for example, in life story interviews, and occasionally in therapeutic interviews. Of course, this is not entirely true. There indeed are occasions, although these cannot be characterized as typical everyday and mundane situations either, in which people opt for something like a life story in an attempt to do damage control to their (public) image.[1] Here I use one such incident to show how life stories provide a welcomed repertoire that on one hand seemingly opens up the narrator's subjectivity, displaying genuinely personal information, but on the other hand does exactly the opposite: counteracting and undermining its goal of displaying openness and ingenuity.

In our ongoing discussions with Mark Freeman, in which we push for the investigation of small stories (Bamberg 2007; Freeman 2007; Georgakopoulou 2007b), we also have argued that work with narrative in the domain of identity analysis can no longer be restricted to the textual, referential level of what a story is about. Instead, narrative analysis, as exemplified in small story analysis, should aim to increasingly incorporate how the choice of linguistic devices is contextualized.[2] In other words, suprasegmentation, facial expression, and gesture—all in coordination with how language is put to use—need to be scrutinized in as much detail as possible. However, most of the time, there is no camera, or even set of cameras, that record the interaction from different angles—let alone on those rare occasions when life stories are shared.

The story I have chosen for analysis in this chapter, however, has been videotaped and is publicly available. It surfaced in the form of an interview that the politician John Edwards gave to Bob Woodruff, a reporter for ABC News, and was aired

August 8, 2008, on ABC's television newscast *Nightline.* In this interview Woodruff probes questions into Edwards's personal and private affairs. And as the interviewer makes clear to the audience at the beginning, Edwards is not only willing to answer these very private and personal questions but had also *asked* for them *to be asked*—to be able, as he states: "*to tell the truth so they* [the American people] *know the truth and they . . . know it from me.*"

This, as it appears, presents an interesting case from a big story orientation using narrative data to pursue identity analysis. We do have the usual constellation of an interview in which the interviewer asks the interviewee the who-are-you question. However, in contrast to the typical biographical setup, the interviewee has approached the interviewer, so that he, the interviewee, can answer the who-am-I question. In other words, we do not have to train the interviewer in techniques that tease out the answer to the who-am-I question; rather, the interviewee will volunteer the answers and the interviewer can lean back, be his normal, average self, and ask the kinds of questions anyone else would ask in this kind of situation.

The Data: The Interview and Its Context

The place of the interview is the Edwards's home in North Carolina; at least three cameras are present: Camera 1 presents the interviewer and interviewee as equally visible; camera 2 shows a close-up of the interviewer—with the interviewee's back partly visible; and camera 3 presents a full facial close-up on the interviewee. What actually was aired on August 8 has been pieced together into a 16½-minute exchange of answers and questions; that is, the viewer sees excerpts and does not know whether these excerpts were shot in sequence and how these segments were cut and edited into the final version. What was seen in the final edition on August 8 was a rotation between the three different camera angles, predominantly focusing on Edwards's face, particularly when he was speaking. In addition, ABC published a transcript on its website (www.abc.com). However, incorporated in the transcripts are excerpts that were not included in the aired interview. In addition, there were passages in the aired interview that were not included in the transcript.[3]

For the reader who is not familiar with the events that preceded this interview, John Edwards is a former North Carolina senator. He was a leading Democratic presidential candidate in 2004 and in 2008, and he also ran for vice president in 2004 in the election campaign with John Kerry. Until recently he was widely considered one of the leading voices in the Democratic Party, and then he was reported to have had an extramarital affair in 2006 while his wife Elizabeth's cancer was in remission. He had repeatedly denied the affair, but on July 21, 2008, he was confronted by reporters for the *National Inquirer* when leaving the Beverly Hilton Hotel, where he had met with the woman with whom he was alleged to have had the affair—which, in addition, was said to have resulted in her having a baby.

After the interview was aired, in the next four days, discussions erupted in the media. A number of blogs popped up, reflecting a large public interest in the story.[4] Though at the beginning the discussions centered on the moral question of Edwards's actions, they quickly shifted to whether he is trustworthy in that interview or lying, and what made him go on television and volunteer this interview in the first place.

In sum, the public became intrigued with the *real* John Edwards—the man who is married to a woman with cancer, who had an affair with another woman, who ran for vice president, and who gave that interview on *Nightline.* Monday, three days after the interview, this discussion raged across morning shows, and the same night, during *Inside Edition,* a "body language expert," Tonya Reiman, declared "I can tell you he's being honest when he was talking about *I didn't think I was ever going to get caught,* because there's not much changing in his facial expression, there's no movement." And she continued: "The expression that really surprised me was the smile. . . . He's coming out to discuss that he's an adulterer and he starts out by laughing, so my impression is that he's trying to mask the true emotions that he has: guilt, remorse, shame."

In contrast to discussing the topic of his honesty, here I focus on three brief excerpts from the interview and analyze how the interviewee's excursion into biographical detail can be taken to constitute attempts to answer the who-am-I question, and I conclude that biographical detail may be the wrong device for occasions like this. The segments chosen for analysis are three brief passages in which Edwards talks about his life and the person he is. Excerpt (i) surfaces almost two minutes into the aired interview and lasts 1 minute, excerpt (ii) follows 12 seconds after segment (i) ends, and excerpt (iii) lasts 5 seconds and ends 25 seconds before the end of the interview. Obviously, the viewer of the whole interview (or reader of the transcript) has more than these three excerpts to form an opinion vis-à-vis Edwards's identity. However, the three excerpts are the ones in which he explicitly makes claims as to what kind of person he is, how he came to be who he is, and his involvement in this as an agent and/or victim. In other words, he claims to *explain* how he became who he is, laying out his biography—although only briefly: the consistencies and changes across his life course, his own agentive involvement in these changes, and how he differs from others but at the same time is the same as everyone else.

Identity, Sense of Self, and the Who-Am-I Question

Although designing characters as protagonists and antagonists in fictitious time and space can open up new territories for identity exploration—with the potential to transgress traditional boundaries and test out novel identities—narratives of factual past events are dominated by a rather different orientation. The delineation of what happened, whose agency was involved, and the potential transformation of characters in the course of events are firmly in the service of demarcating and fixing the identity under investigation. If past-time narration is triggered by the *who-am-I question*—that is, having the quest for identity or sense of self of the narrator as its goal—then there is no space for ambiguity, boundary transgression, and the exploration of novel identities. On the contrary, the goal is to condense and unite, to resolve ambiguity as much as possible, and hopefully come up with an answer that lays further inquiry into one's own past and identity to rest.

However, the reduction of identity to the depiction of characters and their development in what the story is about leaves out the communicative space within which identities are negotiated and the role that narration takes in this space. Reducing narratives to what they are about irrevocably reduces identity to be depicted through the referential or representational level of speech activities—disregarding the real life in which identities are under construction, formed, and performed. However, it is within the space of everyday talk in interaction that narration plays an important function in the formation and navigation of identities as part of everyday practices and for its potential function to orient toward "the human good." Nevertheless, although identity and our sense of who we are both are necessarily acquired in our everyday practices, there seem to be some overarching dilemmas, if not aporias, that need to be tackled.

The three most pressing dilemmas center on (1) issues of "*continuity and change,*" posing the question how it is possible to consider oneself to remain the same across time, let alone a lifetime, in the face of constant change; (2) issues of "*uniqueness and conformity,*" whether it is possible to consider oneself as unique in the face of being the same as every other person (and vice versa); and (3) around issues of "*agency* and *construction*" (or "*who is in charge*"), asking whether it is the person, the *I*-as-subject, who constructs the world the way it is, or whether the person (*me*) is constructed by the way the world is, in which *I* (as undergoer) am subjected to it. And although these dilemmas may sound at first quite abstract, they surface in every turn in making sense in interaction with one another.

Attempting to resolve these dilemmas in terms of positing an intrinsic dialectic between (1) constancy and change, (2) uniqueness/specificity and generality/universality, and (3) the two directions of fit, from person to world and from world to person, points up correctly that the three dilemmas are linked with each other in a number of illuminating ways. Constraining the analysis of identity and identity formation to one of the dilemmatic areas will not suffice. Empirical work in the domain of identity research faces the task of tying these three contradictions together: Viewing the narrating subject (1) as not locked into stability nor drifting through constant change, but rather as something that is multiple, contradictory, and distributed over time and place but contextually and locally held together; (2) as positioning self in terms of membership claims vis-à-vis *others;* and (3) as agentive, though simultaneously situated and contextualized in a sociocultural context. Along these lines, identity is not confined by just one societal discourse and can change and transform and consequently better adapt to the challenges of historical change and their increasing cultural multiplicity in an increasingly globalizing environment.

Starting from the assumption that narration is a verbal act that is locally performed in situated interactional contexts, its function in identity formation processes cannot be reduced to the verbal messages conveyed. Rather, the local interactional contexts in which narrative units emerge form the foundation for the inquiry of identity formation and sense of self. Though transformations from oral to written forms of text traditions are widely studied within the long-standing frame of the hermeneutic cycle, work with transcripts from audio records is relatively new. Much newer, and becoming rapidly more sophisticated, are concerted efforts to audiovisually record narrations and to analyze how they emerged in interaction, including the sophisticated ways in which they were performed. Audiovisual material, of course, can be more microanalytically scrutinized in terms of the contextualized coordination of narrative form, content, and stylizations of performance features in the service of identity formation processes.

An Analysis of Edwards's Story

Excerpt (i) (shortly after the opening of the interview): Having stated for the overhearing audience that people have an enormous sympathy for Edwards's wife Elizabeth and that she (also) was going through cancer, the interviewer ended with the question "how could you have done this?"—with a falling intonation—framing his turn to be followed up by the interviewee as an act of defense.

W: . . . how could you (.5) have done this ↓ =
E: =can I explain to you what happened ↑ (0.5) uhm eh
first of all it happened during a period
after she was in remission from cancer
that's no excuse in any possible way for what happened
this is what happened ↓
I grew up as a small-town boy in North Carolina
you know
came from nothing
worked very hard
eh dreamed that I'd be able to do something hopeful eh
helpful to other people with my life
I became a lawyer
ehm through a lot of work and success I eh got eh some
acclaim as a lawyer
people were telling me
oh he's such a great person
such a great lawyer
such a talent
you're gonna go no telling what you'll do
and this is when I was thirty thirty-one years old
then I went from being a senate young ↑ senator
to being considered for vice president
running for president
being a vice presidential candidate
and becoming a national public figure
all of which <.5> fed <.5> a self-focus
and egotism
and narcissism
that leads you to believe
that that you can do whatever you want
you're invincible
and no and there'll be no consequences
and//
W //so you
E nothing <.5> nothing could be further from the truth
W so your assumption was . . .

I will briefly work through the first excerpt with a focus on the management of the three identity dilemmas mentioned above: Edwards reacts to the interviewer's challenge of his moral standards (line 1) by asking (back) for permission to *explain* (2)—which is hearable as a deferential act though framing his upcoming account as an explanation. After a brief excursion into the time frame when *it* happened (3–5), he repeats his preannouncement from line 2, reannouncing that there is a string of events that will serve as an explanation (line 6). It is of interest that he chooses to give an account in terms of what happened, that is, a chain of events that can be taken to serve as the answer to Woodruff's initial question, instead of, for instance, a simple character description (e.g., *because I sinned* or *I am bad;* or worse: *I was born bad and I didn't change*).

Starting with line 7, Edwards launches into a narrative that positions himself as a character in the remote past of his boyhood (7), coming *from nothing* (9) but working *very hard* (10) and having dreams of doing good to others later on in life (11–12). Using his childhood and North Carolina as the spatiotemporal setting, he presents himself as a character who is agentively moving himself in an upward trajectory from childhood to adolescence, as someone who anticipates a future and makes it happen; and in all this work and success are stressed as the factors that made this possible, all the way up to a lawyer (lines 13–15).

At this point, however, Edwards's style of self-characterization changes. Subsequent from here, he is presented (presents himself) in a recipient/undergoer position. Others are taking the role of agents; they see something in him and become the incentive force for his *going somewhere* (lines 16–21). This design of self-presentation through the voices of others is maintained for what *became* of him in the years after he turned thirty-something (lines 22–26) and culminates in his summary statement: "*All of which fed a self-focus and egotism and narcissism that leads you to believe . . . you are invincible*" (27–33).

The events recapitulated span the lifetime of a fifty-five-year old: from childhood to a successful adult man. The overarching cohesive device by use of which these events are connected is one of change (in contrast to constancy): from an agentive character toward one that is more passive, from someone who had to work hard for success to someone who was moved into a career in politics. And the position from where this process is stitched together is not only retrospective but one from where success became handed down on a silver platter; symbolizing an inherent negative devaluation for a self—for any self. Though his story started out with the self (his self) in subject position (7–15), the *I* fades into the background, to ultimately be replaced in lines 30–32 by *you.* This use of *you* is most likely to be heard as the "inclusive you" (everyone, including the speaker), marking the change from "who I used to be," a special little boy in North Carolina, to who I am now, someone who is a "national public figure" (26) but ultimately just like everyone else when it comes to being corrupted into self-interest: an ordinary everyone, a *you.* In sum, Edwards navigates skillfully the balancing act with regard to the self/other dilemma: *I* started out special, and although it looked as if I became even more special in my career as a politician and national public figure, when it comes to our egos and narcissisms, I am just an ordinary person—just like you. The membership categories he alludes to (small farm boy, hard worker, becoming a helpful lawyer) are set up and juxtaposed against a career in politics (being *a great lawyer, running for president*), aligning him as speaker with the master narrative of politics and publicity as corrupting otherwise noble characters.

In addition to Edwards's navigation of the identity dilemma of presenting himself as different and same vis-à-vis others, he manages to navigate both other dilemmas equally well: There is change over time. Though the rhetoric of youth in biographical reasoning typically is employed as a time for mistakes, due to immaturity and lack of experience, against which later life can stand out as the quest for an improving (moral) sense of self, Edwards opts for a different trajectory: When you are young, you are less subjected to the complexities of life, particularly the fast pace of a career in the public realm, and therefore much less self-centered and concerned with yourself. Similarly, his agency across his life course is said to have decreased. He constructs a sense of young self that was highly agentive and accountable—where accountability is usually assumed to go along with responsibility—but over time his agency diminished, and this may not only have implications for a claim with regard to responsibility but also with the negative values attributable to the public status of celebrities.[5]

Line 36 has been left out of the analysis thus far because it is not part of the story. Rather, it characterizes an overall evaluative stance—where it is not clear whether Edwards denies the assumption that *you* (as in *we:* everybody) are invincible, asserting that human deeds actually *do* have consequences. This certainly is one possibility; and it actually would explain why he is on *Nightline,* doing just that, explaining. However, the viewer also could interpret this statement to imply that he is taking back his story—that he actually does not see himself as changed. He may not even see himself in terms of diminished agency, and politics maybe isn't all that bad. We will pick up the ambiguity that is not resolved at this point after our discussion of excerpts (ii) and (iii).

Excerpt (ii) (following shortly after excerpt i): Excerpt (ii) follows the first only 12 seconds later and is preceded by Edwards's reaction to Woodruff's question about whether he did not think he would get caught. Edwards responds by alluding to the length of the affair ("it was short") and that it was a judgment mistake. At that point he returns to his life story by orienting the audience to what is important about it (him):

E: and <1.0> and the important thing is
how I could ever get to the place
to that place
and allow myself to let that happen
and I believe the reason it happened
is because I'd gone through this lo::ng process
where I became
at least on the outside
something different

than that young boy who grew up in a small town
in North Carolina
and coz that young boy would never have done this
never thought about doing it to his family to his wife

Although Edwards's life story in segment (i) was foreshadowed twice, his reference to the "important thing" serves as a discursive device to refer back and condense a previous stretch of discourse. Line 2 clarifies that Edwards is referring to the story captured in segment (i). "*The* place" in line 2 is changed to "*that* place" (3) (in parallel to where I let *that* happen line 4), which usually denotes a more distant position, particularly if *that* is made the explicit choice that is supposed to override his previous use of *the.* Starting with line 5, he once more delves into the *reason* for what happened, going back to W's original question "How could you"?—and it is "this lo::ng process" that is given prominence in terms of how this change came about. In terms of how the speaker positions his agency and responsibility, it is the process that is made the semantic agent; and judging from his intonation, the length of that process contributed significantly to what happened.

Here, in excerpt (ii), Edwards skips the details of the course of time laid out in excerpt (i) and orients his audience from the end point of his developmental process (the here and now) back to his beginnings, for which he claims the right family values to be in place. This certainly supports our analysis of excerpt (i) and it also removes an interpretation we were left hanging with above: whether possibly his disclaimer in line 36 was an attempt to take back his story. This interpretation does not seem to hold. Rather, he reinstates his story with its emphasis on change, and he attempts to once more bring it to the point where the claims of change and diminishing agency coincide. However, now with a new concession in line 8: "at least on the outside." This comes somewhat as a surprise; if the viewer is instructed through the details of the story in excerpt (i), and repeated here in its gist of excerpt (ii), to make a distinction between his original self and his now corrupted self, we are told in line 8 that there is a difference between his inside self and an *outside* self. The outside self is the one that is apparent to the superficial onlooker who sees change where there actually may be constancy, and who may lay blame to the internal self while other agentive forces may have forced themselves onto the outside self—leaving the internal self untouched. Thus, underneath or behind this *outside* is the internal self—and presumably it is *the real* one, lingering on from his childhood—something politics, success, and narcissism were not able to replace?

Excerpt (iii) (close to the end of the interview): Excerpt (iii) follows up on the interviewer's question about how Edwards's supporters who thus far trusted him would see him now. Implied in this question is an underlying assumption that the change claimed by Edwards is posing a challenge to the public's sense of a continuous identity, a challenge that requires the interviewee again to address his position on change versus constancy. Edwards briefly reiterates the purpose of the interview "to tell the truth"—which the public will hear from him. Then, he summarizes his position on the constancy/change dilemma in the following two lines:

1 E: I am no different from the person they knew
2 I'm at my core exactly the same person

These claims come as a surprise when compared with the claims Edwards made in the previous two excerpts with regard to how he had navigated constancy and change thus far, and what he claimed had caused that change—even though Edwards already hinted at a difference between what may be visible from the outside and what *is* inside. Here, the claim is that the core, his *real self* at the inside, never changed. The small boy is alive—and even more so, it is claimed to be his core, true, and authentic self. We will revisit this seeming contradiction below.

Analysis of Edwards's Storying Performance

As I argued above, to reduce answers of the who-am-I question to people's verbal responses, and the analysis of identity to the analysis of those responses, would not do justice to the ways selves and identities express themselves and navigate everyday situations. In the remainder of working toward a better understanding of how biographical identities are made use of in interview situations, I focus on one other important nonverbal means of communication: facial expression. Unfortunately, the use of gestures, particularly the use of the hands, is not available from camera angle three from where the focus is on John Edwards's face (see figure 9.1).

In response to Woodruff's "*how-could-you* challenge," Edwards leans slightly forward into the interviewer, with raised eyebrows, gazes fully toward Woodruff, and asks back "can I explain what happened" (line 2). His demeanor is deferential—not defensive—but he assertively presents a knowing sense of self, inviting the audience into his "knowing position." When he repeats this introduction for his biographical tour through his life stages in line 6, the camera focuses for a moment on the interviewer—suggesting that some other piece or pieces of what has been said may have been edited out. Starting from his boyhood, he works himself into a narrative style that is oriented toward the interviewer. With line 16, Edwards

Figure 9.1 The Focus on John Edwards's Face as He Says *"Can I Explain What Happened,"* Excerpt (i), Line 2

Source: Clip from the interview with John Edwards on *Nightline*, ABC Television Network, August 8, 2008.

Figure 9.2 The Focus on John Edwards's Face as He Says (on the left) *"People Were Telling Me,"* Excerpt (i), Line 16; and (on the right) *"Such a Great Person,"* Excerpt (i), Line 17
Source: Clip from the interview with John Edwards on *Nightline*, ABC Television Network, August 8, 2008.

changes his posture into a more upright and erect position; he moves his head back, pulling his eyebrows down so that his eyes become narrow (figure 9.2). This facial expression is joined by a slight headshake; and this facial demeanor is maintained all the way to line 21. Overall, facial expression, head shaking, and his move into a backward, more erect posture join forces with verbally deferring agency to others—what they have made of him. As such, these lines contrast starkly with his forward orientation and open face expression when talking about himself as young agent (lines 7–15).

With the following lines, where he refers to his career as a politician (lines 22–26), he returns to what we could call his narrative baseline: leaning slightly into the interviewer, no frown, no headshake. However, when he refers to the three negative features (*self-focus, egotism, narcissism*), which mark the outcome and the high point of his career development, the same kind of skepticism and distance return to his bodily demeanor and facial display. Then, in line 36, this distance is replaced by a light and short smile, coinciding with the second mention of *nothing,* and a bit stronger with *further* (figure 9.3).

Figure 9.3 The Focus on John Edwards's Face as He Says (on the left) *"Nothing,"* Excerpt (i), Line 36; and (on the right) *"Further,"* Excerpt (i), Line 36
Source: Clip from the interview with John Edwards on *Nightline*, ABC Television Network, August 8, 2008.

Figure 9.4 The Focus on John Edwards's Face as He Says (on the left) *"Never Have Done This,"* Excerpt (ii), Line 12; and (on the right) *"Exactly the Same,"* Excerpt (iii), Line 2
Source: Clip from the interview with John Edwards on *Nightline*, ABC Television Network, August 8, 2008.

What his facial expression can be taken to index is a personal distancing vis-à-vis what others have done to his "original" identity. His life as a boy and his accomplishments for which he claims agency are told in a style that indexes comfort; in contrast, the influence of others on him is indexed as causing discomfort. When he appeals in line 36 to *the truth,* he returns to the narrative style of signaling "comfort"; his bodily cues signal a frame from boyhood (back then) to the truth (the here and now), providing continuity to his biographical self.

This interpretation is confirmed by a closer look at excerpt (ii). Referring to how he became different from *that young boy* and how he would have acted (lines 9–13), Edwards leans forward, raises his eyebrows, and again invites the audience into his "knowing position." His eyes then become narrow and display a critical distance and disapproval of the actions alluded to (e.g., adultery). Finally, in excerpt (iii), Edwards's display of a light smile, comfortably leaning back, and closing eyes seal his biography: He confidently shows (and tells) that the young boy and he speaking in the here and now are one and the same person. His smile, contextualized this way, may be taken as masking guilt, remorse, or shame, as suggested by "body language expert" Tonya Reiman. However, if we pay close attention to the sequential display of facial and verbal expression, it is more safe to interpret his smile as providing a local cue for how he positions himself as confidently underscoring the moral stance he has taken vis-à-vis *what happened:* I *explained* what happened—and *myself.* My position is one of continuity: I am the same person I used to be (figure 9.4).

Summary and Conclusions

Before I launch into a brief and final discussion of the analysis thus far, it should be clear that both analyses—the analysis of the text as well as of facial expressions—could have been more refined and elaborated, and, in addition, supplemented by the analysis of other expressive modalities, providing more evidence for the overall orientation suggested in this chapter. Though one aim here is to demonstrate how small story analysis begins to incorporate multimodal forms of analysis into identity research, the second aim is to demonstrate the limits of biographical material.

Returning to Edwards's navigation of the three identity dilemmas, he characterizes himself as a young boy in highly agentive terms, and he claims this sense of who he was as pertaining to the here and now. It is his *inside* or *core self,* as he calls it, that always was in place—and is brought out back into the open in this interview—fully visible to the viewers. In terms of differentiating himself from others, he marks himself as a member of two categories: (1) the North Carolinian, hard-working male who works his way up the sociopolitical ladder; and (2) the young overachiever who gets catapulted by others into popularity and celebrity status. Being a member of the second category causes him discomfort, and he displays his critical distance by way of verbal and facial (physical) means. Remember that it is his membership in this category that he framed as the cause for *what happened.* So he marks it off as imposed and antithetical to his *real* identity. Now, if we as onlookers of the interview or as interpreters of biographies are looking for a coherent presentation of someone's sense of self, the data are contradictory. Either Edwards changed—and his explication stands: He went from good to bad, but his bad was imposed by others. Or he did not change, and he is still the same boy he used to be—but in this case, what happened should never have happened. How can he have it both ways?

The answer lies in the functions that biographies can serve—and what they may not be good for; as the brief excerpts from Edwards's interview document, navigating identity is profoundly dilemmatic. Asking the who-am-I question—or, with the data at hand, being confronted with the who-are-you question as in Edwards's case—is business that results in navigating at least three dilemmas, continuity/change; sameness/difference with respect to others; and last but not least, agency (who's to blame). This means that answers in the form of identity narrations will never be simple or clear, especially when having to do some heavy-duty moral accounting.

This has two sets of consequences, one for the use of biographical data in appeals to the public, the other for biography and biography research more generally. The first can best be put forth in the form of a piece of advice: The attempt to answer the who-am-I question in a way that attempts to reaffirm who I really am—that is, to make a claim to authenticity and truth—is problematic. Factual narratives work within the same boundaries and presuppositions as fictional narratives. They are excellent means to test out identities, to explore, and to revise. And this can be done—with a helpful interviewer—in therapy or research settings, or in everyday interactions, where we have demonstrated repeatedly the function of small stories in positioning identities, taking them back, and revising them—in short, in testing out boundaries and engaging in identity practices. Laying claim to and positioning a real or authentic self in narratives distorts and deflects from what narratives "are good for." In navigating identity dilemmas, (i) setting up boundaries between *I* and *you* and simultaneously flattening them, (ii) maintaining that we are the same young boy we used to be but having to account for our actions in adult-like categories, and (iii) navigating agency in terms of credit and blame are excellent territories for identity formation processes—maybe even for truth seeking—but problematic for holding claims to authenticity and truth.

NOTES

1. Being reminded that some people sit down to write their life stories, because they "have a life" that *needs to be told*—or, for that matter, have others write their life stories, is a very different situation that would require a separate discussion.
2. There seem to be some serious misunderstandings of what the terms "context" and "contextualization" stand for. Context is not the surroundings of language and text! Rather, language and texts are aspects of how speakers contextualize, i.e., cue how they want to be understood in situations (contexts).
3. It appears that the transcript has been made from excerpts that were originally considered to be aired but then dropped for a more refined and "cleaned-up" version.
4. Between August 8 and 12, www.abc.com counted 1,160 people who posted an opinion on their Blotter, and 60 more who commented on the transcripts from the interview.
5. It may be noteworthy that Edwards's appeal to the equation of (his) celebrity status and (shallow) ethical values in his interview occurred in the same days as John McCain's endorsement to present Barack Obama side by side with protocelebrities Britney Spears and Paris Hilton.

REFERENCES

Bamberg, Michael. 2007. Stories: Big or small—Why do we care? In *Narrative: State of the art,* ed. M. Bamberg, 165–74. Amsterdam: John Benjamins.

Bamberg, Michael, and Alexandra Georgakopoulou. 2008. Small stories as a new perspective in narrative and identity analysis. *Text & Talk* 28:377–96.

Freeman, Mark. 2007. Life "on holiday." In *Narrative: State of the art,* ed. M. Bamberg, 155–63. Amsterdam: John Benjamins.

Georgakopoulou, Alexandra. 2007a. *Small stories, interaction and identities.* Amsterdam: John Benjamins.

———. 2007b. Thinking big with small stories in narrative identity analysis. In *Narrative: State of the art,* ed. M. Bamberg, 146–54. Amsterdam: John Benjamins.

10

Reflection and Self-Disclosure from the Small Stories Perspective: A Study of Identity Claims in Interview and Conversational Data

ALEXANDRA GEORGAKOPOULOU
King's College London

IN THIS CHAPTER I examine the close association of reflection (henceforth R) and self-disclosure (S-D) within biographical studies with the storyteller's explicit, and by extension "evaluative," ascriptions and statements about self (cf. Bamberg, in press). In other words, how do tellers *propositionalize* about their lives? The association of R and S-D is part and parcel of certain assumptions, in particular that, in order for tellers to reflect on their lives and selves and to open up (self-disclose) to an interviewer, they must have a critical distance from the reported events and be given the opportunity to piece them together in a life story within an interview situation (cf. Freeman 2006).

Thus, once storytellers start talking about their internal states and feelings, likes and dislikes, and themselves as being "X" or "Y," analysts take those statements to be signals of "who" they are in a more or less "continuous" or "stable" way, and also of what value social identities (e.g., gender, class, ethnicity) have for them. As we will see below, this association has not been without its critique. However, my aim here is to take it on board and interrogate its validity and applicability to a corpus of both interview and conversational stories. Specifically, I examine self-ascriptions and other-ascriptions, assessments/characterizations, and categorizations of the kind that social science interview analysts tend to focus upon, what I call *self-identity claims* and *other-identity claims.* To do so, however, I align with the assumptions, concerns, and tools of small stories research, as I outline them below. My questions are: How do the occurrence and sequential management of identity claims differ in the interview versus the conversational narrative data? What interactional actions do identity claims perform in each environment? And what do such differences tell us about the ways in which tellers do self? Finally, what are the implications of such differences for the ways in which R and S-D have been conceptualized with the biographical studies paradigm?

Small Stories Research

In recent work, my colleagues and I have proposed small stories (Georgakopoulou 2006, 2007; Bamberg and Georgakopoulou 2008) as an alternative to canonical narrative studies that sets out to include certain underrepresented activities in the focal concerns of narrative and identity analysis. Space restrictions here do not allow the discussion of the definition and identification of small stories (but see Georgakopoulou 2007, chap. 2). Here, however, I briefly list the four main points of divergence of small stories from biographical work assumptions:

1. Emphasis on breaking news, stories of the future, and hypothetical and shared events in contrast to the emphasis on stories of past, personal, nonshared events. This was the starting point of small stories research, namely, the frequency and salience of certain types of stories that departed from the Labovian prototype of past, personal experience told in nonshared stories in conversational settings (Labov 1972). In particular, in my study of Greek female adolescents (Georgakopoulou 2007), stories of projected events were by far the most salient type of conversational story.
2. Emphasis on interactional, co-constructional aspects as opposed to a focus on representational aspects. My suggestion here is that the commonly found bias within narrative interview research in favor of the representational aspects of the stories and the claims in them (cf. Atkinson and Delamont 2006) may be overstating them as self-construction resources as well as skewing the ways in which they are intimately linked with the interview as talk-in-interaction. We have shown (Bamberg and Georgakopoulou 2008; Georgakopoulou 2008), instead, that storytellings are integrally connected with their local interactional context and therefore should not be taken as unmediated or authentic records of self.
3. Emphasis on other-identity claims as opposed to self-identity claims. This suggests that the excessive emphasis on stories and statements about self in interview situations underestimates the wealth of identity work done when the focus is on discursive representations of others (see Georgakopoulou 2007, chap. 5).
4. Emphasis on the historicity of stories versus the view of stories as a single event. As I have shown (Georgakopoulou 2007), storytelling events among intimates draw irrevocably on lived and/or shared experience. Stories of shared events are thus part of a trajectory, an interactional history that can be drawn upon argumentatively; for example, claims and views based on this history may be accepted, contested, refashioned, and the like. This is normally obscured in interview narratives, where primacy is given to the single event and the researcher's extrapolation of dominant discourses at play from that event.

Data and Methods

This chapter is based on data collected for a project funded by the Economic and Social Research Council titled Urban Classroom Culture and Interaction, 2005–8.[1] The project employed the methods of ethnographic sociolinguistics and collected data from a group of fourteen- and fifteen-year-olds in a comprehensive school in London by means of participant-observation, radio-microphones (180 hours in total), interviews, and retrospective participant commentary on extracts from the radio-microphone recordings and video recordings. We also drew on school policy and media documents to set this in a wider context. Overall, we employed a multifaceted methodology so as to capture the sociospatial orientations of the phenomena under study, that is, who orients to what, where, how, and why. Also, a goal was to capitalize on the relative strength and exigencies of each method in order to chart individuals' identity profiles across time and space. For instance, whereas the radio-microphone recordings of spontaneous interaction were crucial to our interest in the ways in which aspects of the participants' social identities were intricately interwoven in everyday social interaction and life at school, the interviews and playback sessions allowed us to access the hitherto unvoiced and to ask about issues that informants did not routinely talk about in everyday activity.

The data for this chapter come from the audio-recorded interactions (in the classroom) and interview of one of our nine focal participants, who we call Nadia. When the recordings started, Nadia was fourteen years old. Her native language is English, and she describes her background as mixed race. Her mother is mixed-race South African, and her father is Armenian. Nadia is a leading member of the girls' popular group and an academically strong student who nonetheless, as we will see, finds "school a bit boring" (for a detailed profile of Nadia, see Georgakopoulou 2008). I focus on Nadia and the other female students' conversations and interviews with the aim of exploring how they locally report (e.g., as stories) their popular culture and new media engagement, ranging from mobile telephone calls and text-messaging to songs and soap operas, personal computers, the Internet, electronic games, fashion, and body care. I also document the kinds of metarepresentations and metadiscourses (e.g., on ethnicity, youth, gender, and schooling) that participants draw upon when asked to reflect on this engagement and on other issues of analytical importance.

Analysis: Nadia's Stories about One "Sweet Talker" and Two "Annoying" Teachers

In our analysis of conversational and interview stories, we did not set out to privilege small stories. Our aim was, however, to ensure that our analytic lens paid due attention to them and did not fail to capture them alongside the full-fledged stories. Small stories are abundant in the classroom data (on average, there are eight stories per period) and occur amid other activities, so they are in tune with people attending to many things simultaneously. Yet they are clearly marked with certain framing devices (e.g., addressee-oriented questions such as "Did I tell you?" and temporal adverbials such as "yesterday"). They also tend to become focal topics, in that they would be taken up again, if momentarily exited from (e.g., when students have to orient to the classroom agenda), with minimal marking. We can see how Nadia signals return to the story in the data at hand in lines 35 and 36 below, with the marker "anyways" and with the reference "he" (instead of a full name, i.e., Adam): "Anyways yea:h he text me yesterday."

Small stories told in the classroom typically involve reports of recent mediated interactions with boys (e.g., on the internet site MSN, by texting, which I call *breaking news*). The sheer act of a boy making contact is tellable in these cases; it is the interaction (who said what and how) that therefore becomes the crux of event-ness in the reports. Breaking news frequently leads to small stories of *projected events (projections);* these involve (near) future encounters with the men-talked-about, and the telling of both is interspersed with references to shared events.

The data at hand come from a narrative event that comprised two interlocked breaking news stories both told by Nadia during a mathematics period. Both stories involve reports of mediated interactions with two boys/suitors the day before. When telling them, Nadia sits at a small table in the back corner of the classroom with Lisa and Shenice. The first story (called "Adam the Sweet Talker"), an excerpt from which I will analyze here, involves a reported texting communication between Nadia and Adam. In the space of eleven minutes, the story is disengaged and reengaged four times but remains focal. It also typically leads to a projection in which Nadia and her interlocutors Lisa and Shenice plan a face-to-face meeting between Nadia and Adam the following week. Here, I concentrate on the first 131 lines of the story.

Moving to the stories from Nadia's interview, first, I need to note that the interviews were not specifically designed to elicit stories. In one-to-one sessions that lasted for more than one hour, the researcher asked the key informants for their thoughts on issues that were of analytical importance for the project: popularity, school, status in class, friendships, uses of new technologies, and music. Yet numerous stories occurred in the participants' interviews, both full-fledged and small stories, albeit ones that were very different from those occurring in the classroom. In particular, breaking news, projections, and stories of shared events were virtually absent, while *generic* and *habitual* stories figured very prominently. Numerous analysts (e.g., Baynham 2005; Reissman 2002) have stressed the importance and frequency of such stories in interviews, and they have argued for the need to view them as narrative data and include them in the analysis. The boundaries between habitual and generic stories are far from sharp and well delineated, and a full discussion is outside the scope of this chapter. Broadly speaking, I take it that though both recount events that are typical, in that they have happened or do happen, over and over again, generic stories present an absence of specific characters and are normally recounted with referential choices such as "you" or "one" that represent generalized actors.

What is most important in my data, as we will see below, is that generic and habitual accounts can be sequentially contiguous and that they are frequently followed by what I call "once" stories, which serve to illustrate the pattern of events and actions recounted in the preceding generic or habitual story with the telling of one specific episode or series of events involving specific characters. These *once stories* typically open with the adverb once, following "like" or "for example," which serve to emphasize the illustrative function of the story to follow. In this sense, once stories are reminiscent of the type of story that Martin and Plum (quoted by De Fina 2003, 169) called *exemplum.*

The Sequential Management of Identity Claims

Identity claims in both conversational and interview data are actor focused; that is, they refer to personality traits (e.g., physical appearance, modes of conduct). They are also organized relationally, with contrastive and associative relationships, so that a list of positive and negative attributes emerges. Finally, they tend to cluster together and be associated with likes and dislikes and with certain category-bound activities in plots, akin to membership categorization devices (Sacks 1992). Elsewhere, I have postulated a distinction between taleworld and storytelling identity claims and have discussed their interrelationships (Georgakopoulou 2008). Here, I single out one systematic difference in the sequential management of identity claims, that is, with regard to where they occur in relation to the story and what types of stories with which they are routinely associated. In crude terms, in the conversational data, identity claims follow the telling of stories; but in the interview data, identity claims precede the telling of stories—as shown here:

> Conversational data: NARRATIVE [breaking news—references to shared events—projections] + Identity Claim

In example 1, we can see this pattern in Nadia's first narrative:[2]

Example 1: 1 Mathematics: 8.55—9.40 AM (identity claims are in *italics*)

1 N: ((excited and quietly)) oh: Adam text me yesterday 12.31 minutes ((into the lesson))
2 d' you know what he said:?=
3 L: = Re:ally?
4 N: he was gonna come and see me (.) yesterday
5 Mr. O: Fo:lks you haven't got time to talk
6 N: and then I says why didn't you?
7 he was like (.) cos I got lost
8 he said (.) I was gonna come down to your school
9 I was like hh ((high pitched))
10 and you never come becau:se↑'
11 he's like (.) I didn't know where I was going
12 > I was like< ((high pitched)) *oh::: you're so lovely*
13 I love you (.) oh my <u>Go:d</u> 12.52 minutes
35 N: Anyways yea:h 14.49 minutes
36 he text me yesterday h—
37 oh yeah (.) I didn't forget my phone by the way ((going through messages to find it, while teacher is taking registry)) ((further down))
46 N: I goes—he text me and he was like hey girl ((Teacher taking registry))
50 let me know when you get this
51 >I was like< who the fuck is this? ((Teacher still taking registry while Nadia is expanding on the text message))
63 N: he's like you forgot me already (.) it's Adam

((Continues with the story. Teacher calling Nadia's name in the registry))

75 so he said he's gonna come next week to see me
76 I was like YE:S!
77 (4) ((reading text)) yeah just cochin now
78 dad was on it (.) I miss you still
79 *o:hh he's so sweet*
80 ((shift in tone)) *bu:t (.) I don't like sweet talkers*
81 (2)
82 do you fall↑ for sweet talk?
83 L: hmm↑
84 N: Do you fall for sweet talk?
85 L: Not really
86 N: Do you?
87 don't lie to me Shenice ((Lisa interrupts to ask how "multiples" is spelled))
94 N: If a brere says one nice thing to you you're like
95 ((high pitched)) *>oh he's so sweet he's so lovely<*
96 S: I've never said that to you
97 N: Oh yes you have
98 like if you get chirpsed on road
99 like remember you called me
100 to tell me 'bout that time you was with Laura ((Lisa asks again about "multiples"))
103 S: I didn't say they were *(lovely)*
104 I said *they were butt ugly*
105 N: Yeah I know but like
106 if a brere says something sweet to you
107 you think *he's lovely*

((Teacher interrupts asking them to do their homework))

111 S: I don't know
112 cos a brere has never said something sweet to me
113 N: don't lie
114 S: I swear to God=
115 N?: =sure
116 S: Not that I can remember
117 N: Dan said he loved you
118 that's sweet=
119 S: =(that's) different
120 N: How is it different
121 S: It's different
122 N: (Okay) ((They briefly interrupt the talk to share crisps))
126 but innit?
127 do you fall for sweet talk
128 on a level? ((8 seconds of silence))
131 N: *I'm too smart for sweet talk*

The story begins with the main reportable event "oh: Adam text me yesterday" (line 1). Before Nadia pauses her narration for the first time, it recounts the mediated interaction between Adam and Nadia; it ends with an identity claim about Adam presented as a reported thought by Nadia the character: ">I was like< *oh you're so lovely*" (line 12). The story is resumed in lines 35–36: "Anyways yeah he text me yesterday," and Nadia elaborates on the already reported interaction, which she ends this time with a telling identity claim about Adam: "*Oh he's so sweet but I don't like sweet talkers*" (lines 79–80). As we will see below, this identity claim prompts a negotiation between Shenice and Nadia around the topic of falling for sweet talk, which ends with Nadia's self-identity claim "*I'm too smart for sweet talk*" (line 131). The above shows how identity claims in this case follow upon the story's reported events and (inter)action.

In contrast, in the interview stories, the pattern is reversed:

Interview data: Identity Claim + NARRATIVE [habitual or generic story +/or once story]

To be specific, forty-eight (out of fifty-five) stories told by Nadia were preceded by identity claims or social positions. The pattern of sequencing in these stories was as follows:

In twenty-seven stories: identity claim plus habitual story

In eleven stories: identity claim plus generic story

In eight stories: identity claim plus generic or habitual story plus once story

In two stories: identity claim plus once story

In example 2, we can see the above pattern at work in relation to Nadia's stories about "two annoying teachers," whom I call Mr. Harris and Mr. Templer:

Example 2

I: So and (.) just really about you so (.) tell me a bit about yourself=
N: =Ooh there's a lot to tell °wow° um (.) I just like (.) coching with
my friends and listening to music really (0.5)
I: Ok (1)
N: And (.) going out (1) school is a bit boring (.) the teachers can
make it more interesting but they just choose not to (.)
especially Mr. Harris (0.5) *he's <u>really</u> boring*
but (.) I suppose (.) actually I feel sorry for us next year
we have him for humanities as well for <u>two</u> years oh gosh (.)
I: Um why: don't you like him as a teacher?=
N: =because *he's bo:ring* (.) he's like ((imitating his voice))
you have three minutes to do three questions it's like <u>OK</u> (.)
when you're half way through the question he's like ((imitating))
>if you haven't finished< you'll get a chance to go back
to it (.) and then he's like (.) a:h *he's just annoying* (.) if you-
he - he'll say (.) everyone work silently and

then you're working quietly and then (1) this girl (.) Lily (.)
she needed help (.) and Bhadra was trying to explain to her
but she didn't understand (.) so I explained to her
>and then he came over and started shouting at me< just 'cause I was
trying to help her (.) and I was like (1) *you're not a very nice person*
I: OK >so you said< it's boring (.) so how do you think it c- could be
(.) made more interesting=
When we get teachers like Mr. Templer it does not help (1) a:h *he's*
just annoying (.) re:ally (.) because he moans at you a::ll the time (.)
he thinks he's doing something good but it's just n:ot it's like (.) he
goes he says stupid things that makes you think w- why did you
say that↑ who g- who (.) who started with you for you to say that
it's like you (.) started the argument and then when you retaliate
he gets you in trouble y— you just can't win (1) with him by (1)um
(.) we'v— we then we got two form tutors (0.5) 'cause our class
was struggling (.) Mr. Templer and Mr. Andrews (.) everyone likes Mr.
Andrews (.) *everyone thinks he's (.) funny and safe and all*
that (.) but everyone kinda hates Mr. Templer 'cause he's (.) *he's*
↑*strict* he just likes to start on people for no reason and he HE (0.5)
teachers aren't supposed to lie just to get you into trouble but HE does
like one time (.) Jabir had a pi- um (.) he was on report (.)
and Jabir's hand was on his report and he was looking that way
(.) and Mr. Templer comes over yea:h (.) ((Story continued))
like one time (.) Jabir had a pi- um (.) he was on report (.)
and Jabir's hand was on his report and he was looking that way
(.) and Mr. Templer comes over yea:h (.) ((Story continued))

Mr. Harris is introduced with an identity claim ("*he's really boring,*" line 7). This is repeated in line 11 ("*he's boring*") and followed by a generic story (lines 11–15). Another telling identity claim ("ah *he's just annoying,*" line 15) punctuates the beginning of another brief generic account (lines 15–17), which leads to a "once" story (lines 17–21), starting as: "and then this girl Lily," line 17. In this case, the identity claim ("and I was like *you're not a very nice person,*" line 21) comes to reinforce the already stated identity claims ("*he's boring, . . . he's annoying*"). In the same vein, Nadia further down utters an identity claim about Mr. Templer ("ah *he's just annoying,*" lines 24–25), followed by a generic story (lines 25–30). Nadia at that point brings in Mr. Andrews as a teacher who is "*funny and safe*" (lines 33–34), in contrast to Mr. Templer, for whom she utters another identity claim ("*he's strict,*" line 35), followed by a very brief generic account (lines 35–37) and then by a "once" story, lines 38–46: "like one time (.) Jabir" (line 40).

Identity Claims and Co-Construction

Breaking news in the data tends to grant storytellers strong telling rights on the basis of experiential primacy, and so the actual events are not often contested. However, there is much co-construction around identity claims, particularly the telling identity claims that are normally produced in relation to a story's evaluation. Identity claims therefore provide spaces for co-construction between teller and interlocutors and a joint exploration of moral frames. We can see this in Nadia's question at the end of the reported texting interaction with Adam: "Do you fall for sweet talk?" (line 82). This question immediately follows a telling identity claim (*he's so sweet*) and the dislike associated with it (*but I don't like sweet talkers*). This leads to an extended sequence of negotiation between Nadia and Shenice (lines 82–131), which I have analyzed in detail elsewhere (Georgakopoulou 2008).

Due to space restrictions, it suffices to say here that the sequence illustrates how identity claims may be confirmed or refuted by prior (shared) experience and may be qualified as a result. This happens with Shenice whom Nadia accuses of "lying" (line 87) about not falling for sweet talk and gradually gets her to backtrack from that statement by bringing in two hypothetical scenarios (lines 94–96, 106–7) and two references to shared events (lines 97–104, 117–21) as argumentative devices. The sequence ends with Nadia uttering a telling self-identity claim "*I'm too smart for sweet talk*" (line 131). In the ensuing talk, which I do not present here, Nadia defends this claim against Shenice's challenge. Thus identity claims in the conversational stories routinely become the object of negotiation and (re)fashioning.

In contrast to this pattern, the main narratives in the interviews unfold without interruptions from the interviewer, who engages in supporting the narrative flow as an attentive, sympathetic listener. This does not imply that there is no co-construction. In fact, identity claims in the interview data serve as responses to invitations by the interviewer to the interviewee to self-report as well as to pose questions for elaboration, explanation, and justification; for example, What do you think about X? Why do you think that? In this way, they provide an account and further evidence for views already stated. We can see how the interviewer's invitation to Nadia in line 1 ("tell me a bit about yourself") leads to statements of likes (lines 3–4) and then to the general claim about school being boring (line 5) that is specified by the telling identity claim about Mr. Harris ("*he's really boring,*" line 7). This identity claim is restated by Nadia and further accounted for by the stories that follow from line 10 onward, in response to the interviewer's question "Um why: don't you like him as a teacher?" (line 10).

In addition to the above, the storyteller's identity claims are normally not contested by the interviewer, but more evidence may be requested. We can see this in the interviewer's question in lines 22–23: "OK >so you said< it's boring (.) so how d' you think it c- could be (.) made more interesting?" The interviewer here latches on to the claim already offered by Nadia regarding the school and Mr. Harris. In response to her question for further elaboration then, Nadia launches a related identity claim ("*he's just annoying,*" lines 24–25), this time about another teacher, Mr. Templer, and as suggested, backs the claim up with two generic stories and a once story.

Identity Claims and Modes of Self

As briefly shown in this chapter, our study examines focal participants' identities and self-projects from a number of standpoints and with different data so as to chart profiles and self-projects for them over time. In light of this, I am not suggesting that we can reduce this complex endeavor to the sequential placement of identity claims. However, I am arguing that the differences in the sequential environment and co-construction of the identity claims, as well as in the type of story to which they are related, are linked with differences in the storytellers' modes of experience and self-presentation. To be specific, in the conversational data, the emphasis is on the recent and newsworthy, whereas in the interview data, the emphasis is on the durative and habitual and the accompanying typicality and generalizability (cf. Baynham 2005; Reissman 2002). In this respect, "once" stories that reinstate the condition of uniqueness and singularity of events suspended by generic or habitual accounts come to stress those events as being emblematic of what has already been described as typical.

This difference in the type of stories employed in each case is closely linked with the sequential placement of the stories in relation to the identity claims. In the case of the conversational stories, identity claims follow on from the plot and, in some cases, become consequential for further emplotment, whereas in the case of the interview data, it is the stories that support and provide evidence for the already-stated identity claim(s).[3] This has implications for how identity claims are presented. In the case of the conversational data, identity claims are presented as "emerging" from—and in light of—the story and the reported events. Their joint fashioning and negotiation with the interlocutors also mean that they appear as if they were still in the making and not entirely fixed.

In contrast, in the interview data, the identity claims are presented as settled, as spaces that have been arrived at and inhabited by the storytellers. The stories that follow the identity claims thus come to account for them, whereas the stories in the conversational data that precede the identity claims come to announce them. In this sense, the self is presented as retrospective and reflected upon, whereas in the conversational stories the self is presented as prospective (i.e., "Where do I go from here?") and in the making.

Conclusion: Revisiting the Paradigm of Reflection and Self-Disclosure

In this chapter I have reported connections not only between identity claims and the type of story but also between the sequential placement of stories within interviews and conversations. If we look at these findings in the light of R and S-D, we find that it is mostly the interview stories (and storytellings) that are more recognizably linked with the biographical work on R and S-D—in the sense of both doing R and S-D and doing them in ways that highlight a "measure of distance" on the teller's part from the reported events and claims and that perpetuate an image of identity that is continuous and stable (Freeman 2006, 142).

My aim in providing evidence for this close link between R and S-D with interview stories is not to cast doubt on such stories as a valid way of understanding the social organization of experience and of making sense of self in specific environments but rather to urge further studies that will try to unpack assumptions that can be taken as inherently connected with the telling of stories in general. Unpacking assumptions here was linked with a change in the focus of inquiry; through the lens of small stories, I have included in my analysis stories that have not traditionally informed the ideas of R and S-D and looked at the local actions that they perform in relation to the identity claims that occur in their context.

It is somewhat tempting to accept that the conceptual apparatus associated with R and S-D applies only to specific outlook on a specific set of narrative data and should thus be left behind by revisionist moves within narrative studies such as that of small stories. Conversely, there is a case for attempting to extend and redefine some of the conventional vocabulary, both in order to systematize it further and so as to facilitate the much-needed constructive dialogue between—crudely speaking—"big" and "small" stories' analysts (cf. the plea by Freeman 2006).

In this respect, in the spirit of Ochs and Capps's definition of narrative (2001), we can argue for a view of R and S-D not as all or nothing but as more or less de-essentialized and multidimensional concepts that come with different possibilities in different contexts. This view would allow for R to bc found in the more fluid processes of exploring rather than "reifying" self and other, of meaning making through negotiation and contestation rather than through "stepping out of the flow" of the "quotidian" (Freeman 2006, 144). It would also open up the scope of S-D beyond the narrator disclosing self to the interviewer (who tends to be a stranger) to capture the more gradual revelatory process of (re)making self in connection with what is already known.

NOTES

1. The project was part of the Identities and Social Action Programme (www.identities.org.uk). The team comprised Ben Rampton (director), Caroline Dover, Alexandra Georgakopoulou, Roxy Harris, Constant Leung, and Lauren Small.
2. Transcription conventions:

//	the point in a turn where the utterance of the next speaker begins to overlap
=	two utterances closely connected without a noticeable overlap
( )	speech that cannot be deciphered
(text)	analyst's guess at speech that's hard to decipher
(( ))	stage directions
(.)	micropause, not timed
(1.)	approximate length of a pause in seconds
CAPITALS	emphasized speech
> <	faster-than-normal speech
::	extended speech
?	rising intonation/question

3. Space restrictions do not allow me to show here how the identity claim "I'm too smart for sweet talk" becomes consequential for the projected story that follows.

REFERENCES

Atkinson, Paul, and Sara Delamont. 2006. Rescuing narrative from qualitative research. *Narrative Inquiry* 16:173–81.

Bamberg, Michael. In press. *Twice-told stories.* www.clarku.edu/~mbamberg/publications.html.

Bamberg, Michael, and Alexandra Georgakopoulou. 2008. Small stories as a new perspective in narrative and identity analysis. In special issue of *Text and Talk: Narrative Analysis in the Shift from Texts to Practices,* ed. Anna De Fina and Alexandra Georgakopoulou, vol. 28, 377–96.

Baynham, Mike. 2005. Network and agency in the migration stories of Moroccan women. In *Dislocations/Relocations: Narratives of displacement,* ed. Mike Baynham and Anna De Fina, 15–35. Manchester: St. Jerome.

De Fina, Anna. 2003. *Narrative and identity: A study of immigrant discourse.* Philadelphia: John Benjamins.

Freeman, Mark. 2006. Life "on holiday"? In defence of big stories. *Narrative Inquiry* 16:139–46.

Georgakopoulou, Alexandra. 2006. Thinking big with small stories in narrative and identity analysis. *Narrative Inquiry* 16:129–37.

———. 2007. *Small stories, interaction and identities.* Studies in narrative interaction 8. Philadelphia: John Benjamins.

———. 2008. "On MSN with buff boys": Self- and other-identity claims in the context of small stories. *Journal of Sociolinguistics* 12:597–626.

Labov, William. 1972. The transformation of experience in narrative syntax. In W. Labov, *Language in the inner city: Studies in the Black English vernacular*, 354–96. Philadelphia: University of Pennsylvania Press.

Ochs, Elinor, and Lisa Capps. 2001. *Living narrative.* Cambridge, MA: Harvard University Press.

Reissman, Catherine K. 2002. Doing justice: Positioning the interpreter in narrative work. In *Strategic narrative,* ed. Wendy Patterson, 193–214. Lanham, Md.: Lexington Books.

Sacks, Harvey. 1992. *Lectures on conversation, vols. I and II,* ed. Gail Jefferson. Oxford: Blackwell.

11

Negotiating Deviance: Identity, Trajectories, and Norms in a Graffitist's Interview Narrative

JARMILA MILDORF
University of Paderborn, Germany

LIFE NARRATIVE RESEARCH in personality psychology has focused on narrative trajectories and on how dispositional traits (what your personality is *usually* or *typically* like) and characteristic adaptations (i.e., more particularized and context-sensitive aspects of one's personality) are combined to form integrative life stories (McAdams 1985). However, life stories can also go awry. This calls for revisions of assumptions such as continuity. Mishler (2006, 41) argues that the conception of a plurality of subidentities "points to another problem with temporal-order models of progressive change: the tendency to treat identity development as a unitary process, as if each life could be defined by a single plot line." Life narrative research can no longer take linear narrative trajectories for granted. Furthermore, life stories need to be considered within the contexts in which they are told. McAdams (2007, 23) contends that "stories are made and remade, performed and edited, instantiated, contoured, and lived out in the social ecology of everyday life and with respect to the norms of narrative content, structure, and expression that prevail in a given culture." Three points McAdams mentions here will be of interest to the present case study: performance, narrative norms, and culture.

This chapter addresses this question: What happens if the life story told hinges on the creation of an identity generally associated with deviance and crime? I examine, as a case study, narrative excerpts from an interview conducted with a graffiti writer in the city of Stuttgart in 2006. I look at the ways in which this graffiti writer oscillates between discursive strategies that can be attributed to the demands placed on him as a member representing a deviant subgroup of society and those required by the interview situation.

Deviance, Youth Subcultures, and the Graffiti Scene: A Brief Overview

The study of deviance has shifted from the perception of deviance as an attribute or as part of a person's individual psychology (e.g., in social pathology theories or criminology) to theories that take into account wider social patterns and the role of stigmatization and labeling for constructions of "deviance" (Scott and Marshall 2005). Though deviance in statistical terms simply means that someone or something is significantly different from the mean or average of a comparable group, the decision about what counts as "deviant" is by no means simple; one first needs to establish what is "normal behavior" (Lemert 1951, 30). Labeling theorists have pointed out that actions or behavior only become "deviant" when they are so labeled by others. Becker (1963, 9) argues that "deviance is *not* a quality of the act the person commits, but rather a consequence of the application by others of rules and sanctions to an 'offender.'"

This emphasis on labeling is of particular interest to sociolinguists because the implication is that deviance has to be negotiated on a discursive level. As far as graffiti is concerned, it can be seen as deviant behavior because there are laws that forbid it. Tagging is illegal. Ironically, however, graffiti was partially adopted by mainstream culture when galleries started to exhibit graffiti as subcultural art, and graffiti on canvases began to be marketed and disseminated through magazines (Lachmann 1988, 245–48). In a sense, graffiti becomes acceptable if viewed within the "art context." This will be important for our understanding of the graffiti writer's narrative presented here.

Another helpful notion is "career." Graffiti writers follow certain career paths, which usually begin with interest in the hip hop culture and graffiti scene and recruitment by already practicing writers. The graffiti subculture, like any subculture, is also marked by inherent codes of practice and rewards, such as the recognition from their peers that writers can obtain. As Ferrell (1998, 605) points out, "The subculture exists not only as a residue of shared physical space but as a larger community of meaning, an exploding cultural universe of collective symbolism and style that in many ways transcends space and time." Codes and rules are not necessarily visible to people outside the subculture, and they thus need to be communicated in (self-)presentations of the subculture. Agar and Hobbs's (1982) analysis of a drug addict's story of how he became a burglar demonstrates how the informant uses different types of coherence to achieve both local and global goals in telling his life story. Interestingly, the addict shows "commitment to straight morality standards, even though his actions are dictated by street morality" (Agar and Hobbs 1982, 27). We will see that the graffiti writer uses similar strategies to negotiate his deviant position vis-à-vis the interviewers.

Two further studies have informed this research: Widdicombe and Wooffitt's (1995) study of the language of youth subcultures, and Macdonald's (2001) investigation into the graffiti subculture in New York and London. Whereas Widdicombe and Wooffitt are rooted in conversation and discourse analyses and therefore set out to investigate *how* youths talk about who they are, Macdonald takes a more content-analytical approach by focusing on *what* the graffiti writers have to say about themselves. Macdonald shows how graffiti writing enables youths to find a voice, to demonstrate their masculinity, and to gain status among their peers. Widdicombe and Wooffitt (1995, 226) found that their respondents raised issues that are also dealt with in the social science literature on subcultures, namely, "conformity, authenticity, the political dimension of membership, categorization, the relationship between the individual and the group, the identity of self and the constitution of the group."

Methodology and the Data

The data for this study emerged as part of a student project within a seminar, "Contemporary Poetry and the City," held in the summer of 2006 at the University of Stuttgart. Four students explored the theme of "city and culture" in and for the city of Stuttgart. They conducted interviews with art students, a dramaturge, a slam poet, a rap singer, and a graffiti writer. The interview with the graffitist, Mo, was taped and videorecorded. Because Mo wished to remain anonymous, he was filmed with his back turned toward the interviewers and a hood over his head. The interview lasted for about twenty minutes. Mo had been given possible questions in advance so that he had time to reflect on his answers before the interview took place. This procedure had an influence on the overall trajectory of the interview and on Mo's manner of speaking. In a sense, he had time to plan a "performance of self" (cf. Thornborrow and Coates 2005, 13). Furthermore, the interviewee and the two interviewers were of approximately the same age. Mo, who was twenty-four years of age at the time of the interview, spoke to two students in their early twenties. At the same time, their educational backgrounds differed. While Achilles and Julia study at the university with a view to becoming high school teachers, Mo dropped out of high school around the age of seventeen. He never trained for a job and has sporadically earned a living by doing odd jobs. He has already been convicted several times for graffiti writing and for substance abuse. This information has implications for the data obtained in this student project.

Discussion

For my discussion I have selected three excerpts from the interview conducted with Mo. The first excerpt is taken from the very beginning of the interview. Beginnings in interviews are important, because this is frequently the place where identities are established for the first time in the interaction. I demonstrate to what extent Mo's self-portrayal follows conventional life narrative trajectories. The second excerpt contains Mo's response to the question about his motivations for being a graffiti writer. Following Agar and Hobbs (1982) in their emphasis on coherence and thematic integration in life histories, I show here how Mo creates macro-level coherence for his personal development on the micro level of his discourse. I will especially pay closer attention to the linguistic features that constitute this micro-level discursive work. In the third excerpt, Mo talks about the issue of illegality. This is of particular interest for my initial question because here the respondent has to negotiate deviance. We will see that surprisingly, or perhaps not so surprisingly, Mo draws upon common cultural values to recast his illegal activities in a more acceptable framework.

Initiation Stories and Interviews: Narrative Trajectories

Mo's narrative follows the conventional teleological pattern of life histories, which begins at the beginning—that is to say, at Mo's birth. In the opening lines to the interview, Mo provided all the information he deemed relevant in the interview situation: his name, his place of birth and where he lived at the time, his age, and the activity around which the whole interview revolved: graffiti writing. This indicates that right from the beginning of the interview, he "staged" himself for an unknown audience, which also involves passing on relevant biographical data. Throughout the interview, his turns, which never overlapped the interrogative turns of the interviewers or vice versa, invariably began with an affirmative and phonetically emphasized "yes//JA" or with a repetition of the interviewer's question (e.g., "Warum ↑sprüh ich. Ja // Why do I tag. Yes"; see excerpt 2). Let us have a look at how Mo presented his initiation into graffiti writing:

Excerpt 1

1. JA, mit sechzehn ↑siebzehn (.) hab ich: angefangen mich für HipHop zu interessieren und alles was so dazu gehört.
2. Hab die typischen ↑Filme angeschaut, Menace II Society,
3. und bin mit Freunden dann eher ↑zufällig eigentlich auf: auf ne Dok- Dokumentation gesto- gestoßen,
4. *Style Wars* heißt die,
5. da gehts um die New Yorker (.) HipHop: Geschichte und um die vier Elemente des HipHops, M↑Cing, DJing, Breakdance, und Graffiti,
6. und das hat mich einfach (.)↑tierisch das hat mir tierisch gut gefallen,
7. und hab: dann auch in der Schule >immer wenn mir langweilig war eigentlich< versucht, so ähnliche Dinge (.) zu zeichnen,
8. hab mir dann irgendwann (.) mit n paar Freunden einfach Spraydosen ge↑kauft
9. und hab zu Haus versucht, selber zu sprayen,
10. und *seit*dem bin ich eigentlich darin: ge↑fangen mehr oder weniger
11. und (.) kann einfach nich mehr (.) davon lassen.

[1. Yes, at sixteen seventeen I developed an interest for hip hop and everything related to it. 2. I watched the typical movies, Menace II Society, 3. and then I more or less incidentally came across a documentary, 4. it's called Style Wars, 5. which is about the history of hip hop in New York and about the four elements of hip hop, MCing, DJing, break dance and graffiti, 6. and I was *really,* I was *really* impressed with that. 7. And then in school, whenever I was bored basically, I tried to draw similar things, 8. and then one day some friends and I simply bought some spray cans 9. and I tried tagging myself at home. 10. And since then I've been all caught up in it, 11. I just can't give it up.]

Mo's speech is highly monitored as can be seen, for example, in its relatively monotonous intonation pattern with occasional but regular rises in intonation and pauses in speech. Nevertheless, typical features of spontaneous spoken conversation also occur. For example, Mo self-corrects the case of the personal pronoun from accusative "mich" to dative "mir" in line 6 because he is obviously searching for the right verb to use here and accordingly has to adapt the verbal subcategorization frame ("das hat mich einfach (.)↑tierisch das hat mir tierisch gut gefallen // I was *really* I was *really* impressed with that"). In line 3 we see a repetition in "auf: auf" and two cut-offs in "Dok- Dokumentation gesto- gestoßen // stumbled upon a documentary." The indefinite article "ein/eine" is mostly reduced to "ne" ("ne Dok- Dokumentation," line 3) or to clitic "n" ("mit n paar Freunden // with some friends," line 8), and the final plosive "t" is deleted in the negative particle "nicht → nich//not" (line 11). Interestingly, Mo does not use dialectal forms even though a weak Suebian accent is noticeable, especially in his slightly more closed and palatalized diphthongs. I will argue later that the respondent's attempt to speak a standard variety of German can be attributed to the interview format on the one hand, but also to the fact that the graffiti subculture is informed especially by American role models and that speakers therefore perhaps gravitate less toward regional linguistic patterns, at least if they perform their subculture to outsiders.

If we apply Labov and Waletzky's (1967) analytical model for narratives of personal experience, Mo's narrative appears very orderly. The narrative begins with a brief orientation in line 1, where Mo tells the interviewer about his age when he began to be interested in hip hop; a lengthy complicating action sequence ranging from lines 2 to 7, in which a number of activities are mentioned that led up to Mo's increasing engagement with graffiti writing; the resolution in lines 8 and 9, which describes the point in time when Mo actually started writing graffiti himself; and a coda in lines 10 and 11, where this whole process of initiation into the subculture is evaluated in retrospect as inevitable and irreversible. Widdicombe and Woofitt (1995, 84–85) also found that their respondents almost invariably began the interview by offering an identification of themselves. They attribute this to the interview format in which the interviewer's initial question was intended to elicit such a response.

The interview format certainly has to account for the linear order of Mo's opening self-narrative. However, I would also see it as the respondent's attempt to mirror the inherent logic in his personal development, as he describes it in his story. Much in the same way that the narrative progresses in linear fashion, the events in Mo's life that led to his career as a graffiti writer are also presented as following logically—that is, temporally and causally—from one to the other. This logic is indicated through the connector "dann//then" (lines 3, 7, and 8) but also through the sequential ordering of events in what are mainly narrative clauses conjoined by temporal juncture. The only clauses that deviate from the pattern are the coordinate clauses in lines 4 and 5, which give background information about the documentary that Mo mentions as one of the main sources of motivation for his subsequent career, and the restricted clause in line 6, which provides a more emotional reason for Mo's increasing involvement in this subculture: "Das hat mir tierisch gut gefallen // I was *really* impressed with that."[1]

Two further lexical choices are worthy of comment because they support on the linguistic level the presentation of the events in Mo's life as matter-of-fact and essential: the particles "eigentlich//basically" (lines 3, 7, and 10) and "einfach//simply" (lines 6, 8, and 11). They tone down the syntactic elements to which they are adjoined (Eisenberg 2006, 233). "Eigentlich" not only modifies the adverbial phrase in "eher ↑zufällig eigentlich // rather incidentally basically" (line 3) or the parenthetically embedded subordinate clause in "immer wenn mir langweilig war eigentlich // whenever I was bored basically" (line 7), but it also becomes a discursive device that invites the listener to accept the explanations the speaker offers as regards his actions. "Eigentlich" suggests that things could have been different but this is how they were "basically" or "in essence." The threefold repetition of "eigentlich" emphasizes the inevitability of how things came about in Mo's life: He became interested in graffiti because of the documentary he happened to watch, and he started his first drawing because he was bored in school.

"Einfach" fulfills a similar function. It also expresses how compelling certain things are: "Und das hat mich einfach (.) ↑tierisch das hat mir tierisch gut gefallen // and that simply *really* that *really* impressed me" (line 6); "hab mir dann irgendwann (.) mit n paar Freunden einfach Spraydosen ge kauft // then one day I simply bought some spray cans with some friends" (line 8); "und (.) kann einfach nich mehr (.) davon lassen // and simply can't give it up anymore" (line 11). Furthermore, short pauses are used in these clauses to set apart individual phrases and thus to give more phonetic, as well as semantic, weight to subsequent phrases. In other words, Mo's lexical choices, in combination with marking prosodic features, support the rationale underlying his life narrative and are used to convey to the interviewer a picture of his initiation into the graffiti subculture as something brought about by "outside forces" rather than his own agency or volition, as it were.

Motivation and Danger: Telling a "Good" Story

In the second excerpt from the interview, Mo answers the question: "Why do you tag?" Rather than following Labov and Waletzky's (1967) narrative syntax for line breaks here, I now chunk the narrative into intonation units to give a flavor of the performance side of the story:

Excerpt 2

1. Warum ↑sprüh ich. Ja.
2. Also auf jeden Fall in erster Linie nich um irgendwas zu beschmutzen oder zu beschädigen,
3. °das is (.) ein: Nebeneffekt°.
4. Ich sprühe eigentlich in erster Linie wegen dem künstlerischen ↑Anspruch ich will *schön*e Bilder malen
5. ich will (.) will den Leuten ↑zeigen was ich ↑kann
6. wie wie ↑gut ich des kann
7. nur irgendwann reichts dann natürlich auch nich mehr ne kleine Hauswand zu besprühen
8. dann will man ↑mehr
9. dann will man das perfektion↑ ieren
10. will des ↑*schön*er machen will des ↑*größ*er machen (.) sucht sich dann ↑*neue* Stellen sucht sich *größ*ere Wände ge↑*fähr*lichere Wände
11. und (.) s is einfach (.) also (.) je ge↑*fähr*licher des is desto *mehr* Kick dahinter is wenn man so n großes Bild fertig gestellt hat
12. >des is wie im Rausch wenn einem richtig der Arsch auf Grundeis ging und man dauernd dachte Oh jetzt könnt gleich jemand kommen<
13. aber ich *muss* des jetzt fertig machen,
14. >dann hat man dann einfach auch so n Adren- Adrenalinstoß<,
15. >ich *muss* des jetzt hier fertig machen und ich *muss* des perfekt machen<,

16. und natürlich je ↑größer und per↑fekter und ge ↑fährlicher des war desto Res- *Re*↑ *spect* kriegt man auch von: von den andern entgegen gebracht
17. und man kann sich da nen ↑Namen erarbeiten.

[1. Why do I tag? Yes. 2. Well, at any rate not primarily to muck something up or to destroy something, 3. that is a side effect. 4. I spray primarily because I want to be an artist, I want to paint nice pictures. 5. I want to show people what I can do, 6. how well I can do it. 7. The only thing is that one day it's no longer enough to paint a small wall of a house, 8. you then want more, 9. you want to perfect it, 10. you want to make it nicer, make it bigger, you search for new places, search for bigger walls, more dangerous walls. 11. And it's simply, well, the more dangerous it is the greater the thrill when you have finished such a big picture. 12. It's like being intoxicated when you're shit scared and you keep thinking "oh, someone might be coming along any minute now 13. but I have to finish this now," 14. then you simply feel the adrenalin kick in, 15. "I must finish this here and now and I must make it perfect," 16. and of course the bigger and more perfect and more dangerous it was the more respect you earn from the others 17. and you can make a name for yourself.]

In comparison with excerpt 1, this excerpt displays a livelier response, which can be seen especially in the way Mo speeds up his speech (lines 12, 14, and 15). The pace of Mo's speech is also increased through rhythmical devices such as regular rises in pitch, for example, in lines 4 to 6, or in line 16, and through parallel syntactic constructions marked by a repetition of short clauses in which the subject is partially elided: "Dann will man ↑mehr dann will man das perfektion ieren will des ↑*schön*er machen will des ↑*größ*er machen (.) sucht sich dann ↑*neue* Stellen sucht sich ↑*größ*ere Wände ge *fähr*lichere Wände // then you want more, then you want to perfect it, [you] want to make it nicer, want to make it bigger, [you] search for new places, search for bigger walls, more dangerous walls" (lines 8–10). The effect is almost that of a musical cadence that imprints itself on the listener's mind. As I mentioned above, Mo's speech throughout the interview remained more or less monotonous. By speeding up his speech in this sequence, Mo reenacts for the interviewer his sense of excitement and agitation when he is out tagging. He describes the thrills involved in writing graffiti and how he is driven toward ever-bigger and -better pictures.

In line 11, Mo takes time to reflect on how he can further explain these emotions, which can be seen in the three short pauses of speech, the false start in "s is einfach (.) // it's simply (.)," and the discursive particle "also//well," which signals to the listener that an explanation is to follow. He then verbalizes his feelings as "mehr Kick // greater thrill." In line 12, Mo's self-monitoring is further lessened; he uses the regional reduced form "des" of the demonstrative pronoun "das//that" (also in lines 6, 13, 15, and 16) and the slang proverbial expression "wenn einem richtig der Arsch auf Grundeis ging // when you're really shit scared." Interestingly, this lapse into slang and regional variants is incongruent with Mo's rather formal usage of the preterit form in "ging//went" and "dachte//thought." The preterit is uncommon in spoken German, especially in southern varieties, where the perfect tense is preferred for talking about past events (Fabricius-Hansen 2005, 520).

What emerges at this point is what I would perceive as a conflict between two narrative demands—namely, to speak authentically about one's personal experiences with the subculture on the one hand, and on the other, to convey a positive self-image in the interview, which includes adherence to the commonly assumed rules of this formal speech event. Put differently, even though Mo obviously makes a great effort to monitor his speech, he gets carried away here. We must also not forget that he spoke to peers who were equal in age but different in educational background and prospective social standing. In this light, his depiction of his activities can be interpreted as an attempt at not only recounting but also, in fact, performing his subculture favorably by converging toward the speech of the interviewers.

Coupland, Garrett, and Williams (2005, 71) contend that "the performance frame establishes a relationship between the meanings co-articulated in the performed event and the meanings that define the wider cultural formation. This relationship and the duality of meaning is laid open to scrutiny when in some sense relevant cultural practices are performed or referred to in a particular event." In this interview, Mo performs as an informant with insider knowledge of a specific subculture. He also performs as a storyteller who relates key developments in his own life. More important, he performs all this to recipients who are not "in the know," and his performance has to negotiate between the values of his subculture and those of the mainstream culture, which considers the subculture's activities illegal. We will see in the third excerpt that one way of coming to terms with this "duality of meaning," as Coupland, Garrett, and Williams have it, is to import values from the mainstream culture into one's own discourse.

In the present excerpt, the strategy seems to lie more in a satisfactory execution of the performance as such, that is, in performing well as a storyteller. For example, Mo uses direct speech to convey his mixed feelings of anxiety and excitement when he is out tagging: "Oh jetzt könnt gleich jemand kommen< aber ich *muss* des jetzt fertig machen // Oh, someone might be coming along any minute now but I must finish this now" (lines 12–13), and in line 15: "Ich *muss* des jetzt hier fertig machen und ich *muss* des perfekt machen // I must finish this here and now and I must make it perfect." A long research tradition has focused on the dramatizing effect of direct speech in oral storytelling (Clift and Holt 2007, 7). Mo's use of direct speech with its first person deixis ("ich muss . . . // I must, . . ." "jetzt hier // here and now") makes the scene he depicts livelier and brings it closer to the listener. At the same time, direct speech here conveys something of his emotional state.

The urgency of Mo's wish to complete his task is conveyed in the threefold repetition of the verb "müssen//must" (lines 13 and 15), which in addition receives phonetic stress. This discursive strategy of personalizing the related experience is in stark contrast to Mo's use of the generic third person pronoun "man//one" in lines 8, 9, 11, 12, 14, 16, and 17. The generic pronoun presents the events as if they could relate to anyone or to no one in particular. Although Mo talks about his own feelings of compulsion, anxiety, and adrenalin-induced excitement, he at the same time speaks about and on behalf of other members of his subculture. They experience similar things when writing graffiti, as his use of "man" suggests.

The values of the graffiti subculture are then summed up in lines 16 and 17: "Und natürlich je ↑größer und per↑ fekter und ge ↑fährlicher des war desto Res- *Re↑ spect* kriegt man auch von: von den andern entgegen gebracht und man kann sich da nen ↑Namen erarbeiten // and of course the bigger, more perfect and more dangerous it was the more respect you earn from the others and you can make a name for yourself." Gaining respect from other graffiti writers and making a name are central achievements in the graffiti subculture and are presented by members of this subculture as their main reasons for writing graffiti (Macdonald 2001, 68ff.). Mo reinforces these values by repeating the adjectives "größer//bigger," "gefährlicher // more dangerous," and "perfekter // more perfect" over and over again, in both their positive and comparative forms (lines 10, 11, 15, and 16). Moreover, he signals his immersion in this subculture by pronouncing the word "respect" (line 16) the English way. The lexical item "respect" thus not only captures an important value but also becomes a linguistic token for an "imported" subculture whose rules and language assign to the German-speaking graffiti writer a hybrid position. This position also needs to be negotiated vis-à-vis the interviewer. As I argued above, one strategy for doing so is possibly Mo's repression of dialectal speech and colloquialisms, which in present-day Germany are increasingly reserved for familial or intimate contexts (Niebaum and Macha 2006, 172).

Illegality and Fitness: Negotiating Deviance

One last feature in the second excerpt already leads me on to the topic that predominates in the third excerpt below: illegality and the discursive negotiation of deviance. In line 2 of excerpt 2, Mo interestingly first defines the reasons for why he tags *ex negativo:* "Also auf jeden Fall in erster Linie nich um irgendwas zu beschmutzen oder zu beschädigen // Well, at any rate [I tag] not primarily to muck up or to destroy something." Labov (1972, 381) treats negatives as comparators and sees their narrative power in the fact that they "provide a way of evaluating events by placing them against the background of other events which might have happened." In our example, Mo starts by using negatives as disclaimers to counteract potential criticism on the part of the interviewers, who can be seen as representing the mainstream culture. This mainstream culture perceives graffiti as an illegal activity, and Mo implicitly refers to what many people probably think of graffiti: that it damages and devalues buildings, train cars, and so on. By indirectly "quoting" such views and by immediately negating them in the presentation of what he does, Mo reframes his graffiti writing and assigns to it more positive values. He claims that he wants to be an artist ("Ich sprühe eigentlich in erster Linie wegen dem künstlerischen ↑Anspruch ich will *schöne* Bilder malen // I tag primarily because I want to be an artist I want to paint nice pictures," line 4) and that he earns respect through his work ("man kann sich da nen Namen erarbeiten // you can earn a name for yourself," line 17).[2] This discursive revaluation is particularly strong toward the end of the interview and can be seen in this excerpt:Excerpt 3

1. JA (.) Legalität is so ne Sache.
2. Das is der Grund warum ich jetzt mit m Rücken und dieser tollen ((touches his hood)) Ka↑ puze zu euch sitz.
3. S ↑is halt einfach nich legal, Graffiti sprayen,

4. und wird auch (.) in Deutschland ziemlich hart besch-bestraft.
5. =Also ich hab da auch schon so meine Erfahrungen mit gemacht,
6. hab (.) ehm, Reinigungskosten zahlen müssen oder Sozialstunden ableisten.
7. JA, ma ma wird fit als Graffiti Sprayer wenn ma man immer mal wieder (.) schnell wegrennen muss, über Hecken springen.
8. Man is *fit,*
9. man kommt *nie* zur Ruhe.
10. Des is zwar auch ne gute Voraussetzung für dann (.) weitere (.) Verfolgungsjagden.
11. Ma is eigentlich immer fit (.) und immer gefordert.
12. Muss sich fit halten, ja.

[1. Yes. Legality is a tricky question. 2. That's the reason why I am now sitting with my back to you and with this wonderful ((touches his hood)) hood on. 3. It's simply not legal, tagging, 4. and you're quite severely punished for it in Germany. 5. Well I've had some experiences with that too, 6. I had to pay for cleaning and do some social work. 7. Yes, you get fit as a graffiti writer when you have to run away quickly every once in a while, jump over hedges. 8. You are fit, 9. you never have a break. 10. It's true that this is also a good prerequisite for further chases. 11. You're always fit really and always under pressure. 12. You have to keep fit, yes.]

Again, Mo begins his answer with the phonetically louder, affirmative particle "JA//yes," which signals his readiness to respond. He then hesitates before he comments, in a mitigating way: "Legalität is so ne Sache // legality is a tricky question" (line 1). The demonstrative particle "so" here assumes a modifying function used to convey the speaker's attitude. The implication is that he does not fully agree with other people's views of graffiti. It is also important in this context that Mo does not use a noun like "Problem//problem" to talk about illegality, for example, but the neutral "Sache//thing." When he mentions the illegal status of graffiti in Germany in lines 3 and 4, the modal particles "halt einfach," together with the pitch rise on the verb "is," again imply that even though illegality is a fact, Mo does not see it that way. The ironic remark in line 2 concerning the measures he has to take to remain anonymous ("mit m Rücken und dieser tollen ((touches his hood)) Ka puze zu euch sitz // sitting with my back to you and with this wonderful hood on") underline his disapproval.

Between lines 4 and 5, the response switches from a general assessment of the issue of illegality to a more personal story, and the latch indicates that Mo is quite keen on relating his personal story. Interestingly, the personal narrative is then made less personal again through the usage of the partially reduced, regional form of "man//one," "ma" (lines 7, 8, 9, and 11). As in excerpt 2 above, the generic pronoun presents the experience as something that other graffiti writers also experience. This evokes a sense of group identity. The speaker immerses his personal identity expressed in the first person pronoun "ich//I" (lines 2 and 5) in the more generalized identity of his subculture.

The most striking feature in this excerpt is the usage of the adjective "fit," which occurs four times (lines 7, 8, 11, and 12) in this short response. Its frequency, as well as the fact that it is phonetically stressed in line 8 and set apart through a subsequent pause in speech in line 11, assign discursive significance to this lexical item. It seems rather odd that a graffiti writer should talk about his activities as "keeping him fit." In the study by Macdonald (2001, 106), for example, the respondents mainly talked about the dangers involved in tagging rather than about their physical prowess, even though one respondent drew a comparison between the pressures involved in tagging and those you have to endure when participating in a sports competition. The fact that Mo emphasizes physical fitness can be interpreted as his attempt to lodge graffiti in a more acceptable cultural framework. Rather than talking about what makes graffiti illegal and unacceptable in the eyes of mainstream culture, he highlights an aspect that has an important standing in contemporary German society: namely, to keep fit and healthy. He thus discursively assigns a new value to graffiti and turns fitness into part of its "symbolic capital" (Macdonald 2001, 65).

Conclusion

In my analysis of the interview data, I have tried to give credit to both what Mo said and how he said it. As I showed, Mo's discourse participates in larger cultural narratives of self both thematically and as far as the very design of his self-narration is concerned. The interview begins with a conventional life narrative pattern marked by a chronological as well as causally linked sequence of events. The linear narrative trajectory underlines the respondent's attempt to make sense of his career as a graffiti writer both in retrospect—that is, when looking back on his life—and also in the interview situation vis-à-vis the interviewers. In a sense, we discern here what McAdams (2007, 19) postulated in his life story model of identity, namely that "people . . . construe their lives as evolving stories that integrate the reconstructed past and the imagined future in order to provide life with some semblance of unity and purpose."

The influence of the interview situation must also not be overlooked. The formality of this speech event contributes to the fact that Mo spoke in a highly monitored way, which can be seen in the regular, relatively slow, and monotonous cadence of his speech, as well as in self-corrections and a careful choice of lexical items. Interestingly, however, formal language features such as the use of the preterit also clashed with slang words and colloquial or dialectal speech forms. This stylistic slippage particularly occurred at moments in the interview when Mo talked about his tagging activities and about the dangers involved in them. I interpreted this as an indication of a conflict between two discursive tasks. First, he had to accommodate to the formal requirements of the interview situation; second, he also had to represent and to perform his graffiti subculture. The latter, I argue, requires linguistic sincerity, which includes an authentic rendition of the subculture's activities, for example, the usage of verbal tokens such as the English word "respect." To use Agar and Hobbs's (1982, 15) words, Mo also had to synthesize "the street world and the straight world" for the interviewers.

This aspect of negotiating the world of one's subculture and the values and expectations of the mainstream culture became especially salient in the way deviance was verbalized in the interview. As I demonstrated, Mo used two strategies of coping with conflicting views concerning graffiti. First, he shielded himself from potential criticism by negating mainstream views of graffiti as destructive and disorderly behavior and by recasting his own activities as "art" or "work." This theme recurs in other parts of the interview, where he expressly denies his participation in "nasty" forms of graffiti writing such as "etching," which involves the usage of acids to burn patterns into surfaces. Second, he imported values from the mainstream culture in order to revaluate graffiti writing. Rather than presenting it as a criminal offence, he talked about the way it keeps you "fit."

What emerges is a discursive strategy of converging toward the main culture's narrative expectations, both on the micro level of narrative form and features and on the macro level of sociocultural values and rules. The close analysis of prosody, lexical choices, disclaimers, and narrative trajectories demonstrated how Mo positioned himself vis-à-vis the interviewers within the subculture of graffiti artists, trying to create involvement and to gain approval. He redefined tagging within the boundaries of acceptable social behavior. In a sense, then, the counternarrative thus created ironically made use of the same strategies of the established discourse it indirectly sought to attack.

NOTES

I thank my students: Sarah Bauer, Beate Fleischer, Achilles Siouzios, and Julia Stahl. I also thank Mo for participating in this study and for allowing the interview to be published.

↑ and ↓ indicate rising and falling intonation.

1. Note that the lexical item used to express the strength of Mo's emotional response, "tierisch," receives phonetic emphasis through a rise in pitch. The adjective "tierisch" literally translates as "animal (*attr.*)" but in its adverbial form is used figuratively in German slang to add emphasis to the subsequent adjective.
2. The verb "erarbeiten" contains the verb "arbeiten" = to work. Again, the graffitist reframes his activities in terms of work.

REFERENCES

Agar, Michael, and Jerry R. Hobbs. 1982. Interpreting discourse: Coherence and the analysis of ethnographic interviews. *Discourse Processes* 5:1–32.

Becker, Howard S. 1963. *Outsiders: Studies in the sociology of deviance.* New York: Free Press.

Clift, Rebecca, and Elizabeth Holt. 2007. Introduction. In *Reporting talk: Reported speech in interaction,* ed. Elizabeth Holt and Rebecca Clift, 1–15. Cambridge: Cambridge University Press.

Coupland, Nikolas, Peter Garrett, and Angie Williams. 2005. Narrative demands, cultural performance and evaluation: Teenage boys' stories for their age-peers. In *The sociolinguistics of narrative,* ed. Joanna Thornborrow and Jennifer Coates, 67–88. Amsterdam: John Benjamins.

Eisenberg, Peter. 2006. *Der Satz: Grundriss der deutschen Grammatik.* Stuttgart: Metzler.

Fabricius-Hansen, Cathrine. 2005. Das Verb. In *Duden: Die Grammatik,* ed. Matthias Wermke, Kathrin Kunkel-Razum, and Werner Stolze-Stubenrecht, 395–572. Mannheim: Dudenverlag.

Ferrell, Jeff. 1998. Freight train graffiti: Subculture, crime, dislocation. *Justice Quarterly* 15 (4): 587–608.

Labov, William. 1972. *Language in the inner city: Studies in the Black English vernacular.* Philadelphia: University of Pennsylvania Press.

Labov, William, and Joshua Waletzky. 1967. Narrative analysis: Oral versions of personal experience. In *Essays on the verbal and visual arts,* ed. June Helm, 12–44. Seattle: University of Washington Press.

Lachmann, Richard. 1988. Graffiti as career and ideology. *American Journal of Sociology* 4 (2): 229–50.

Lemert, Edwin M. 1951. *Social pathology: A systematic approach to the theory of sociopathic behavior.* New York: McGraw-Hill.

Macdonald, Nancy. 2001. *The graffiti subculture: Youth, masculinity and identity in London and New York.* Basingstoke: Palgrave.

McAdams, Dan P. 1985. *Power, intimacy, and the life story.* New York: Guilford.

———. 2007. The role of narrative in personality psychology today. In *Narrative: State of the art,* ed. Michael Bamberg, 17–26. Amsterdam: John Benjamins.

Mishler, Elliot G. 2006. Narrative and identity: The double arrow of time. In *Discourse and identity,* ed. Anna de Fina, Deborah Schiffrin, and Michael Bamberg, 30–47. Cambridge: Cambridge University Press.

Niebaum, Hermann, and Jürgen Macha. 2006. *Einführung in die Dialektologie des Deutschen.* Tübingen: Niemeyer.

Scott, John, and Gordon Marshall. 2005. Deviance, sociology of. In *A dictionary of sociology: Oxford reference online.* Oxford University Press, www.oxfordreference.com/views/ENTRY.html?subview=Main&entry=t88.e574.

Thornborrow, Joanna, and Jennifer Coates. 2005. The sociolinguistics of narrative: Identity, performance, culture. In *The sociolinguistics of narrative,* ed. Joanna Thornborrow and Jennifer Coates, 1–16. Amsterdam: John Benjamins.

Widdicombe, Sue, and Robin Wooffitt. 1995. *The language of youth subcultures: Social identity in action.* New York: Harvester Wheatsheaf.

12

Interaction and Narrative Structure in Dementia

LARS CHRISTER HYDÉN AND LINDA ÖRULV
Linköping University, Sweden

TELLING STORIES involving ourselves is one of the most important ways we have of telling others who we are—and of who we want to be. Listening to this type of autobiographical story generally makes it possible to infer something about the storyteller, both in the present and in the past.

During their lives most people frequently tell this kind of story, in various settings and to different audiences. They are stories that generally have the storyteller as the main protagonist, and the point of the story has to do with the teller and his or her handling of those events that in some way deviates from what is expected. Generally they are also stories with an "extended reportability"; that is, they can be "told and retold over the course of a long period of time" (Linde 1993, 21). Put differently, people tend to have sets of stories about themselves that function as resources for telling stories at various to times to different audiences.

People with Alzheimer's disease (AD) experience a slow loss of linguistic and cognitive skills. Persons with AD are challenged first by having to remember new things and later on by also having to retrieve memories about the past. As a consequence they face an increasing number of challenges in using language and remembering things from the past, something that also especially affects their ability to tell stories. Losing cognitive functions makes it difficult to organize stories temporally, and the same stories tend to be told repeatedly during the same speech event. Losing linguistic functions also results in word-finding problems, and eventually in problems with constructing meaningful linguistic units, which makes it difficult to tell stories at all.

Although much of the research on AD has focused on the loss of skills, several researchers have recently pointed out that people with AD also make attempts to use their remaining cognitive and linguistic resources (see especially Sabat 2001). What have traditionally been viewed as symptoms of decline and lessening skills could be regarded from this perspective as creative attempts to present a positive self-identity. To tell and retell the same autobiographical stories may be a way to show important aspects of the teller's self and identity. Several researchers have pointed out that repetition of stories or fragments of stories may capture something important in the way the person makes sense of his or her life (Ramanathan 1997; Mills 1997). The repetitions and the way these stories are organized may thus be approached as creative solutions rather than as mere symptoms.

Several researchers have shown that persons with mild and moderate AD actually are able to both participate more or less fully in conversations and to tell stories—if they receive support from other participants, especially those without AD. In this case persons without AD can act as *vicarious voices* (Hydén 2008) scaffolding the telling of the story—to use a concept from Jerome Bruner (Wood, Bruner, and Ross 1976)—by helping to organize both the story and the telling by using for instance speech support or small questions.

In the following we use storytelling events where a woman with AD tells the same story to two different audiences. We do this in order to discuss the different ways the audience, and more specifically the interaction between teller and audience, affect the organization of the narrative and hence the various identity functions of the stories. We also argue that at least some of the difficulties in telling stories by persons with AD can be handled by using smaller ready-made narrative units.

Language and Alzheimer's Disease

Persons with AD have declining cognitive and linguistic functions that make it more difficult to do things like telling stories (Hamilton 1994). Much of the research on the way people with AD tell stories is either experimental in nature, measuring for instance their performance in retelling a story just heard, testing comprehension by answering questions about a story (Welland, Lubinski, and Higginbotham 2002), or telling a story about given pictures (see Ehrlich, Obler, and Clark 1997; Duong, Tardif, and Ska 2003). Other studies draw on interview material where the interviewer prompts the interviewee to narrate stories about his or her life, either to the interviewer or to a spouse (see Usita and Herman 1998).

In these studies it is generally found that persons with AD have problems producing stories and telling stories about topics that others suggest (Usita and Herman 1998). They need a lot of interactional support in order to produce a narrative (Ramanathan 1995). Usita and Herman (1998) also found that narratives told by persons with AD tended to be less chronologically organized. Events were repeated, fewer salient events were mentioned in telling life stories, and certain life stages were nebulously represented. A problem with most of these studies is that the way these experiments are organized and conducted makes it difficult for persons with dementia to tell stories. In a review of language function in AD, Sabat (1994) pointed out that much of the relevant research is hampered by an experimental design, which precludes an analysis of the interaction between researcher and subject. Furthermore, in experiments the subject must talk about topics outside his or her everyday contexts, making the task psychologically unfamiliar and hence artificial. As a result, in these situations, persons with AD tend to perform less well than they would in familiar everyday situations. Researchers tend to ascribe this lower performance to the disease and hence assume that the person is suffering from AD's malignant properties (Kitwood 1998).

For persons with AD, the ability to tell narratives is affected by the deterioration of linguistic and cognitive skills. Several researchers have pointed out that the effects of the loss of cognitive and linguistic abilities are not absolute but depend on the social context, and especially on the attitude of other conversational partners without AD (Sabat 1991; Kitwood 1998). Sabat has pointed out that persons with AD are actually able to pursue conversations and tell narratives if they get interactional support.

The Driver's License Story

In an attempt to avoid some of these methodological limitations, data were collected in one care unit at an elder care facility in Sweden. This care unit served eight residents, seven of whom were diagnosed with some form of dementia, mostly AD. For a period of five months, video recording was done in communal areas at the elder center (data collection by L.Ö.). In total about 150 hours of recording were collected. All these residents had consented, together with their next of kin, to taking part in the study. (All the data are in Swedish and have subsequently been analyzed in relation to Swedish language use. Only the examples used in this chapter have been translated into English.)

Storytelling between persons with AD without staff present was observed mainly between two female residents, Martha and Catherine, diagnosed with AD four to five years ago and seven to eight years ago, respectively. Both have midrange AD, although Martha is distinctively more inclined to hold the floor in conversations and generally less impaired in linguistic capabilities. In small talk and in commenting on other persons' stories, Catherine's difficulties are sometimes negligible, but they become more evident as she tries to construct a story of her own. In spontaneous storytelling situations, Martha is almost always the teller of the story while Catherine is her confidante. Martha's stories, told spontaneously to her friend Catherine, often are autobiographical, are emotionally involved, and contain evaluative statements.

We have identified one story that is told several times by Martha on different occasions, in various contexts, and with shifting audiences. The story is organized around a set of reportable events. The actual story is then adapted to these different contexts and audiences and is therefore told in different ways (cf. Linde 1993; Norrick 1998). We call this "The Driver's License Story." It is about how Martha in her past, perhaps as a young person, decided to learn to drive and to get a driver's license, and then to buy her own car. Her husband questioned her ability, both to learn to drive and to save up for a car by herself, but he was proved wrong. In the summer Martha and her family went for a long car ride, visiting relatives in various places. Martha surprised her sister and mother by being able to drive, and she later on discussed with her sister about being a married woman and learning to drive.

In one sense this is a story about the different reactions encountered some decades ago by a woman wanting to be able to drive and to have her own car. It is a story that portrays Martha as not only challenging the values of her generation about what women could and ought to do but also overcoming them, going her own way, and making a statement about herself.

In the following we analyze this story and the way it was told in two storytelling episodes. Episode 1 takes place within the framework of reading from the day's newspaper and conversing together. This group activity involves one assistant nurse, Martha, her friend Catherine, and four other residents. Martha's story lasts for almost six minutes. Episode 2 occurs about a month later. Martha and Catherine are on their own, commenting on their surroundings. This time the storytelling goes on for over 25 minutes.

The Structure of the Story

During the two storytelling episodes, Martha basically tells about her decision to learn to drive and buy a car, and about her first vacation with her car, driving with her husband to see her family. Analytically, some aspects of Gee's (1986) model for the production of narrative discourse were used. Gee suggested a way of transcribing and analyzing oral narrative, taking its point of departure in the prosodic organization of the narrative. He argues that stories are organized around some basic units that are marked by changes in prosody, like raising the voice, stressing, pauses, and the like. A narrative is divided into main *parts, strophes,* which are organized around happenings or events, and finally *lines,* which are the basic elements expressing ideas. The teller prosodically marks various elements in a narrative, helping the listener to follow and understand the story as he or she hears it; this makes it possible to identify what the teller thinks important, funny, noteworthy, or connected.

Using this model, it could be argued that the stories about getting a driver's license are organized around a set of strophes, for instance "deciding to learn to drive," "the driving instructor encouraging Martha to learn to drive," "Martha decides to buy a car," and so on (table 12.1). The strophes generally have a clear beginning, some sort of complicating action, and an evaluation (Labov and Waletzky 1997). The strophes are variations of more general *themes* that could be considered *parts* of the story; for instance, "getting a driver's license," "buying a car," and "driving on vacation." Taken together, the strophes and the parts constitute a set of temporally progressive events.

The strophes are nested together into stories, and in this way the stories that are told on the two occasions emerge. It is unclear whether the stories that emerge from the nesting process are supposed to be heard as continuous stories—although it is possible to listen to the narrations in that way. The strophes could most probably be thought of as a set of autobiographically reportable events. They are also apparently events to which Martha has access. From the fieldwork we know that Martha had problems accessing memories in general and that she tended to use a small number of stories in different types of situations as a way of creating meaning (Örulv and Hydén 2006).

The strophes are made up of lines that are often organized around certain phrases. Quite often Martha uses the same line (or phrase), although in two different contexts. This is especially true about lines that express some important emotional or moral content. Some of these phrases can be found in both storytelling episodes.

It turns out that Martha organizes the nesting of the strophes into a larger story in different ways, depending on the storytelling setting. When she is telling the story without staff present, the emerging story lacks a temporal progression of events. As a consequence, strophes can be told several times without comments, or events can be told in reverse order or without any temporal order at all. When Martha tells her story with a staff member present, the assistant nurses support Martha's storytelling,

Table 12.1
The Units of the Driver's License Story

	Part I: Martha's Getting a Driver's License
1:1	Martha decides to learn to drive
1:2	The local driving instructor encourages the young Martha to learn how to drive
1:3	Martha's husband questions her ability to learn to drive
1:4	Martha passes her driving test easily
	Part II: Buying a Car
2:1	Martha decides to buy a car (VW)
2:2	Martha's husband questions her ability to save up for a car
2:3	What the car looks like (VW)
2:4	Getting help to buy a car
2:5	Martha plans how to pay for the car
2:6	Making a down payment to get the car right away
2:7	Martha buys a car
2:8	Getting the car (right away)
	Part III: Driving on Vacation and Meeting the Family
3:1	Practicing before going away
3:2	Making a detour (700 kilometers)
3:3	Surprising her sister (later: mother): the absent husband/driver
3:4	Advising her sister about learning to drive: never drive with one's husband
3:5	Competing with her husband for the driver's position
3:6	Stopping along the road, picking berries and flowers
3:7	Driving for several days, visiting other relatives on the way

resulting in a temporally well-organized story. The relationship between the interactional setting and the structure of the story will be analyzed further.

Storytelling Activity in the Absence of Staff

After lunch the two women are moving along the corridor talking, and eventually they sit down on a bench. Quite early on in the stroll, Martha starts to reminisce and gradually starts to tell a story about her driver's license. Catherine goes along and sits close to Martha on the bench. Martha tells her story for about 30 minutes. At that time the staff starts to move around, and the two women hear snatches of the conversation between the staff. The storytelling comes to an end, resulting in a long pause (nearly 2 minutes). After some brief comments about the staff, the two women start to comment on the lights in the corridor. The storytelling episode is over.

Example 1 is from near the end of the episode—that is, after some 25 minutes. It is a typical example of the way the storytelling is organized and of the kind of stories Martha tells. This is the third time during the episode that Martha tells the story about her decision to buy a car. Just before the example starts, she has been telling about making a down payment on a car. In line 1, Martha makes a general comment about that summer, followed by an "and then" (line 2) indicating that new events will be added to the story. On line 4 Martha repeats the "and then" and the new story part organized around a new theme starts:

Example 1

1	Martha:	it was it was such a lovely summer
2		[and then —]
3	Catherine:	[yees you] were lucky
4	Martha:	=and then I got and then I (. . .)
5		the instructor he asked me (.)
6		"would you like me to accompany you looking for a (.) car—"
7		'cause he did understand [(xx)]
8	Catherine:	[yes]
9	Martha:	"'cause they won't cheat you then" he said
10		and then he said
11		"I can accompany you and (..) look for a car 'cause I could pick the best one"
12	Catherine:	yes that's true
13	Martha:	yes "If you want to" he said
14		"yes I would like that" I said
15		"I've got—my brother has got a driver's license but (. . .)
16		but he eh (.)
17		it's better I get to learn from eh someone who's a real instructor"
18	Catherine:	yes that's true
19	Martha:	=yes "You are really careful, you really are" he said
20		((*takes hold of Catherine's arm, leans forwards towards her and looks her in the eye*))
21		"so you'll get along okay" he said
22		[((*leans back and laughs*))]
23	Catherine:	[well that was a nice compliment]
24	Martha:	((laughs)) *yees*
25		((*laughter in her voice; points to Catherine*))
26	Catherine:	she got a nice compliment!
27	Martha:	*yes
28		((makes a pointing gesture toward Catherine again and keeps it during the rest of the utterance))
29		he said that
30		yees*
		((nods and then exchanges a knowing look with Catherine)) ehh
31	Catherine:	yes I believe so (xx xx)
32	Martha:	=yes

In general the telling of the story in the example is interactionally well organized. Both women position themselves in the turn taking as tellers and listeners, changing positions so as to leave room for comments. Catherine frequently supports Martha's storytelling with small interjections or comments (lines 8, 12, 18, 23, 26, 31). There are no gaps in the turn taking, or long pauses or outright misunderstandings that cannot be solved. In the telling there are some small pauses generally having to do with word-finding problems (most notably in lines 15, 16). Thus, there is little indication of problems in the organization of the interaction.

From line 19 and onward to line 31, an evaluative section of the story can be identified. During this stretch of talk, it is noticeable that simultaneous talk appears. The simultaneous talk underlines that both participants have recognized and appreciated the evaluation of the events in the story. In this way closeness between the two women is displayed around some points in the story (for a further analysis of this aspect and its relevance, see Hydén and Örulv 2009). The simultaneous talk is further supported by bodily display of closeness and hand gestures; Martha puts her hand on Catherine's arm, leans forwards, gazes at Catherine, points, and so on (lines 20 and onward).

Discursively the telling is organized around a dialogue between two of the story's main protagonists, Martha and the driving instructor. The dialogue is replayed and dramatized. The quotations are generally prefaced or followed by expressions like "he said," "and then he said," "I said," and the like. Martha's narrative voice is found only at the beginning of the story (lines 1, 2, 4, 5) and in the small comments in the evaluative part of the story (lines 21, 24, 25).

There is a problem with unclear word references and sometimes confusing pronouns. In line 4, for instance, Martha says, "and then I got and then I," and in line 6 she quotes her driving instructor. What she probably meant to say is that she got her driver's license and then considered buying a car. In lines 15 and 16, Martha evidently has problems finding words. She resolves this problem by using a phrase that she has used several times previously: "It's better I get to learn from eh someone who's a real instructor." This solution introduces a third problem, namely, the fusion of two storylines.

In line 15, Martha introduces a circumstance that probably is important to her: the fact that her brother has a driver's license. Potentially, he could help her select and buy a new car. When she has talked about her brother previously, it had to do with her not letting him teach her how to drive. It is this storyline she continues in line 17, that she wants the professional instructor to teach her how to drive. She then continues the storyline by quoting her instructor's approval of her choice. The fusion of two different storylines in this ways happens several times during the storytelling episode.

In general, during the whole storytelling episode when Martha nests the strophes together she does not organize her telling around a temporal progression of the events. Normally it would be expected that this type of autobiographical story would be organized around a set of events that are temporally ordered; the order of the events in the telling corresponds to the order in which it is told (cf. Labov 1972). This would make it possible for the listener to pose the question "What happened then?" to the unfolding narrative, and to listen for the next. What happens when Martha tells her story is that she changes the order of the events and repeats certain events and parts of the story several times, making certain that events appear again and again without relating them to the temporal sequence of events.

Normally, a storyteller has to indicate very specifically if new information and events are added to the story told so far. This happens if the teller has *forgotten* to mention some important information, making subsequent events unintelligible or pointless. The reason for the teller to indicate the addition of new information is that the listener then has to reinterpret what has been going on in the story because there will be a new answer to the listener's ubiquitous question "and then what happened?" Martha does not indicate that she is adding new events, and Catherine as a listener does not signal any problems with understanding the unfolding story. One possible reason for adding the new events and strophes could be that they are in some way thematically connected to something in the preceding strophe.

Telling the Story with Staff Present: Scaffolding

In the video-recorded material, the driver's license story is told twice when staff is present. Generally the story is organized as a number of narrative units organized around strophes that are then nested into a larger story, similar to what happened without staff present. The main difference has to do with the fact that the assistant nurses actively support the telling of, and help to organize, the stories through questions and other means.

Example 2 is from an episode where six of the persons with AD and a nurse are sitting around a table while the assistant nurse reads aloud. The assistant nurse has just been reading an article involving cars, and one of the participants asks the assistant nurse if she has a car. This starts a more general discussion among the participants about cars, different types of cars, and so on. After some further discussion, the assistant nurse turns to Martha and Catherine and asks them if they used to have driver's licenses. (Unfortunately we do not know whether the assistant nurse in this particular case knew about Martha's story and hence wanted her to tell the story, although this is a common strategy in the data and occurs in relation to this very story later on with another assistant nurse.)

In response to the assistant nurse's question, Martha tells about acquiring her driver's license and how she and her husband went for a vacation (example 2). They went north from their home, on small roads, in order to visit Martha's sister and her family and other relatives, and Martha was eager to be at the wheel.

Example 2

Martha: and then we drove up to eh
X-county an' an' an' [further up] ((1))
Catherine: [X-county?] ((1)) [(xx xx)] ((2))
Martha: [to X-county and further up] ((2))
I drove 700 kilometers then
[(xx xx)]

7	Asst. nurse:	[wow]
8	Martha:	I was so afraid Edward ((*her husband*)) would get ahead of me to the wheel
9		so I eh was in an awful hurry whenever we were to drive off ((*laughter in her voice at the end of this line*)) ((*laughter*))
10	Asst. nurse:	but did you drive all the way by yourself?
11	Martha:	=yes I did
12	Asst. nurse:	=wow
13	Catherine:	=you were stubborn
14	Asst. nurse:	yeah
15	Catherine:	but then you managed [that]
16	Asst. nurse:	[but] then you made many rest stops?
17		did you stop ma—?
18	Martha:	=well we stopped here and there and had berries an'
19		and there were lingonberries and bilberries too
20	Asst. nurse:	=ye:ah
21	Martha:	•yeah
22		and then we had relatives along the route too
23	Asst. nurse:	yes, okay ((*nodding*))

As we can see in this example, the assistant nurse actively supports Martha in her telling in various ways. She uses sustainers prompting Martha to go on (lines 14, 20, 23), evaluative utterances (lines 7, 12), and she requests further information (lines 10, 16–17). When further information has been provided, she signals understanding (line 23).

When Martha drives home a point (line 9) about hurrying to get behind the wheel before her husband, she laughs. At this point the assistant nurse requests further information when she asks what happened next: "But did you drive all the way by yourself?" This request helps Martha to present some more information about her driving—and she gets appreciation from both Catherine and the assistant nurse. The assistant nurse again requests more information (lines 16, 17), and in response to this Martha continues her story.

The intervention of the assistant nurse helps Martha tell the events in a progressive order and also to avoid repetitions. In this way it is easy to follow and understand what once took place and what events Martha wants to tell about. The assistant nurse's requests underscore Martha's accomplishment, giving her fellow participant Catherine the opportunity to affirm Martha as both stubborn and capable (lines 13–15). They also put the events in order. Having clarified the fact that they had relatives along the route, Martha is then able to move on to tell about meeting her sister (subsequent to the excerpt) and surprising her by being able to drive, and the parts of the story are linked together in a smooth and unproblematic way.

When a staff member is present, it also seems that the active support from the assistant nurses is a very effective way of helping Martha in her storytelling. They scaffold Martha in her storytelling (Wood, Bruner, and Ross 1976), in two ways. The first way is providing a framework to enable Martha to tell a shorter anecdote that fits into the conversation, and the second is helping Martha tell the events in a progressive temporal order. In the first episode the small story illustrates a point already made by the assistant nurse, and Martha does not need to explain why she tells this story. Nor does she need to establish its relation to other events over a longer period of time, which would be more problematic, but can stick to this single anecdote, embracing only one situation.

In the example, Martha is given the opportunity to present herself in a certain way to an audience. That is, she presents herself without having to establish on her own all the contextual information that the listener is usually provided with in autobiographical storytelling (cf. Moore and Davis 2002; Usita and Herman 1998).

The Story Told Twice

In these examples it is evident that for Martha, telling about getting a driver's license, buying a car, and getting to drive on her own—and being capable of doing so—is a way for her to remember events that are somehow central to her identity. This is probably true even if she is only able to tell parts or fragments of the story on her own, that is, in a sequence that makes sense logically. A constantly recurring theme is her ability to do things on her own and follow her own mind, even if other people are critical or might disapprove of her actions. Apparently, retelling these memories is a way for her to sustain her identity as an independent and capable woman who knows her own mind.

Although combined differently, there is an overall similarity between the two versions of the driver's license story as to what units are included. The parts seem to fit together in more than one way, some of which notably diverge from the chronological structure but still add up to a recognizable story—even with instances of almost identical linguistic phrases. Taken together, this indicates that Martha is using a number of kindred themes, closely related to getting a driver's license and to the consequences of this. In this respect her way of telling has a close resemblance to traditional oral storytelling. In the 1960s Albert Lord pointed out that traditional storytellers did not so much recite lengthy stories from memory as they—in their "reciting"—*composed* the tales, using traditional verbal formulas (Lord 1960). Gee (1986) argues in a similar fashion. Stories that stand out from standard patterns, he claims, become comprehensible when viewed as *oral* stories rather than as literary stories.

In previous articles (Örulv and Hydén 2006; Hydén and Örulv 2009) we have argued that the frequent retelling of stories organized around a common overall theme—often used to make sense of the current situation even when not quite applicable—could have to do with having limited access to certain cognitive themes, resulting in a reuse of those accessible themes. We used the term "story lines," that is, genres of narrative plots that organize the stories and render them meaningful as being part of that particular genre and often of a certain moral theme. These genres are also connected to certain ways of presenting a positive self-identity.

In line with this, it can also be argued that difficulties in telling autobiographical stories can be handled by (re-)using smaller ready-made units that somehow illustrate a meaning-based connection between events (Ramanathan 1997, 115). That is, one reuses more or less flexible resources that can be combined in a variety of ways, although still in line with the same moral theme, to compose autobiographical stories. In this way the referential aspects of the composed story do not quite add up as comprehensible when scrutinized, but the point or the moral theme remains intact (see Örulv and Hydén 2006). As a consequence it becomes possible to use these moral themes to sustain the teller's identity.

One important finding in this study is that it is possible for a person to relate actively to a loss of memory by using his or her remaining narrative elements in creative ways, and with some support. Thus, Martha is capable of combining a set of narrative events, characterized by their tellability and evaluative points, into a storytelling event. That is, memory loss is not a simple loss of memories but a loss of a possibility to combine and use memories in telling stories that are recognizable by others.

It also turns out that the most important thing is not necessarily the progressing temporal organization but the tellability of the story and its evaluative points. As long as this works, the teller with AD can use the telling of stories to present and negotiate his or her identity.

Transcript Key

(1)	Line numbers are organized so as to reflect the rhythm of the speech and actions.
((*italic text*))	nonverbal actions and clarifications
underlining	emphasis
[text]	Brackets indicate the start and end points of overlapping speech (numbered within double parentheses when two such instances occur next to each other).
:	elongated syllable
=	following previous utterance in immediate succession
•hh	audible inhalation
•yeah	inhalation speech
"text"	reported speech, marked explicitly or with paralinguistic measures such as change in voice quality
—	interrupted speech
?	question intonation
(xx xx)	inaudible speech
(text)	unclear speech

REFERENCES

Duong, Ahn, Andreanne Tardif, and Bernadette Ska. 2003. Discourse about discourse: What is it and how does it progress in Alzheimer's disease? *Brain & Cognition* 53:177–80.

Ehrlich, Jonathan S., Loraine Obler, and Lynne Clark. 1997. Ideational and semantic contributions to narrative production in adults with dementia of the Alzheimer's type. *Journal of Communication Disorders* 30:79–99.

Gee, James P. 1986. Units in the production of narrative discourse. *Discourse Processes* 9:391–422.

Hamilton, Heidi E. 1994. *Conversations with an Alzheimer's patient: An interactional sociolinguistic study.* New York: Cambridge University Press.

Hydén, Lars Christer. 2008. Broken and vicarious voices in narratives. In *Health, culture and illness: Broken narratives,* ed. L. C. Hydén and J. Brockmeier, 36–53. New York: Routledge.

Hydén, Lars Christer, and Linda Örulv. 2009. Narrative and identity in Alzheimer's disease: A case study. *Journal of Aging Studies* 23:260–74.

Kitwood, Tom. 1998. Toward a theory of dementia care: Ethics and interaction. *Journal of Clinical Ethics* 9:23–34.

Labov, William. 1972. *Language in the inner city: Studies in the Black English vernacular.* Philadelphia: University of Pennsylvania Press.

Labov, William, and Joshua Waletzky. 1997. Narrative analysis: Oral versions of personal experience. *Journal of Narrative and Life History* 7:3–38. Orig. pub. 1967.

Linde, Charlotte. 1993. *Life stories: The creation of coherence.* New York: Oxford University Press.

Lord, A. 1960. *The singer of tales.* Cambridge, MA: Harvard University Press.

Mills, Marie A. 1997. Narrative identity and dementia: A study of emotion and narrative in older people with dementia. *Ageing and Society* 17:673–98.

Moore, Linda A., and Boyd Davis. 2002. Quilting narrative: Using repetition techniques to help elderly communicators. *Geriatric Nursing* 23:262–66.

Norrick, Neal R. 1998. Retelling stories in spontaneous conversation. *Discourse Processes* 25:75–97.

Örulv, Linda, and Lars Christer Hydén. 2006. Confabulation: Sense-making, self-making and world-making in dementia. *Discourse Studies* 8:647–73.

Ramanathan, Vai. 1995. Narrative well-formedness in Alzheimer's discourse: An interactional examination across settings. *Journal of Pragmatics* 23:395–419.

———. 1997. *Alzheimer discourse: Some sociolinguistic dimensions.* Mahwah, NJ: Lawrence Erlbaum Associates.

Sabat, Steven R. 1991. Facilitating conversation via indirect repair: A case study of Alzheimer's disease. *Georgetown Journal of Languages and Linguistics* 2:284–96.

———. 1994. Language function in Alzheimer's disease: A critical review of selected literature. *Language and Communication* 14:331–51.

———. 2001. *Experience of Alzheimer's disease. Life through a tangled veil.* Oxford: Blackwell.

Usita, Paula M., and Keith C. Herman. 1998. Narrative intentions: Listening to life stories in Alzheimer's disease. *Journal of Aging Studies* 12:185–98.

Welland, Richard J., Rosemary Lubinski, and D. Jeffrey Higginbotham. 2002. Discourse comprehension test performance of elders with dementia of the Alzheimer type. *Journal of Speech, Language, and Hearing Research* 45:1175–87.

Wood, David, Jerome Bruner, and Gail Ross. 1976. The role of tutoring in problem solving. *Journal of child psychology and psychiatry* 17:89–100.

13

Concurrent and Intervening Actions during Storytelling in Family "Ceremonial" Dinners

JENNY MANDELBAUM
Rutgers University

IN ORDINARY CONVERSATION, speakers take turns at talk that usually consist of one turn constructional unit, and then speaker exchange occurs (Sacks, Schegloff, and Jefferson 1974). In telling a story, a speaker produces more than one turn constructional unit. To do this, a prospective storyteller (sometimes in collaboration with prospective recipients), indicates that there is a story to tell, and may be granted the conversational floor for an extended turn (Jefferson 1978; Sacks 1978). As a storytelling proceeds, the ends of turn constructional units may provide opportunities for, or make relevant, turns by recipients. As I discuss below, these recipient turns are usually minimal, and foster or support the ongoing storytelling, both in terms of reserving the conversational floor for the storyteller, and facilitating the action the teller purports to be producing through the telling (Stivers 2008). There are occasions, however, when a recipient produces turns that disrupt or intervene into an ongoing storytelling. It is these recipient responses that are the focus of this chapter.

I describe two ways in which recipients can intervene into storytellings (thereby temporarily suspending or diverting them), and address the import for family relations of the character and placement of these interventions. The first kind of intervention involves attending to local material matters. The second involves recipients producing nonaligned responses. Both practices are widespread in my data set.

This chapter draws on more than forty videotapes of family dinners, most of them holiday dinners, and approaches these data from the perspective of conversation analysis (cf., e.g., Atkinson and Heritage 1984). The data are videotapes of events that would have occurred whether or not they were videotaped. Families signed informed consent forms, and they agreed to videotape "ceremonial" dinners (e.g., Thanksgiving, Easter, or Passover dinners) by setting up a video camera before dinner in a position that included all participants in the camera's view, turning the camera on, and letting it run until the end of the dinner. The interaction preserved on these tapes was examined for possible orderly practices and sense-making processes in interaction through which participants produce actions.

For conversation analysts, once a candidate phenomenon is identified, a collection is built of multiple possible instances of the phenomenon. These are then analyzed in detail, and they are compared in order to discern regularities in the operation of the piece of action being examined that operate across multiple instances and thus constitute a stable practice for performing that action. (For further details of conversation analytic methods, see Atkinson and Heritage 1984; Pomerantz and Fehr 1997). Drawing on the database of forty videotapes, this chapter summarizes an initial examination of two kinds of recipient interventions into storytelling—attending to material, non–storytelling-related matters, and producing nonaligned recipient responses. Each was widespread in this data set, and provides an opportunity to consider the role that family relationships may play in the organization of the telling of a story.

Research has shown that storytelling can play an important role in family life (Blum-Kulka 1997; Ochs and Taylor 1995). However, conversation analysts are wary of assuming that constructs from outside of interaction—such as culture, context, gender, relationship, family or anything else—are to be taken to be relevant to the organization of the actions that are being performed in it. The burden of relevance is on the interactants. That is to say, for the *analyst* to take it that some construct from outside of the interaction is procedurally relevant (Schegloff 1987) to its unfolding, the analyst must show that and how interactants are demonstrably oriented to that particular construct at that particular moment. Though the majority of the interactions in my collection of Thanksgiving, Easter, and Passover dinners are fellow family members, it is not always "family" that is procedurally relevant or demonstrably oriented to in such a way as to shape the unfolding interaction.

Recipient intervention into storytellings is a well-documented phenomenon. Sacks (1978) suggested that any recipient turns during a storytelling constitute a kind of interruption of it, because storytellings involve the floor being yielded to one party for an extended turn at talk. But other work has indicated that recipient turns can either foster the ongoing storytelling or impede it. Schegloff (1982) showed how crucial recipient "continuers"—such as "mmhm," "uh huh," and "yeah"—are to the ongoing storytelling. He demonstrated that they have a robust role as indicators that a recipient is attending to the story but is not taking up or preparing to take up the floor at the end of a unit of the telling.

Similarly, Goodwin (1986) described how the precise placement of recipient continuers and assessments can provide for the continuation of the ongoing storytelling. Unless they are misplaced or misaligned, continuers and assessments do not constitute interventions into storytellings, but rather can provide indications from recipients of what they take to be the current state of the storytelling, in terms of both its progress and its import. There are things that recipients can do that can intervene into, or compete with, the storytelling, however—and actions of this kind are the focus of this chapter. Goodwin (1997, 78), drawing on Goffman, described what she called "byplay": teasing, heckling, or playfully dealing with a description or story. Mandelbaum (1989) described how recipients can produce questions during the course of a storytelling that can fundamentally redirect or reconstitute the story.

In this chapter I describe two other intervention practices, each falling on different ends of the social solidarity scale. One is "material interventions": a recipient intervenes in a storytelling to pursue temporarily some material matter, such as asking for or about food. The other is where a recipient produces responses in such a way as to indicate a different upshot and/or trajectory for the storytelling than the one indicated by the teller. I noted above that for conversation analysts, invoking such discourse-extrinsic concepts as "family" is usually avoided unless they can be shown to be procedurally relevant. In each of the cases examined below it is possible to invoke family relationships as at least partially implicated in the interventions that occur. After laying out the practices and discussing them, I return to a discussion of the extent to which "family" can be invoked in understanding how these recipient responses unfold.

The first practice we examine involves a potential story recipient producing a first pair part request of someone at the table, seeking a material object such as food. These requests need not become the focal action of talk; they can be dealt with nonverbally, for instance by indicating an item of food to be passed, followed by the passing of it by a fellow interactant. When they do become focal actions, however, their precise placement in ongoing talk may indicate the social or relational "job" that they may be, at least in part, designed to accomplish. The second practice is the production of nonaligned recipient responses. These responses take up an element that is available in the storytelling, but they take it in a direction that differs from the one for which the storyteller appears to have built the storytelling. In the instances examined in this study, these nonaligned recipient responses are also disaffiliative.

In instance (1) there is a food solicitation and a food offer, but they are produced in ways that both intervene in between the soliciting of a storytelling and its production, and also seem oriented to "rescuing" the potential storyteller, a child, from her father's requests for and assessment of the storytelling. That is, here the placement of alternate focal actions, the solicitation and offer of a roll, seems designed by the mother, who solicits a roll for herself and then offers a roll to the child, to provide what we might loosely call social support for the child from whom the storytelling has been solicited:

(1) [Stew Dinner]
1 DAD: [So Ci:n (0.2) tell me
2 about your day.
3 (0.5)
4 CIN: Uh::h
5 DAD: Wha'd=ju (d) learn.
6 (1.0)
7 DAD: [O:^::H yeah (we) went to thuh- we went to uh: (.)
8 CIN: [Uh:m-
9 CIN: Claim Jumper.
10 DAD: Claim Jum[per today.
11 MOM: [(>uh huh<)
12 MOM: May I have a roll [please,
13 CIN: [For uh field trip.=
14 DAD: =Sure.
15 DAD: An' may I have thuh- butter please.

16 MOM: Yes.=hh
17 (0.5)
18 CIN: Went to Claim Jumper for (our)/(uh) fie:ld trip.
19 DAD: Yiea:h, an'- an'- tell me about it.
20 (0.5)
21 MOM: °°Cindy want uh roll,°°
22 (1.0)
23 CIN: Mm[::_
24 MOM: [(It's soft, it's good,)
25 DAD: Come on,
26 CIN: Ye[ah.
27 DAD: [Describe this thing to me,
28 CIN: Uh:m_ .h It was fu:n¿
29 (0.3)
30 DAD: No.
31 (.)
32 DAD: You're gonna h(h)afta do uh lot [better than that.]
33 MOM: [Well she's-] she'll s- she's-
34 DAD: Hey [(shh:)
35 MOM: [(just starting.) [°She's just starting.°
36 DAD: [Don't: defend 'er:,
37 DAD: [I wanna hear this from °her.°
38 MOM: [( ) ((high pitched mumble))
39 MOM: °She'll do fine,°
40 (0.5)
41 CIN: Uhm_ (2.0) What's this?
42 (1.0)
43 MOM: Uh garbanzo bean.
44 CIN: Ew:.
45 DAD: It's uh bean.
46 MOM: You don't haft[a eat that part. Just eat the vegetable(s).
47 DAD: [It's just uh type of bean.
48 DAD: [And- [tell me-
49 CIN: [(m) [(m)
50 MOM: °Can I have the butter please,°
51 DAD: Sure.
52 (3.5)
53 DAD: Cin¿ Go ahead. You're up.
54 MOM: (°Take your knife °)
55 (1.5)
56 CIN: They took us on uh tou:r through the kitchen.
57 CIN: An' my favorite (0.2) part was going in thuh z- (0.3)
58 uhm_ thuh z:ero freezer. Zero below.
59 (0.5)
60 DAD: [O:h. (It was) zero degrees in there?

Here, Mom, Dad, and nine-year-old Cindy are beginning dinner together. In line 1 Dad solicits from Cindy an account of her day: "So Cin tell me about your day." After a brief gap in line 3, during which Cindy leans forward, Cindy begins a turn with "Uh::". Simultaneously she puts a forkful of food in her mouth. Though eating does not have to substitute for talking, here it apparently does. So this is one kind of material intervention into a storytelling—the storyteller may, at least temporarily, substitute eating for talking.

In line 5 Dad produces a more specific solicit of the telling from Cindy, "Wha'd=ju learn". In line 6 Dad takes a roll. Next, in lines 7 and 10, Dad recalls what Cindy did: "O:::H yeah (we) went to thuh- went to uh: Claim Jumper today." Mom offers confirmation in line 11. (As the tape proceeds, we learn that she chaperoned the field trip). At this point, Cindy could be about to produce her storytelling. In line 12, however, Mom asks for a roll. This may be prompted by Dad having just taken a roll in line 6. Next, Dad asks for the butter in line 15. Despite Cindy's "for a field trip" in line 13, completing Dad's turn and perhaps beginning the solicited report of her day, in line 14 Dad is fully oriented to Mom's request, granting it with "Sure" in line 14, then passing her the bag of rolls, while issuing a related request in line 15. He builds it as related or reciprocal with the "and" that begins his turn, "An' may I have the butter please." He is fully involved with the material matter of food allocation then, and is not currently aligned as a recipient of Cindy's incipient story (that he has solicited). Mom says "yes" in line 16, then passes the butter. Cindy treats the reciprocal exchange as complete here, as in line 18 she puts together her utterances from lines 9 and 13, "Went to Claim Jumper for uh field trip." She produces this as though it is a complete turn constructional unit. In line 19, Dad solicits more from Cindy, treating this as an incomplete account: "Yiea:h, an'- an'- tell me about it."

At this point, Dad has clearly solicited a report of Cindy's day. It should be produced immediately next. As Cindy straightens up in her seat though, during the (0.5) gap in line 20, in line 21, in a whisper, Mom offers Cindy a roll: °°Cindy want uh roll,°°. Dad has taken a roll in line 6, and is currently attending to buttering it. Simultaneous with Dad's solicitation of Cindy's story in line 19, "Yiea:h, an'- an'- tell me about it," Mom has extracted a roll for herself from the bag. Her hand immediately dips back into the bag during the (0.5) second silence in line 20, during which Cindy has not begun to respond to Dad's solicitation, and she extracts another roll. In terms of the food allocation procedures of the meal, then, giving Cindy a roll is a possibly relevant next action, since Dad has one, Mom has just taken one, and Cindy is therefore the only one at the table who does not yet have a roll.

That Mom produces her offer sotto voce may indicate that she takes it that this action should be produced and treated as a subordinate activity—that is, there is some primary activity to which this should be subordinated. Presumably it is Dad's strong solicitation of Cindy's account of her day, making relevant a story from Cindy to which the offer of the roll is produced as subordinate by whispering it. However, it is important to look at the placement of the offer. It comes after Dad's third solicitation of an account from Cindy, and at a point where Cindy could or should have started her account but has not. In producing her offer *here,* it is possible that Mom may be oriented to some difficulty Cindy may be having in producing the story indicated by recurrent delays in starting at lines 3, 4, 6, 8, 17, and, most recently, line 20. The offer of a roll may provide a temporary alternative primary focus (produced as a temporary alternative *subordinate* focus via the whisper). The offer could provide for a "legitimate" delay in Cindy beginning her story.

During the one-second silence in line 22, Cindy is oriented to the roll, and she appears to be considering it. This is further indicated in line 23 in her "Mm," which could be heard to be enacting thinking or considering. At this point Cindy needs to respond to two quite different first pair part initiating actions: her father's solicitation of a story, and her mother's offer of a roll. It is possible that her "Mm" in line 23 can be heard to be responding to either initiating action by enacting "thinking." In lines 24 and 25, both parents solicit her further. In line 24, Mom provides positive assessments of the roll, "It's soft, it's good" thus renewing and upgrading the offer. In line 25, Dad prompts Cindy to tell her story with "Come on." That he says no more about what he is expecting from Cindy indicates his understanding of the force of his earlier story solicit to make relevant a story next.

In line 27, in overlap with Cindy's "Yeah" in line 26, when she takes the roll from her mother, Dad produces another more specific solicit of a story from Cindy: "Describe this thing to me." There is considerably more recipient intervention as this story proceeds, some of it from Dad quite negative, as in Dad's assessment of the story so far in line 32, "You're gonna have to do uh lot better than that." Space considerations preclude examination of this recipient assessment of the story itself, and the storyteller's own possible diversionary tactic in line 41, inquiring about an object in the stew, "What's this."

In the practices we have examined in this instance, first pair part turns concerned with the material matter of food distribution are produced at points where the storytelling has been strongly solicited by using first pair parts that make a telling relevant immediately next. The intervening turns are positioned just at the juncture where Cindy appears to be struggling with the production of the storytelling. They may thus be seen to give Cindy a legitimate alternative activity she "should" participate in, perhaps as a way to "protect" Cindy from her father's forceful solicitation of her storytelling. In this way, these material interventions in the particular positions in which they occur may provide a way for Mom to "protect" or "support" Cindy.

In the next instance, we see interventions of a different kind. Rather than being concerned with material matters extraneous to the storytelling, a recipient produces nonaligned responses of various kinds. This extract is taken from a family Easter dinner. Participants are Tim, who is a college student home for the Easter holiday; Mangita, Tim's fellow college student girlfriend; Tim's parents, Dad and Mom; Jon, Tim's brother, who is in high school; and Bobshi, who is Mom's mother, and Tim and Jon's grandmother. Immediately before this excerpt, the family has been reminiscing about a car they had when the boys were younger:

(2) [Easter Soup – Vacation Story 19:47–23:42]

54 TIM: ((addressed aside to Mangita)) That's the one the- (.) the horses
55 shit on the windshield.
56 ( ): (hhh)

(0.5)
JON: and Mom went [through the] ( )
MAN: [O:h yah]
(1.3)
JON: (wall)
(0.3)
MAN: (ehh)(heh)
(1.3)
MOM: [(But-/Bite-) it's sti:ll a- a wonderful fa:mily=
( ): [( )
MOM: =memory.
TIM: iYeh?
JON: (hm) (hm)[(hm) (hm)
TIM: [Yeh (only) I 'on't like the sme:ll.
MAN: heh huh huh huh huh huh
MOM: Then when I pu[t (the) windshield wipers
DAD: [Do you remember your
DAD: [mother turning the windshield wi]pers o:n mm hm
MAN: [hah hah hah hah hah]
DAD: hm hm hm hm [hm hm hm
TIM: [Didn't work very well
MAN: -(hh)huh huh -(h[h)::
DAD: [D'you remember ten minutes (in)
your mother got pulled over by a Virginia
trooper¿
TIM: nI remember she got p[ulled]
MOM: [No:.] I got
pu[lled over by a trooper cz-
TIM: [I- I remember her getting pulled over a lo:t.
DAD: No she got pulled over by a Virginia trooper. You
guys were in the ba:ck seat. (0.5) and this
Smokey [the Bear guy,]
TIM: [All the other-] All the other cars le:ft,
(0.5)
TIM: and [she's
DAD: [Ye:s.
(0.5)
TIM: [Pulled over]
DAD: [Well this] Smokey the Bear guy sticks 'is head
in the window n says we're lu:cky that we have
extradition otherwise he would've taken 'er in
jail. (.) And you two who were >little at the
time< started baw:ling crying cause they were
gonna jail your mother¿
(0.5)

TIM: I wi:sh they ha:d.= ((through a mouthful))
MOM: =and I was going <si:xty two: mi:les an hou:r.>
(0.3)
TIM: Why:¿
(1.4)
DAD: We were [keeping up with traffic as a m(h)atter=
MOM: [Why¿
DAD: =of fact. they just- (0.5) d-=
TIM: =are you the [only ( )]
DAD: [They took us to a justice (a) the
peace hou:se. He said "You fo:ll[ow me]

The family has been reminiscing about a Pontiac Bonneville that they had. In line 54, Tim has identified the car to Mangita in the following way: "That's the one the- the horses shit on the windshield." Tim's responses to his parents' talk resist aligning with them. When Mom, in line 65, somewhat jokingly proposes this as a "Wonderful family memory," Tim contests it with a questioning "Yeh?" in line 68, and in line 70 he formulates an exception: "Only I don't like the smell." The family continues to reminisce about this occurrence, with Dad in lines 73–74 soliciting the boys' memory with "Do you remember your mother turn the windshield wipers o:n:." While, in lines 75 and 76, Mangita and Dad laugh, Tim treats the matter seriously with "Didn't work very well" in line 77.

Although much could be said about Tim's nonaligned responses to the family's reminiscences at this point in the interaction, here I focus on three different subsequent nonaligned responses. First, in response to his father's reminiscence solicit (Lerner 1992) in line 79, rather than producing or coproducing the solicited reminiscence, Tim produces a slightly different one that resists Dad's projected reminiscence and is also condemnatory of his mother. Second, in response to his father's telling of the reminiscence, Tim offers a markedly different reaction than the one his father reports. Again, this response is hostile toward his mother. Finally, when his mother reports her traffic "violation" in a way that presents it as self-evidently nonblameworthy (thus indicating that she was stopped unnecessarily by the trooper), Tim treats the violation as accountable, thus rejecting her claim of self-evident innocence. Each response thus intervenes in the ongoing reminiscence by resisting its projected trajectory and import.

First, Tim produces a different kind of reminiscence than his father's reminiscence solicit projects. In line 79, Dad solicits Tim and Jon's memory of what happened next after their mother turned on the windshield wipers: "D' you remember ten minutes in your mother got pulled over by a Virginia trooper¿" As Lerner (1992) points out, reminiscence solicits are a way to begin a storytelling about a shared event. In lines 83–84, Mom appears to be about to set the record straight, rejecting Dad's version with "No": "No I got pulled over by a trooper cz-." In overlap with Mom's turn, in line 85 Tim uses reminiscence as a pretext for introducing something related but with a quite different trajectory: "I remember her getting pulled over a lot." So he treats Dad's reminiscence solicit as prompting memory not of a particular occasion but of multiple occasions of being pulled over. In this way he participates in the activity of reminiscing, but he builds his response not by assisting in bringing the storytelling to the floor (as can be prompted by a reminiscence solicits) but by prompting a different kind of memory that contains a critique of Mom. Though this is an available direction in response to Dad's reminiscence solicit, it draws a somewhat different import than that which Dad's turn projected.

Next, Tim makes relevant next further talk regarding Mom being pulled over recurrently, rather than regarding this particular occurrence. In this way he introduces a critique of Mom as though this is the solicited response. In producing a related yet divergent response in second position, Tim directs talk toward critique of Mom rather than reminiscencing about the family event Dad has invoked. This direction is different both materially, in terms of what gets addressed, and relationally—in two senses. First, it deals with a critique of Mom, and it is thus potentially disaffiliative with her. Second, it disjoins Tim from the solicited reminiscence of a shared family event, and thus it separates his memory from the shared family memory that Dad has projected. Further, it projects the abandonment of reminiscing about this particular occasion, in favor of remembering Mom being pulled over recurrently. Note, however, that it is formulated as reminiscing. Dad has solicited their remembering with "Do you remember." Tim uses the "remembering" format in line 85 with "I remember her getting pulled over a lot." In this way he preserves the activity format, reminiscing, but invokes a remembering that does not involve a story but rather a more general indictment of Mom's driving.

In line 86, Dad expeditiously dismisses this direction for conversation made available by Tim by beginning his next utterance with "No," followed by a report of the event regarding which he was apparently soliciting reminiscence: "No she got pulled over by a Virginia trooper. You guys were in the b<u>a</u>:ck seat. (0.5) and this Smokey the B<u>e</u>ar guy. . . ." This perhaps attests to the interactional rights to the floor of a storyteller who has projected a story to tell, and it displays the kind of interactional resources that can be deployed to resist recipient intervention.

Throughout the ensuing telling, Tim resists the import of his parents' reminiscences. We next examine his resistance to the import his Dad draws from the recounted reminiscence. In lines 95–100, Dad proceeds to report the event. The punch line is that the children, Jon and Tim, were crying because they thought that their mother was about to be taken away by the trooper. The story is formulated as addressed to Jon and Tim via "you two" and "your mother" and via Dad's gaze being directed toward them. In line 101, there is no uptake of the apparent punch line of the story. In line 102, Tim says "I wish they had," apparently indicating, contrary to the implications of his reported "bawling crying," that he would have preferred it if his mother had been jailed. This reaction contrasts strongly with that portrayed in the telling. In addition to not taking it up as a reminiscence, it indicates the opposite reaction to the prospect of his mother being arrested than the one recalled by his father. In this way, Tim does not take up his father's story as a reminiscence; nor does he take up the available hearing of it as an amusing story about their youth. Further, he actively counteracts the implication of fondness for or concern about their mother.

When his mother, in line 103, produces a turn that relies on recipients to collaborate with her in her claim of self-evident almost-innocence, "and I was going <si:xty two: mi:les an hou:r," Tim treats the claim as accountable (Heritage 1984; Scott and Lyman 1968), by asking "Why:¿" in line 105, thus rejecting her claim of self-evident innocence. In her tone of voice, she indicates strongly that she takes this to be ridiculous, and presumably self-evidently so. In portraying the ticket as ridiculous, she also implies that she was not blameworthy. However, in line 105, Tim does not treat it as self-evidently ridiculous. Rather, he asks "Why," indicating that he takes going at 62 miles per hour to be something that needs justification, and is thus a problem rather than self-evidently not a problem. In line 107, after a long gap in line 106, Dad provides an account for the speed, formulating it as a safety-related matter: "We were keeping up with traffic as a matter of fact." He formulates this turn as contesting by including "as a matter of fact," indicating that this is contrary to the expectations embodied in the "Why" in line 105.

Notice, then, that here Tim resists his mother's apparent project of indicating that she was stopped unnecessarily by contesting that which she indicates she takes to be self-evident. This has consequences for the storytelling, because it results in further talk regarding the occurrence devoted to showing how his mother was in fact not culpable. It also has relational consequences, in that Mom proposes herself as blameless, and Tim resists this, thereby implicating her as blameworthy.

Here, then, we see a different kind of recipient intervention into a storytelling structure. The storytelling structure is a reminiscence—a format that is widespread in family dinners. Reminiscences of shared events are plausibly particularly susceptible to recipient intervention and redirection, or, to put it a little differently, are likely to involve multiple participants who could be "co-storytellers" and who could legitimately provide knowledgeable contributions or responses to the storytelling. So reminiscences may provide for access to the production of the storytelling in a much more liberal way than is typical of other kinds of storytelling. Likewise, they also invoke a special array of "proper" responses.

We know from years of research on storytelling in everyday conversations that recipient responses play a key role in the ongoing construction of a storytelling. For unknowing recipients (Goodwin 1981), a key part of responding to a storytelling is discerning, taking up, or resisting the "project" that the story may be designed to enact (Stivers 2008). Despite the fact that the reminiscence solicits indicate the expectation that he is in fact a *knowing* recipient—one who is already privy to the events to be told, and therefore possibly aware of their import—we see this kind of resistance produced persistently by Tim. In addition to having the potential to derail or redirect the reminiscences and storytelling, Tim's responses position him antagonistically vis-à-vis his parents. From this instance we learn something about the interactional construction of families.

In various ways, reminiscence of shared family events may provide a particularly powerful opportunity for a family to enact being a family by producing the appearance of a group with distributed roles and perspectives of particular kinds of events that form a shared history. Shared assessment and alignment on the meaning of those events is clearly optional. However, resisting parents' interactional projects—not only by treating a projected reminiscence about a particular event as invoking recurrent instances of that occurrence (rather than a reminiscence about a particular event) but also by contesting parents' inferences about these shared events—enacts a particular kind of disaffiliation and independence. Agreeing on the import of a particular memory may embody a family that is unified in the past and the present, and may invoke a shared, affiliative history. However, nonaligned responses of different kinds can be destructive of, or at least threatening to, social solidarity. They imply contested memories, disagreement, and even hostility.

In addition, then, to making relevant attempts to redress his apparent efforts to take reminiscing in a different direction, and thus having the potential to redirect the ongoing storytelling, Tim's responses here introduce an additional layer of quite active disaffiliation with his mother. The practices he recruits in resisting his parents' implications are not particular to being a mother or son but appear to form part of the collection of practices through which these roles/identities/relationships (and presumably others) are enacted. They may also have important implications for the construction and management of the "independence" that is a standard adolescent developmental phase. There is, however, something deeply family-relevant in reminiscing about the past. Tim's resistance to his parents' reminiscence-related projects constitutes one kind of intervention into an ongoing story or reminiscence. His divergent responses threaten to undermine their emergent interactional projects. As this instance also indicates, however, storytellers are not without resources in addressing recipient interventions of this sort, and they may provide for the ongoing interactional construction and management of the development of teenagers' identity and independence.

In instance (1) we saw recipient interventions of a quite different kind: food solicitations and an offer. Though Mom's requests and offer are clearly not storytelling related—and could thus be taken to be disaffiliative with the storyteller and as disruptive of Cindy's ongoing project of telling about her day in response to her father's solicitations—they do seem to be precisely placed to intervene at moments where Cindy is exhibiting trouble, and they are thus supportive of Cindy, and apparently sensitive to her. This is perhaps just the sort of special sensitivity a parent should be able to enlist on his or her child's behalf.

Note that a lack of buy-in to the storytelling—through interventions attending to material matters such as understanding a referent in the storytelling or having food passed—can be interactionally neutral. But in instance (1), we saw that dealing with food distribution during the storytelling can actually be affiliative and thus can foster social solidarity by "supporting" a fellow interactant, whereas instance (2) showed that resisting aligning with a storytelling, being aligned as a story recipient, and treating the storytelling as a storytelling but pursuing a disaffiliative set of responses can all be destructive of social solidarity. Thus we see that concurrent and intervening actions during storytellings of different kinds may be affiliative or disaffiliative, and may be strongly implicated in the production and management of family roles and relationships.

Transcription Key

.	indicates falling intonation (not necessarily end of sentence)
(0.5)	indicates amount of silence, in tenths of seconds
_	underlining shows a sound that is stressed
:	indicates that the preceding sound is extended or "stretched"
^	indicates raised pitch
(h)	indicates laughter incorporated into a word
?	indicates rising intonation (not necessarily a question)
[&]	marks the beginning and ending of overlap
hhh	marks an audible outbreath; hh marks an audible inbreath
°	encloses speech that is produced quietly
-	indicates a cutoff in the course of production

REFERENCES

Atkinson, J. Maxwell, and John Heritage, eds. 1984. *Structures of social action.* Cambridge: Cambridge University Press.

Blum-Kulka, Shoshana. 1997. *Dinner talk: Cultural patterns of sociability and socialization in family discourse.* Mahwah, NJ: Erlbaum.

Goodwin, Charles. 1981. *Conversational organization: Interaction between speakers and hearers.* New York: Academic Press.

———. 1986. Between and within: Alternative sequential treatments of continuers and assessments. *Human Studies* 9:205–17.

Goodwin, Marjorie Harness. 1997. By-play: Negotiating evaluation in story-telling. In *Towards a social science of language: Papers in honor of William Labov,* ed. Gregory R. Guy, John Baugh, Deborah Schiffrin, and Crawford Feagin, 77–102. Philadelphia: John Benjamins.

Heritage, John. 1984. *Garfinkel and ethnomethodology.* New York: Polity Press.

Jefferson, Gail. 1978. Sequential aspects of storytelling in conversation. In *Studies in the organization of conversational interaction,* ed. Jim Schenkein, 213–48. New York: Academic Press.

Lerner, Gene H. 1992. Assisted storytelling: Deploying shared knowledge as a practical matter. *Qualitative Sociology* 15:247–71.

Mandelbaum, Jenny. 1989. Interpersonal activities in conversational storytelling. *Western Journal of Speech Communication.* 53:114–26.

Ochs, Elinor, and Carolyn Taylor. 1995. The "father knows best" dynamic in family dinner narratives. In *Gender articulated: Language and the socially constructed self,* ed. Kira Hall and Mary Bucholtz, 97–121. New York: Routledge.

Pomerantz, Anita, and B. J. Fehr. 1997. Conversation analysis: An approach to the study of social action as sense making practices. In *Discourse as social interaction,* ed. Teun A. van Dijk, 64–91. London: Sage.

Sacks, Harvey. 1978. Some technical considerations of a dirty joke. In *Studies in the organization of conversational interaction,* ed. Jim Schenkein, 249–69. New York: Academic Press.

Sacks, Harvey, Emanuel A. Schegloff, and Gail Jefferson. 1974. A simplest systematics for the organization of turn-taking in conversation. *Language* 50:697–735.

Schegloff, Emanuel A. 1982. Discourse as an interactional achievement. In *Analyzing discourse: Text and talk,* ed. Deborah Tannen, 71–93. Washington, DC: Georgetown University Press.

———. 1987. Between micro and micro: Contexts and other connections. In *The micro-macro link,* ed. Jeffrey Alexander, Bernhard Giesen, Richard Munch, and Neil Smelser, 207–34. Berkeley: University of California Press.

Scott, Marvin B., and Stanford M. Lyman. 1968. Accounts. *American Sociological Review* 33:46–62.

Stivers, Tanya. 2008. Stance, alignment, and affiliation during storytelling: When nodding is a token of affiliation. *Research on Language and Social Interaction* 41:31–57.

14

Truth and Authorship in Textual Trajectories

ISOLDA E. CARRANZA
National University of Córdoba and National Council for Scientific and Technological Research (Consejo Nacional de Investigaciones Científicas y Técnicas), Argentina

THE TWO TERMS in the title of this chapter, "truth" and "authorship," have long been central topics in narrative research. They remain ineludible because they are not only core elements of narrativity but also raise key questions about the roles of narrative in social life. The chapter seeks to show how truth and authorship are shaped by the path taken by witnesses' depositions within the institutional meanders of the justice system. It does so by focusing on the multilateral character of storytelling in institutions and the complex processes of entextualization, decontextualization, and recontextualization.

Historical truth and claims of veracity have been classical preoccupations in narrative studies (Barthes 1981) that have not been confined to the discourse of history or the study of historiography. White (1980), for example, establishes a link between a moral authority and the truth claims inherent in the narrativized world of any account of reality. Based on the understanding that "narrative truth" in the storyworld is dependent on point of view or perspective, analysts of literary narrative have distinguished between an author/storyteller's, narrator's, and character's reliability (Phelan and Martin 1999). Conversely, Doležel (1999) argues that truth in nonfictional narrative, as in history, is expressed in constative speech acts contingent on the historian's ability to gain evidence about the past and to make plausible conjectures that are scrutinized by the scientific community. The treatment of truth has also surfaced in studies of autobiography. Schulster (2001), for instance, ascertains the lack of historical truth and the effect of mythical self-presentation in an autobiographical account, which itself constitutes a historical document with real consequences for the construction of identity. Likewise, in criminal law, the construction of a given version of the past as real and true reflects the essence of storytelling and its products—the texts.

Issues of authorship can be seen to comprise an extremely wide range of facets, from the multiplicity of voices in the text (Bakhtin 1981) to the social actor's changing footing in the production of a text (Goffman 1981; Levinson 1987). In studies of conversation, Duranti's (1986) article on the audience as coauthor is emblematic of interactional discourse analysts' long-standing awareness of the fact that the textual surface, the plot, and the interpretation of a story are joint achievements. For more than a decade, narrative phenomena, like many other objects of research, were mostly considered in scenarios of interactional cooperation and friendly interpersonal relationships, mostly based on solidarity. Although confrontation and conflict over different versions of the past have been less investigated or explained, they can have tangible and long-lasting effects on a person's life as a citizen and on his or her relations with state institutions. To complicate matters further, the authorship of stories told in institutions involves additional dimensions, such as the storyteller's social responsibility for parts of content, selection of the facts, composition of the form, reproduction of the text, change of medium, and so on. In the administration of criminal justice, these aspects of storytelling have concrete legal consequences for the institutionally defined storyteller, the individuals presented as characters, and sometimes others as well.

The joint and coordinated generation of an emergent text is viewed here as a process that is conditioned by the identity, the resources, and role of participants in the social encounter. Particularly useful here are the insights provided by Bauman and Briggs (1990) and Briggs and Bauman (1992) on social actors' agency and the ways in which intertextual strategies reflect and reproduce social power. In institutional contexts, the rights of different categories of interactants to narrate and to transform what was said condition the processes of entextualization, decontextualization, and recontextualization. Therefore, the network of social positions and the specific power relations have to be part of the present analysis of story trajectories in the administration of criminal justice. The data I present come from a very large corpus of oral criminal trials for homicide in a large city of a Spanish-speaking country. All the trials were observed and recorded from beginning to end, and in each case, a copy of the dossier was collected.

Some direct antecedents of the present study of textual trajectories are found in work by Blomaert (2001) on asylum seekers' narratives in bureaucratic procedures in Belgium and in work by Briggs (1997) on the construction of an indigenous woman's "confession" in Venezuela. Like those studies, the present one deals with communicative situations in which there are deep gaps between the participants' communicative skills and experiences, and in which the power asymmetry conditions the way in which utterances circulate across institutional contexts. The specific research questions considered in this chapter are, Where is truth? Who is its author in a criminal trial? The search to answer them takes us onto a path similar to Kroskrity's (2000) and Silverstein's (1998) and leads us to deal with ideologies about texts.

The Emergence of the Official Tale (Coding Time 1)

A person who has witnessed a crime or alleged crime produces a deposition before a member of the police department or before an assistant to the investigating attorney in the court. The verbal interaction between them is carried out with the witness spinning a narrative—interrupted and at times guided by questions—whose pace allows the clerk to type what will become the official record of the oral version. The institutional role of the police or court clerks entitles them to direct the interaction. In that respect, they are the superordinate participants.

The deponents can possess a varied range of linguistic resources and communicative skills, but they seldom have familiarity with the resources and skills that this institutional environment sanctions as normative. Then, there is usually an asymmetrical relationship between deponents and court clerks regarding their competence in the register that is typical of police or court depositions.

The dynamic process of generating the deposition makes the clerk the composer (Levinson 1987) of the form. Most of the deponent's utterances are not registered word by word—only those that stand out for their importance for the assignment of responsibility or the peculiarity of the deponent's lexical choice. Expressions that assign responsibility, or seem idiosyncratic, are captured as a textual quote between inverted commas. The rest of the content—or more precisely, the "denotational text," to use Silverstein's (1993) term—is presented as indirect reported discourse introduced by fixed formulas. Thus, the composer may present the deponent as having said, for example, that a suspect was "de rasgos fisonómicos normales sin señas particulares [of normal physiognomic features without particularities]." Most of the utterances display a syntax that is typical of the written medium in the institutional register, with multiple subordination and abundance of gerunds, among other features. Most of the lexical choices are those of the clerk doing the writing.

As a result, the genre known as deposition (by a witness or defendant) has a heterogeneous style that combines expressions that are characteristic of the institutional bureaucracy with expressions that have a colloquial or even vulgar tone. The process of entextualization involves mechanisms of relexicalization, explicitation, and completion of the utterances produced by the deponent.

If we take into account the multiple ways of being an author, we must admit that the role of composer (Levinson 1987) does not fully belong to the deponent, who gets defined, however, as the principal (Goffman 1981) or responsible social actor on account of their signature. The "artifact text" (Silverstein 1993) becomes an object that enlarges a file in a bureaucratic system and a document that legally binds the deponent with its "denotational text" (content). In addition, it fixes a version of the story about the past events. If the criminal suspect is eventually brought to trial, around two years have elapsed between the speech event in which this fixed version of the tale is produced and the courtroom session presided over by a judge in which it becomes interactionally and legally relevant.

Authorial Self versus Authorial Self (Coding Time 2)

The juridical doctrine inculcated in lawyers' education, and incorporated by the law professionals into their perception of the criminal procedure, upholds the advantages and virtues of orality and the principle of immediacy or copresence. The latter prescribes the physical copresence of the judge, accusers, defenders, and defendant in order to gain the best possible knowledge of the facts through the possibility of inferring the degree of certainty in the answers, cross-examining witnesses, getting clarifications, and the like.

In the negotiation between the trial lawyer and the witness (who may be cooperative or uncooperative) over the emergent text, the witness, author of the testimony in progress, is confronted as author of a previous text: the deposition. The procedure of reading this text in the courtroom is called "incorporation of the deposition by its reading," and it is regulated by the Code of Criminal Procedure, which allows it in two types of situations: to help the witness' memory and if the witness contradicts himself or herself.

The reading is not carried out in a nonstop flow, and it is subject to selective segmentation and reentextualization. Sometimes lawyers would alternate from reading isolated fragments to reformulating what they can see on the page. In every instance, this recontextualization serves the lawyer's communicative goal, which is getting the witness to confirm some specific elements of the story version that is favored by the lawyer.

Particularly during the cross-examination of witnesses for the defense, some questions by the prosecutor anticipate an imminent recontextualization of the written deposition. The most usual shape those questions take is "Do you remember what you said at the police station?" This seems to transfer the center of relevance in a testimony from memories and knowledge about the defendant's actions to the memories and knowledge about the text attributed to the witness.

When the recontextualization of the written text does not develop in the direction sought by the interrogator, and the confrontation between incompatible authorship commitments leaves the witness no way out, the trial lawyer often poses a dilemma of the following kind: "Did you lie then or are you lying now?" The witness is well aware of their legal responsibility incurred by taking the oath "to tell the truth and nothing but the truth." In the negotiation about the favored story version, the interrogator usually allows the witness to save face by asking "When did you remember better, then or now?" The earlier written text is always near in time to the facts investigated in the trial, the witness's cognitive states and memory conditions at that moment of entextualization are taken for granted, and the witness provides the commonsense answer—"Then"—interactionally collaborating in this way to make the written text prevail.

The data indicate that although trial lawyers are mere relayers (Levinson 1987) of the written story, when they use it as a disciplinary device, the trial lawyers' storytelling rights exercised in reading supersede the authorship privileges of witnesses. As a result, around two years after the inscription of a fixed story version, control over the tale is achieved through a use of reading in the courtroom, which leads witnesses to ratify the content and the form of what they allegedly stated at the police station or some office of the courts.

The success of the trial lawyers' interactional strategy seems possible due to an underlying force that exceeds the limits of the institution and has the weight of common sense. Urban (1996) examines the notion of "fixed text," which consists in the belief that there exists a single original and that any reproduction will be identical to the original. Beliefs that are widespread in society and shared by concrete coparticipants holding asymmetrical positions allow for the smooth exercise of power by the superordinate participant of the pair.

The changing self, which is endowed with an undifferentiated authorial role, is expected to behave consistently with its previous act of telling. In other words, the institution expects the witness not to change. However, as Bruner (2003, 94; my translation) puts it, "It's not that I cannot tell you (or tell myself) the 'true story, the original one' of my desolation during the sad summer that followed my father's death. Rather, I'll tell you (or tell myself) a new story about a twelve-year boy who 'once upon a time.' And I could tell it in many ways, each modeled by my subsequent life not less than by the circumstances of that summer so long ago." Witnesses are expected to produce copies that do not depart from the original story, regardless of their own changing self, the individuals involved in the production of the original and the copy, and the distribution of roles among them.

Defining What Is Real

The second main finding of this study is that, in the practice of the oral trial, it is those previous, written texts that are perceived, represented, and used as vehicles of truth. The traditional prevalence of written texts is brought to bear in the consideration of the artifact text, which exhibits signatures and lasts over time. The institutional character of this product is enhanced in its courtroom use (although the oral testimony also has this institutional character), and its superiority in precision and exhaustiveness is taken for granted.

The idea that is at play is that of "true text," which brings about epistemological consequences for the activity of trying. The written deposition enjoys the status of legitimated source of knowledge about the facts that motivated the trial, just like the expert witnesses' reports, the seized objects, and the photographs of the crime scene. But in addition, it becomes a privileged source of knowledge due to the use trial lawyers make of it during the examination and cross-examination of witnesses, because the information it contains counts as true.

The speech community shares the fixed-text ideology, that is, the idea that authors are consistently capable of producing copies of their own text without considerable variations or contradictions, regardless of the context of situation and the concrete coparticipant in each particular interaction. This makes the interactional mechanism of opposing the oral text in progress with the written one even more effective for the exercise of power.

Witnesses' communicative skills, and capacity to respond, seldom enable them to challenge the written text's superiority. Besides, they themselves adhere to the expectations of constancy of content. Only in rare cases are witnesses capable of resisting being considered the origin of an assertion. More frequently, witnesses' resistance to ratify certain content is easily overcome by the lawyer by referring to the witnesses' signature on the artifact text.

The most common situation is that in which the witness admits the preeminence of the enunciation that got inscribed earlier. In the exchanges that illustrate this, the witness herself manifests the true-text ideology:

Prosecutor: Efectivamente. Usted dijo que lo— vio que ((reads deposition in the file)) "movía el arma haciéndola girar en un dedo, luego escuchó que hizo un ruido metálico,"

→Silvia: Sí, puede ser. No sé.

Prosecutor: "Como hace un policía al cargar el arma."

→Silvia: Sí ((inaudible)) si está ahí, ((in reference to the file))
Prosecutor: That's right. You said that you saw him— you saw that ((reads deposition in the file)) "he moved the gun making it turn around a finger, then she saw that it made a metallic noise,"
→Silvia: Yeah, maybe. I don't know.
Prosecutor: "in the same way that a police officer charges a gun"
→Silvia: Yeah ((inaudible)) if it there, (.. ..) ((in reference to the file))

The conditional clause "if it's there," with its tacit, idiomatic continuation, "so it must be," indicates the witness's subjection to the privileged representation.

Because the content expressed orally by the interrogated witness is controlled by imposing on it the content and the form of the written text, the lawyer's favored construction of reality prevails. This effect is possible because locating truth in writing is part of the institutional members' system of beliefs, regardless of its congruence with other beliefs, and even if it is in tension with legal principles explicitly defended. It is interesting to detect the predominance of the written document even when trial lawyers expect the oral testimony to provide more and better information.

Storytelling in Social Structures

The effect of the true-text ideology, which includes the officially true story, is a component of every criminal trial; it is functional to the local exercise of power in interaction; and it molds the resolution of the confrontation of the texts attributed to a single author, to the detriment of the oral testimony. Blomaert also found effects of generalized ideologies in his study of asylum seekers' stories in the Belgian bureaucracy; as he states, "both the power asymmetry and the conflict are socially and culturally invisible because of . . . reasons, . . . which have to do with the *pervasiveness* of ideologies" (Blomaert 2001, 444; emphasis added).

Consideration of ideologies and the structure of social positions leads discourse analysts to a revised conception of the storyteller. The habitual interest for the individual product, a narrative text, usually isolated from the intertextual chains of which it is made up and separated from its interactional history, has consolidated a view of the teller as an autonomous individual. This individual develops their own narrative plan and calibrates their self-presentation to an immediate copresent addressee, both being considered in a sociostructural, historical, and political vacuum. Conversely, research on more broadly contextualized storytelling has revealed, among other things, narrative variation in shifting contexts (Bauman 1986), cultural scripts (Bruner 1990, 1998), the social distribution of telling rights (Briggs 1996; Hymes 1996), the natural histories of discourse (Silverstein and Urban 1996), and the uses of narrative representation in historical struggles such as nation building (Wodak 2002).

This suggests that research on narratives in interaction risks being reductionist if it is based on a conception of the subject as an autonomous agent who freely represents their private experiences (cf. Carranza 2000), whereas attention to the ways in which storytellers are situated in social structures and their self is conditioned by normative expectations can yield quite different results. Let us notice that in the trajectories and the storytellings considered in this chapter, even the story is shown to be public in a broad sense, and what determines what is real is not the individual's perception and memory but an intersubjectively and institutionally ratified version. Forms of authorship in the data are assigned rather than chosen. By telling stories, creativity, expression, and resistance are laboriously achieved (if at all) by a struggling social agent as they live their life in society.

Conclusion

We have seen that institutional representatives exert control over the telling and the tales, both during the first process of entextualization at the preparatory stage of the trial and during the examination of witnesses in the courtroom. On the former occasion, the deponents ignore at least three things: They will be held responsible for the form as well as the content of the artifact text; it may become more valuable than their later utterances because it can be used to force them to rectify their oral testimony; and it will be prone to transformations if parts of it are reformulated during examination and then during the closing arguments.

In the second moment of control over the telling and the tales, the superiority of the written texts is preserved. Clearly, this is culturally convergent with the traditional prestige of writing, and it is institutionally compatible with the procedural weight that characterizes writing in other branches of the law. Despite explicit legal principles positing the opposite in the interactional dynamics of the testimony, the early deposition acquires, at a minimum, the status of the best statement that can be made of the content, and, more frequently, its use actually takes the shape of an imposition of truth upon falsehood.

The foregoing analysis suggests that only judges who direct a trial conscientiously and counterpart trial lawyers who are interactionally and legally competent can counterbalance these tendencies and give the storyteller direct, online access to the audience made up by the jurors and the judges. In sum, research on narrative benefits from the consideration of the ways stories circulate in society not only because it adds sociological insights to the uses of narrative but also because it throws light on substantial narratological research problems. When the broader social factors that condition storytelling are brought into the picture, the face-to-face interaction and its resulting narrative text are more deeply understood. The present study is a case in point. It has shown that prevalent, shared ideologies about an original text and a true text account for the interactional outcome of the story negotiated in the courtroom. Those ideologies also account for the version of the past that is most likely to be taken up by the judge's sentence and to have effects on human lives in the future.

Transcription Notation

(.. ..)	intraturn pause
—	self-interruption
,	rising intonation
.	falling intonation
→	line under analysis
(( ))	transcriber's comments

REFERENCES

Bakhtin, Mikhail. 1981. *The dialogic imagination: Four essays by M. M. Bakhtin,* ed. Michael Holquist. Austin: University of Texas Press.

Barthes, Roland. 1981. The Discourse of History. In *Comparative criticism: A yearbook,* vol. 3, ed. E. S. Shaffer, 7–20. Cambridge: Cambridge University Press.

Bauman, Richard. 1986. *Story, event and performance. Contextual studies of oral narrative.* Cambridge: Cambridge University Press.

Bauman, Richard, and Charles Briggs. 1990. Poetics and performance as critical perspectives on language and social life. *Annual Review of Anthropology* 19:59–88.

Blomaert, Jan. 2001. Investigating narrative inequality: African asylum seekers' stories in Belgium. *Discourse & Society* 12 (4): 413–49.

Briggs, Charles. 1996. *Disorderly discourse: Narrative, conflict, and inequality.* New York: Oxford University Press.

———. 1997. Notes on a "confession": On the construction of gender, sexuality, and violence in an infanticide case. *Pragmatics* 7 (4): 519–46.

Briggs, Charles, and Richard Bauman. 1992. Genre, intertextuality and social power. *Journal of Linguistic Anthropology* 2 (2): 131–72.

Bruner, Jerome. 1990. *Acts of meaning.* Cambridge, MA: Harvard University Press.

———. 1998. What is a narrative fact? *Annals of the American Academy of Political and Social Science* 560:7–27.

———. 2003. *La fábrica de historias: Derecho, literatura, vida.* Trans. Luciano Padilla López. Mexico City: Fondo de Cultura Económica.

Carranza, Isolda E. 2000. Identity and situated discourse analysis. *Narrative Inquiry* 10 (1): 151–56.

Doležel, Lubomír. 1999. Fictional and historical narrative: Meeting the postmodernist challenge. In *Narratologies: New perspectives on narrative analysis,* ed. David Herman, 247–73. Columbus: Ohio State University Press.

Duranti, Alessandro.1986. The audience as co-author: An introduction. *Text* 6 (3): 239–47.

Goffman, E. 1981. *Forms of talk.* Philadelphia: University of Pennsylvania Press.

Hymes, Dell. 1996. *Ethnography, linguistics, narrative inequality: Toward an understanding of voice.* London: Taylor & Francis.

Kroskrity, Paul V. 2000. Regimenting languages: Language ideological perspectives. In *Regimes of language: Ideologies, polities, and identities,* ed. Paul V. Kroskrity, 1–34. Santa Fe: School of American Research Press.

Levinson, Stephen C. 1987. Putting linguistics on a proper footing: Explorations in Goffman's concepts of participation. In *Erving Goffman: Exploring the interaction order,* ed. Paul Drew and Anthony Wootton, 161–227. Boston: Northeastern University Press,.

Phelan, James, and Mary Patricia Martin. 1999. The lessons of "Weymouth": Homodiegesis, unreliability, ethics, and the remains of the days. In *Narratologies: New perspectives on narrative analysis,* ed. David Herman, 88–109. Columbus: Ohio State University Press.

Schulster, Jerome R. 2001. Richard Wagner's creative vision at La Spezia or the retrospective interpretation of experience in autobiographical memory as a function of an emerging identity. In *Narrative and identity: Studies in autobiography, self and culture,* ed. Jens Brockmeier and Donal Carbaugh. Philadelphia: John Benjamins.

Silverstein, Michael. 1993. Metapragmatic discourse and metapragmatic function. In *Reflexive language indirect discourse and metapragmatics,* ed. John A. Lucy, 33–58. Cambridge: Cambridge University Press.

———. 1998. The uses and utility of ideology: A commentary. In *Language ideologies: Practice and theory,* ed. Bambi Schiefflin, Kathryn Woolard, and Paul Kroskrity, 123–45. New York: Oxford University Press.

Silverstein, Michael, and Greg Urban, eds. 1996. *Natural histories of discourse.* Chicago: University of Chicago Press.

Urban, Greg. 1996. Entextualization, replication, and power. In *Natural histories of discourse,* ed. Michael Silverstein and Greg Urban, 21–44. Chicago: University of Chicago Press.

White, Hayden. 1980. The value of narrativity in the representation of reality. *Critical Inquiry* 7:5–27.

Wodak, Ruth. 2002. Fragmented identities: Redefining and recontextualizing national identity. In *Politics as text and talk,* ed. Paul A. Chilton and Christina Schäffner, 143–69. Philadelphia: John Benjamins.

15

Legitimation and the Heteroglossic Nature of Closing Arguments

LAURA FELTON ROSULEK
University of Illinois at Urbana-Champaign

THE CLOSING ARGUMENTS of criminal trials in the United States are both a persuasive and an argumentative genre in which two lawyers take the same defendant, victim, witnesses, and evidence and use their linguistic and communicative skills to create opposing discourses that are intended to make the jurors decide in their side's favor. In these discourses, lawyers frequently call upon the words or voices (Bakhtin 1981) of others such as witnesses, the law, and cultural products such as the Bible. In this chapter I examine the official trial transcripts of the closing arguments in eighteen felony state district court trials and argue that during the closing arguments, lawyers use the voices of others for several functions, and one is to legitimate the narratives they produce about the crime and the trial. When they use a voice as a legitimation device, the other side has two options: to respond directly (e.g., by recontextualizing the statement, deauthorizing the original speaker, or delegitimizing the statement) or to silence the voice. The two sides are able to create contrasting representations of the same reality partly through the different voices they use to legitimate their arguments.

The Closing Arguments of Criminal Trials

In the court system of the United States, the closing arguments are lawyers' final opportunities to convince the jurors that they should reach a certain conclusion about the defendant's guilt or innocence. Throughout the trial, the prosecution creates a crime story (Heffer 2005)—its depiction of what supposedly occurred during the events in question. The defense then creates its own alternative story or else finds flaws in the prosecution's. The crime stories created by the two sides are the "stories in the trial" (Jackson 1988). They are put together into more cohesive and complete narratives during the closing arguments. Throughout the trial, however, there is also the creation of the trial story (Heffer 2005) or "the story of the trial" (Jackson 1988). During the closing arguments, lawyers thus spend much of their time on the trial story, which includes what the witnesses said, how people behaved, and what other events occurred during the trial (Heffer 2005).

In addition to these two types of narratives, there are also mythopoetic stories. According to Van Leeuwen (2007), these are stories that provide legitimation for the speaker's suggestion that the hearer(s) should behave in a certain way. This type of narrative appears frequently in the corpus as attempts to convince jurors to act in a certain way or to caution them not to, as in this example:[1]

(1) There's a young family with two young children. . . . One child doesn't regularly eat the crust on their toast or their bread and so the parents are trying to teach them proper nutrition and to eat all of the bread including the crust. So one time the father is upstairs in the attic and sees some crust in the attic area. . . . So he goes down and gets one of the children who he believes was the offender, brings them upstairs to the attic and says, "I'm going to make you eat this. You're going to learn to eat crust." The mother happens to be nearby and hears that, runs in and says "No. Stop. That has rat poison on it. I was using that to kill the rats."

In this story, the father was going to use circumstantial evidence, and it would have killed his child. The defense lawyer warns that "that is the danger when dealing with circumstantial evidence" in a closing argument, and if the jurors use it, they may make as important a mistake as the father in the story would have.

Heteroglossia

The closing arguments of criminal trials are heteroglossic discourses (Bakhtin 1981), which means that speakers take on multiple roles in a discourse, and in doing so, they re-create the voices of others either in the form of reported speech or quoted speech. For the purposes of this chapter, the quoted or reported speech will be termed "voices" to draw on the insights of Bakhtin (1981, 1986) that in every discourse, multiple viewpoints and multiple characters' voices are re-created to produce a single discourse. Speakers take on multiple identities or footings (Goffman 1981), and some of these positionings are as characters, speakers from past discourses whose words are reanimated, performed, or constructed (Koven 2002; Tannen 2007). Many of the voices of characters are recontextualized (Bauman and Briggs 1990) in ways that fit the current context and the ideological position of the current speaker.

In the closing arguments, lawyers re-create voices from many characters, including those of witnesses, the judge, the law, each other, and outside characters. However, little has been said in the literature about why lawyers use the many voices of others and, specifically, what functions are served by the different voices other than that they are a means of implicitly evaluating the credibility of the witnesses (Fuller 1993; Heffer 2005). Therefore, this chapter seeks to examine the functions that are served by the inclusion of different voices within the closing arguments of criminal trials, and how the use of these voices contributes to the creation of opposing discourses by the prosecution and defense.

The Data

The data for this analysis come from the official trial transcripts of the closing arguments in 18 felony trials that took place between 1996 and 2006 in a state district court in the Midwestern United States. The defendants were on trial for crimes that included murder, child sexual abuse, sexual assault, controlled substances, robbery, and assault.

The arguments were given by ten defense lawyers (three female, seven male), with one having three arguments in the corpus and five having two. There were nine different prosecution lawyers (three female, six male). One had two arguments in the corpus, two had three, and one had four. The trials themselves were not chosen for any reason, other than availability, so as to not influence the type of results found.

To examine the heteroglossic nature of the closing arguments in the corpus, I recorded all instances of the use of another's voice as either quoted or reported speech. I coded each instance of another's voice by the character whose voice was re-created, the topic(s) discussed in the voice, and if the lawyer agreed or disagreed with the voice as was evident from the surrounding discursive context. For each argument, I then cross-checked the opposing argument for the use of the same voice and the function it served in that argument. By comparing which voices were included in arguments and how they functioned, the types of voices lawyers use and the functions they serve emerged. By comparing the results for pairs of arguments from the same trials, I was able to show how the use of different voices for different functions allow lawyers for opposing sides to create contrasting narratives about the same events.

Functions of Voices

The analysis revealed that reanimated voices serve five different functions in the closing arguments. First, they are used for legitimation when the lawyers quote an authority to use the source's credibility and status as evidence for the veracity of the lawyers' assertions. Second, voices are re-created so that the lawyers can recontextualize or give them a new or altered meaning. Third, voices are used as evidence when the lawyers argue for or against a witness being considered a legitimate authority. Fourth, voices are reanimated when the lawyers deconstruct the truth value of the original utterances. Finally, lawyers re-create the voices of characters in narratives when they describe an event and a key action in that event was verbal in nature. All five functions allow the lawyers to create persuasive arguments while reanimating others' voices.

Legitimation

In the data, the first reason that lawyers use the voices of others is to legitimate their own narratives and conclusions. Legitimation encompasses the reasons, the justifications, and the validations for how things are (Berger and Luckmann 1966; Van Leeuwen and Wodak 1999; Van Leeuwen 2007). In the case of the closing arguments, the lawyers are trying to present a narrative as valid and as necessarily true. The lawyers are utilizing the authority of other speakers as a means of increasing the persuasiveness and legitimacy of their argument.

During the closing arguments, the lawyers present a narrative of the crime and the investigation despite their not having been present for these events. Ultimately, they accomplish this by drawing on the voices of the witnesses who testified about what occurred, as in this example:

(2) [The defendant] got mad at me. . . . He went off on me and shoved headfirst into a furnace. . . . That's why I don't have hair on my arms. He beat me up.

In (2), the lawyer directly quotes the victim of the crime and thus animates a first-person account of the assault she suffered at the hands of the defendant. The effect of this is that the witness, as someone who was actually there, serves as a "personal authority" (Van Leeuwen 2007), which is being an authority due to one's role in the local context. Thus, the voice of the witness provides legitimation to the narrative the lawyer is presenting because someone who was there said that that was how the events happened.

In all the examples in the corpus where the lawyers use the voice of a personal authority, the witness's authority comes from his or her familiarity with the defendant, victim, crime, or investigation, and their having sworn to tell the truth on the witness stand. There are times such as (3) when the authority of the witness needs to be argued by the lawyer:

(3) She said—testified that at the time that she was living at this residence that she was unemployed and was normally home except when she had to go to treatment.

In (3), the witness's authority is constructed by saying that she was present at the time the abuse may have occurred, so she has the authority to testify about what happened during that time.

Other than witnesses to the crime, experts (e.g., medical professionals) frequently testify during trials, adding their explanations of what occurred and why (Mauet 1996; Wilson 1997). During the closing arguments, these witnesses serve as "expert authorities" (Van Leeuwen 2007) through the lawyers' reproduction of their voices. Experts are those whose authority is based on the amount of knowledge and understanding they are presumed to possess. Lawyers have no personal expertise in these areas, so they utilize the words of those who do to legitimate their argument as in examples (4) and (5):

(4) Dr. [X] said that such shaking poses a grave risk of death to a seventeen-month-old child.

(5) Dr. [Y] said children may be convinced or manipulated into saying or believing something is true when it is not.

The physician in (4) was called to testify in a shaken baby case, in which the defendant admitted shaking the baby but the defense argued that that had not caused her death. The voice of a medical expert is thus offered to legitimate the prosecution's claim that it did. In the case in (5), a child claimed to have been abused by a family member, and the defense argued that she was mistaken. They used the voice of this expert to legitimate their claim that it was possible that despite her saying that abuse occurred, it did not.

Frequently, in closing arguments, that the witness is an expert is not discussed, because it has already been granted by the court or discussed during the witness's testimony. However, there are other instances in the corpus where the status of the witness as an expert is discursively constructed during the closing arguments, as in (6):

(6) Then there was Dr. [Y], and I want to talk to you a little bit about Dr. [Y]. . . . He's a man that's published hundreds of works on sexual abuse. He's an international and national presenter on the topic.

That lawyers construct the witnesses as experts as in (6) is important because, as Matoesian (2001) demonstrated, though the status of expert is institutionally granted, it is also reconstructed in the interplay between the lawyer and the witness testifying on the stand. This corpus shows that it is sometimes reconstructed again in the closing arguments.

Other than witnesses, another set of voices that lawyers reanimate to legitimate their conclusions are the "impersonal authorities" (Van Leeuwen 2007) of the law and the judge. According to Van Leeuwen, impersonal authorities are "laws, rules, and regulations" (96). In the American court system, the judge does not serve as an expert but as an impersonal and removed entity who hands down regulations that must be followed. Lawyers use the voices of the law and judge to legitimate their evaluation of the elements of the crime narrative. Examples of this can be found in (7).

(7) Knives which are, in the words of the judge, something that in the manner it is used or intended to be used is known to be capable of producing death or great bodily harm, so the knives are dangerous weapons.

In (7), the lawyer is defining the knife used in the crime as a dangerous weapon, and he uses the words of the judge to legitimate his evaluation of it. Lawyers also use these authorities' voices to legitimate their commands to the jurors. They construct their orders and instructions as not originating with the lawyer but as dictated to them by the law and judge, as in (8):

(8) The law that you have sworn to uphold tells you that you cannot convict a person on speculation, belief, or conjecture.

Here, it is not the lawyer telling the jurors not to convict the defendant based on conjecture; it is the law. Having the law require it of them not only legitimates the command but also might mitigate the face threatening act to some degree.

Additionally, lawyers utilize cultural or symbolic voices, which serve either as "role model authorities" or "voices of tradition" (Van Leeuwen 2007). As examples (9) and (10) demonstrate, this is the object of using a culturally or socially accepted source or norm as an authority:

(9) It brings to mind to me a quotation by Louis Nizer, a well-respected attorney who once said, "When you hear an assertion, compare it against a rule of probability."

(10) There's an old Mexican proverb and it says, "Solo los niños y los barrachos dicen siempre la verdad." That means only little children and drunks always tell the truth.

The quotation in (9) is an example of the lawyer using a role model authority, a symbolic person who by his believing in a statement may make the jurors believe in it as well. In (10), the lawyer quotes a Mexican proverb for which there is an English version as well. The authority of this voice comes from society accepting this traditional voice as a source of knowledge, and with this power, it provides legitimation to the lawyer's statement.

Of particular importance, by quoting a cultural reference, lawyers not only legitimate their claim but also call upon a shared cultural base. For example:

(11) A person also has the ability to do good things, too. I just want to refer you to the adage in the Bible that those who are without sin cast the first stone.

The lawyers use the authority of the cultural product to add credibility to their claims, but by using the references they do, the lawyers also place themselves within the same social group as the jurors. For example, in (11), the lawyer indexes that he is a Christian who knows the Bible. Given the locale in which this trial took place, it is likely that many jurors would also fit into this category. Because Mauet (1980) found that jurors believe lawyers with whom they share a cultural or personal connection, it seems likely that these references will add another layer of persuasive power to the lawyer's argument because they index a common identity.

The final use of others' voices as legitimating authorities functions a little differently because the truth value of the repeated utterance is not important. What is important is that people might have said it. These are hypothetical voices about what people generally do or might do to serve as the "legitimation of conformity" (Van Leeuwen 2007). This type of authority comes either from doing what is "always" done or from what "everyone" or at least "most people" do (Van Leeuwen 2007, 96). They are marked by an abstract subject, such as *we, you,* and *people,* and then a statement about what is the usual course of action, as in the following examples:

(12) We see something on the TV or a magazine, a crime that is, and we tend to conclude, "Gee, this guy looks like a bad guy. A terrible thing he did. I hope they catch him."

The lawyer is not accepting the truth value of the quoted utterance, but he or she is using it to legitimate the thoughts the jurors may have had during the trial or the things they may say during the deliberations as normal.

The common thread among the different sources of authority used in the corpus is that their voices are being used to legitimate the lawyer's argument, to add credence to his or her narrative and evaluations. The lawyers use the words of people whose knowledge of the topic is potentially more acceptable than the lawyer's own—witnesses, experts, judges, society, cultural icons, and so on. A lawyer could omit these sources of information and present the narratives and evaluations as his or her own, but by creating a heteroglossic discourse through direct and indirect quotations, the lawyer utilizes the authority or believability the original speakers may have in the minds of the jurors.

Recontextualization

Lawyers also reanimate others' voices to recontextualize (Bauman and Briggs 1990) or rephrase them. Frequently, this is done so that the voice is understandable to the jurors, such as when lawyers are reanimating an utterance that either is difficult to comprehend (as with the voices of experts or the law) or has multiple possible interpretations. The recontextualization of an utterance that is difficult to comprehend can be seen in this example:

(13) The defendant is guilty of a crime committed by another person [person A], when the defendant has intentionally aided the other person in committing it or has advised or hired or counseled or conspired with or otherwise procured the person to commit it. . . . They were in on it together and the law says that when you're in on it together and somebody else commits a crime, you're liable too.

In this example, the meaning of the discourse legitimates the lawyer's claims that the defendant is guilty by being involved in the criminal act, even if he was not the one who made the fatal blow, but it could be lost on the jurors because it is legalese and quite a lengthy sentence. Therefore, the lawyer restates the law as being "when you're in it together and somebody else commits a crime, you're liable too." Therefore, the lawyer uses the re-creation of the voice as an opportunity to recast it in a way that the jurors may understand more easily.

The second recontextualization process in which lawyers give their interpretation of another voice, be it a witness's or the law's potentially ambiguous statement, can be seen in example (14).

(14) At that time he's coming up with things that, "Hey, look, I, you know, I might have hit her head on the crib a little bit." He doesn't know that that kind of force couldn't have caused the injuries at that time.

In this example, the lawyer is using the words of the defendant to legitimate the defense's claim that he did not know what type of force could have hurt his daughter and thus thought he might have done it during an accident. The lawyer not only uses the defendant's voice to show this, but the lawyer then recontextualizes it to explain what he meant when he said it. As this example shows, the lawyers can use the voice of another not only as evidence of the accuracy of their narratives but also as an opportunity to recontextualize the words in such a way that their interpretation fits their argument.

Additionally, lawyers recontextualize others' voices so they can respond to them in a sort of manufactured dialogue. For example, when one side posed a question to a witness who then answered it or a lawyer posed a question to the jurors during his or her argument and then answered it himself or herself, the other side's lawyers would then repeat the question during their closing argument to frame the discourse and then respond to it even though the question was not initially directed at him or her. For example:

(15) [The prosecution lawyer said] "Why would she be sweating?"

In this example, the defense lawyer is presenting a verbal action, questioning, that the prosecution lawyer performed during his closing argument and is doing so that he can provide a different answer to the question than the prosecution lawyer did. Pascual (2006) showed that lawyers frequently use questions in the closing arguments to present a fictive trilogue among themselves, the jurors, and the opposing lawyer. This is a perfect example of this phenomenon, because the first lawyer asked the question and responded in one way while the second lawyer re-asked the question in the first lawyer's voice and then answered it in a different way.

Authorization/Deauthorization

As discussed above, lawyers often discursively construct the authorities they use as experts. They also frequently spend time deconstructing the authority of the other side's witnesses. In some cases in the corpus, lawyers use the speaker's own words as evidence of their authority or lack thereof. In other words, they re-create a metadiscourse that a witness has provided about his or her own credibility and authority, and in doing so, they rely on a witness's authority as an expert on themselves to legitimate their claims:

(16) When Mr. [D] asked you—or accused her of siding with her daughter, what was her answer? "I'm not siding with anyone. I'm just telling the truth."

(17) If you recall, he even admitted to me that his opinion could be described as an educated guess.

In example (16), the prosecution lawyer allows the witness's own voice to legitimate his and her claim that she is a credible witness. In (17), the defense lawyer claims that the prosecution's expert witness did not meet with the victim and thus did not have the necessary knowledge to give an expert opinion. To legitimate their claim, they reanimated this utterance of his in which he agrees that he is not a complete authority or expert in the case.

Deconstruction

Next, though lawyers often use multiple voices of other characters to legitimate their narratives, there are also many instances when lawyers on one side disagree with what a witness said. This is the case in examples (18) to (20).

(18) He admitted that he would get frustrated by [the victim's] crying. Interesting point with that. When he testified here yesterday he said she very rarely cried, she'd just sleep all day, but that's not what he told the police.

(19) He claimed that he and ____ went to work that day. They worked all day. And we find out from the next witness that no, they didn't go to work that day.

(20) The prosecutor said in his closing statement "[B's] assault on [the victim] doesn't matter." But it does. If [B's] assault on [the victim] could have caused the head injuries that resulted in death, it matters.

In (18), the lawyer uses what the defendant said in earlier statements to contradict what he said during in his testimony. This assumes that what he told the police was the true statement, and it recontextualizes what he said on the stand as false. In (19), the lawyer claims that what the defendant testified to is false because another witness testified to something else. The supposition, then, is that the other witness was telling the truth and the defendant was not, instead of the other way around. In (20), the defense attorney quotes the prosecution lawyer so that she can disagree with him and can show through a sort of logic that what he said was wrong. Overall, by deconstructing the truth value of the original discourse, the lawyers attempt to take away the legitimating power of the words.

Verbal Actions

The final reason that lawyers use the voices of others is to depict verbal actions in narratives. Verbal actions occur in a narrative when the process in which a character engages is verbal rather than mental, physical, and the like. An example:

(21) When asked about what happened to [the victim] his response was, "Sharon who?"

In this example, the lawyer is presenting the narrative of the investigation, and he includes the voice of the defendant when the defendant's feigned lack of knowledge of who the detectives were talking about was a complicating action in the narrative. A voice such as the one in example (2) is classified as functioning as a verbal action when the voice is the re-creation of a complicating action in the narrative, though it is a verbal action. In other words, the function of the voice is to reenact what a person said during an event. The truth value of the statement re-created is not at issue; nor is the authority of the speaker. Additionally, the voice is not meant to legitimate the lawyer's claims. It is simply being used to reenact a verbal process that occurred during an event.

The inclusion of voices as representations of verbal actions is often not neutral. In example (21) above, what the defendant supposedly said is something a small child who is in trouble would say, or so the prosecution lawyer claimed. Verbal actions can also index other social positions, as in this example from Hobbs (2003):

(22) I was waitin' f'r him to start sw-sw-singin' "Swing low, sweet chariot, coming for to carry me home" because this case is all about race. (Hobbs 2003, 284)

In this example, the lawyer evaluates the witness as a person who might have started to sing this spiritual on the stand. By evoking this voice, regardless of the fact that it did not actually occur, she characterizes him as someone who would say such a thing (Hobbs 2003; Fuller 1993). In other words, lawyers often re-create the voices of characters not only because it is important for the sake of the narrative that the character said something but also because what they said or even how they said it marks them as part of a certain social group or as having certain characteristics. This supports the findings of Bakhtin (1981), Agha (2005), Koven (2002), Tannen (2007), and many others.

Lawyers also use what could be called nonexistent voices or a discussion of voices that did not occur to evaluate the characters as well as to present the narrative, as in these examples:

(23) He certainly didn't come out and say, "Yes, I did this to her and I—and I feel terrible."

(24) Where is the "No way, There's no way this happened, I would never, I did not. She's either lying or she's crazy." "I don't know, but I didn't do this, there's no way in the world I did this." Where is that?

In example (23), the defense lawyer is using what the defendant did not say to evaluate what he did admit to as not as bad as it could be. By characterizing what the defendant could have said but did not, the defense lawyer evaluates the defendant's statements as not a true admission. In example (24), the lawyer says that the defendant did not say the things an innocent man would have. By using the negative voice, the lawyer evaluates the defendant as not innocent. Overall, but presenting verbal actions that did not occur in the investigation and trial, the lawyers create narratives that evaluate their not occurring as meaningful.

When speakers presenting a narrative re-create a dialogue such as a verbal action, it can add a level of performance to the narrative (Ferrara and Bell 1995). Constructed dialogues can create a bond between the speakers and the hearers, and they can make characters more lifelike (Tannen 2007). Though it is not being argued here that adding a level of performance to their closing arguments is the conscious intention of lawyers when they reanimate voices that are verbal actions, it could be an effect of this process.

The Construction of Opposing Discourses

The previous discussion highlighted how lawyers use the voices of others to suit their own needs. When arguments are compared for which voices they use and how, it becomes clear that it is in the juxtaposition of the different uses of other's voices that the construction of opposing discourses by the two sides occurs.

There are instances within the corpus when both sides during their arguments take the same segment of discourse and reanimate it in order to legitimate their arguments. When this occurs, each side recontextualizes the voice so its interpretation is in line with their argument. Thus, the same voice legitimates each side's narrative. Cases of this can be seen in examples (25) and (26):

(25) Prosecution—He said and admitted, "I never ruled myself out as a possibility." During the next few minutes I'm going to show you that there's a reason he didn't rule himself out. That reason is because he is the only person who could have, who had an opportunity to, and in fact did commit this crime.

(26) Defense—And when he had stated, "I never ruled myself out as a possibility," that goes to the interviews. . . . What he does is he sits down and he proceeds to tell Officer [B] any and every possibility he could possibly think of how [the victim] could have been injured. . . . He doesn't know that that kind of force couldn't have caused the injuries at that time.

In (25), the prosecution takes the defendant's statement "I never ruled myself out as a possibility" and portrays it as an admission to the crime, in which the defendant legitimated his role as a possible defendant. In (26), the defense takes the same exact statement and recontextualizes it as evidence for their claim that the defendant did not know what kind of force by which the child's injuries were caused because he is an inexperienced parent who was doing anything he could to help the police.

In some instances, one lawyer will use a speaker as a source of authority and the other lawyer will deauthorize that speaker in his or her argument. In some examples, the second lawyer produces a discourse about why the original speaker should not be seen as credible or as knowledgeable about the topic, as in these examples:

(27) Defense—He told you that if this had happened in his jurisdiction—this is Dr. [Z] now, a coroner, a guys whose job it is to make these determinations, just like Dr. [A], if this happened in his jurisdiction he would have called it an accidental injury.

(28) Prosecution—I think you really need to consider in this case with regard to Dr. [Z's] testimony. . . . He admitted that his opinion in this case was written in a letter to a defense counsel before he had ever seen any law enforcement reports. It was based solely upon a limited amount of medical reports.

In this case, the defense had provided an expert witness who was not from the area to counter the claims made by the prosecution's expert witnesses. They legitimate their claim that this was an accidental death by reanimating the voice of the authority who also said this. The prosecution, conversely, counteracts this claim not by saying that what Doctor [Z] said was wrong but by deconstructing his expert status and his authority to make such a judgment.

In other instances when one side uses a voice as a source of legitimation, the other side attacks what the speaker said, not the speaker himself or herself. In these instances, the side opposed to a voice frequently reanimates the same voice and then discusses why it cannot be true, as in these examples:

(29) Prosecution—She said it was impossible, that was her word, impossible for these injuries to result from a short fall based upon her experience, that is, thirty years as a pediatrician.

(30) Defense—Dr. [B] said "It is impossible to get a fatal injury from a short fall; impossible." I asked her about that specifically and I asked her, could she be wrong, and she said, she said "Well, I'm human you know." . . . And in fact Dr. [C] and Dr. [D] agree that it is possible to get a fatal brain injury from a short fall.

In (29), the prosecution uses what Dr. [B] had said to legitimate their claim that it was not possible that the child had received the injuries that killed her from falling, as the defendant claimed. The defense then challenges the truth value of this same utterance in (30) by referring to the fact two other doctors had said it was possible. The prosecution silences the alternative views.

Finally, there are instances when one uses a voice as legitimation and the other side silences that discourse (Huckin 2002). By omitting voices that are antithetical to the narrative, lawyers deny their validity and importance. For example, in one case, the prosecution silenced the entire testimony of the victim's daughter, who observed the altercation between her father and the defendant and who confirmed that the victim, her father, was fighting back. This could have helped legitimate the defense's self-defense claim so the prosecution silence it. The lawyers also silence the testimony of the second victim in the case (the first died; the second did not). He struggled with the truth, but the defense includes him so they can deconstruct what he has said. In this instance, what the victim has said could legitimate the prosecution's claims, but the defense challenges the testimony's truth value, thus attacking his credibility and authority. The prosecution then remains silent about his testimony, erasing its importance in their argument.

Conclusion

This analysis has shown that lawyers reproduce the voices of others in their closing arguments for five main reasons: (1) The lawyers use the authority of the original producers of the voices to legitimate the point they are making; (2) the lawyers are able to recontextualize the voice to suit the argument their side is making; (3) the lawyers use the speaker's own words to authorize or deauthorize him or her as an expert; (4) the lawyers disagree with what a witness said and re-create it in order to deconstruct its truth value; and (5) the voices reenact verbal actions being described in the narrative. Within these processes, they can also position themselves as members of a community with the jurors, all of whom are aware of certain culturally recognized voices. Thus, the heteroglossic nature of closing arguments exists for complex reasons.

Using these different functions, lawyers are then able to build contrasting closing arguments from the same base by drawing upon different voices and by silencing, recontextualizing, deauthorizing the speaker, or deconstructing the truth value of voices the other side used to legitimate their argument. In other words, lawyers pick and choose among what others have said to construct an argument that is in opposition to the other side.

NOTES

A special thanks to Michèle Koven and Rakesh Bhatt, as well as to the Language and Society Discussion Group, for their suggestions and comments.

1. For the purposes of this analysis, any differences between quoted and reported speech will be ignored as they are both attributing the context of the message to the original speaker, regardless of whether the linguistic forms are left intact or changed in the current discourse.

REFERENCES

Agha, Asif. 2005. Voice, footing, enregisterment. *Journal of Linguistic Anthropology* 15 (1): 38–59.

Bakhtin, Mikhail M. 1981. Discourse in the novel. In *The dialogic imagination. Four essays by M. M. Bakhtin,* ed. M. Holquist, 259–422. Austin: University of Texas Press.

———. 1986. *Speech genres and other late essays.* Austin: University of Texas Press.

Bauman, Richard, and Charles L. Briggs. 1990. Poetics and performance as critical perspectives on language and social life. *Annual Review of Anthropology* 19:59–88.

Berger, Peter, and Thomas Luckmann. 1966. *The social construction of reality.* Harmondsworth, U.K.: Penguin Books.

Ferrara, Kathleen, and Barbara Bell. 1995. Sociolinguistic variation and discourse function of constructed dialogue introducers: The case of be + like. *American Speech* 70 (3): 265–90.

Fuller, Janet. 1993. Hearing between the lines: Style switching in a courtroom setting. *Pragmatics* 3:29–43.

Goffman, Erving. 1981. Footing. In *Forms of talk,* ed. 124–57. Philadelphia: University of Pennsylvania Press. Orig. pub. 1979.

Heffer, Chris. 2005. *The language of the jury trial.* London: Palgrave.

Hobbs, Pamela. 2003. "Is that what we're here about?" A lawyer's use of impression management in a closing argument at trial. *Discourse & Society* 14 (3): 273–90.

Huckin, Thomas. 2002. Textual silence and the discourse of homelessness. *Discourse & Society* 13:347–72.

Jackson, Bernard S. 1988. *Law, fact, and narrative coherence.* Liverpool: Deborah Charles Publications.

Koven, Michèle. 2002. An analysis of speaker role inhabitance in narratives of personal experience. *Journal of Pragmatics* 34:167–217.

Matoesian, Gregory. 2001. *Law and the language of identity: Discourse in the William Kennedy Smith rape trial.* New York: Oxford University Press.

Mauet, Thomas. 1980. *Fundamentals of trial technique.* Boston: Little, Brown.

———. 1996. *Trial techniques.* 4th ed. Boston: Little, Brown.

Pascual, Esther. 2006. Questions in legal monologues: Fictive interaction as argumentative strategy in a murder trial. *Text & Talk* 26 (3): 383–402.

Tannen, Deborah. 2007. *Talking voices: Repetition, dialogue and imagery in conversational discourse.* Cambridge: Cambridge University Press. Orig. pub. 1989.

Van Leeuwen, Theo. 2007. Legitimation in discourse and communication. *Discourse & Communication* 1 (1): 91–112.

Van Leeuwen, Theo, and Ruth Wodak. 1999. Legitimizing immigration control: A discourse-historical analysis. *Discourse Studies* 1 (1): 83–118.

Wilson, James Q. 1997. *Moral judgment.* New York: Basic Books.

16

Multimodal Storytelling and Identity Construction in Graphic Narratives

DAVID HERMAN
The Ohio State University

WHEN THEY FOUNDED the field of narratology in the middle to late 1960s, structuralist theorists of narrative failed to come to terms with two dimensions of narrative that constitute focal concerns of this chapter: on the one hand, the referential or world-creating potential of stories; on the other hand, the issue of medium-specificity, or the way storytelling practices, including those bearing on world creation, might be shaped by the expressive capacities of a given semiotic environment. Exploration of both of these dimensions of narrative has played a major role in the advent of "postclassical" approaches to the study of stories (Herman 1999), that is, frameworks for narrative inquiry that build on classical, structuralist models but supplement those models with concepts and methods that were unavailable to earlier theorists such as Roland Barthes, Gérard Genette, A. J. Greimas, and Tzvetan Todorov. As part of this larger program for research, my analysis here focuses on word-image combinations in graphic narratives to explore a particular aspect of the worldmaking process: how texts that exploit more than one semiotic channel trigger inferences about agents within narrated worlds, or storyworlds.[1]

In general, narrative worldmaking constitutes a topic of broad relevance for *cognitive narratology,* or the study of mind-relevant aspects of storytelling practices, wherever—and by whatever means—these practices occur (Herman, forthcoming a). Cognitive narratologists work to enrich the original base of structuralist concepts with ideas about human intelligence, examining various dimensions of narrative structure vis-à-vis modes of sense making; to this end, stories can be studied both as a target for interpretation and as a means for organizing and comprehending experience, a tool for thinking.

In the approach to narrative worldmaking sketched here, the focus is on cognitive processes cued by discourse patterns—inferences, prompted by visual as well as verbal information in graphic narratives, about the ontological status, inhabitants, and spatiotemporal profile of a given storyworld. Storyworlds can thus be viewed as mental models enabling interpreters to frame inferences about the situations, characters, and occurrences either explicitly mentioned in or implied by a narrative text or discourse.

Reciprocally, narratives provide blueprints for the creation and modification of such mentally configured storyworlds.[2] A key question for cognitive narratology is what constitutes distinctively narrative practices of world construction, as opposed to those enabled by readouts from scientific instruments, syllogistic arguments, and other modes of representation.

Meanwhile, questions about medium-specificity fall under the scope of *transmedial narratology* (Herman 2004), or the study of narrative across media. Unlike classical, structuralist narratology, transmedial narratology disputes the notion that the fabula or story level of a narrative (= what is told) remains wholly invariant across shifts of medium (= an aspect of how that "what" is presented). Yet it also assumes that stories do have gists that can be remediated more or less fully and recognizably, depending in part on the semiotic properties of the source and target media. Transmedial narratology is thus premised on the assumption that, although stories conveyed via different media share common features insofar as they are all instances of the narrative text type, storytelling practices are nonetheless inflected by the constraints and affordances associated with a given semiotic environment. Sets of constraints and affordances interact in multimodal storytelling, or forms of narration that recruit from more than one semiotic channel to evoke storyworlds.

In what follows, after laying some additional groundwork for my analysis and providing further details about the three case studies on which I am focusing, I consider how the coordinated use of words and images in graphic narratives bears on three aspects of the profiling of characters in storyworlds: the assessment of the modal status (real or imagined? remembered or anticipated?) of the situations and events that the characters experience; the positioning of characters vis-à-vis one another, interpreters of the story, and broader master narratives circulating in the social domain; and the shaping of identity by a double temporal logic—according to which narrated occurrences are not only localized episodes within a chronology but also complex event-structures whose effects are distributed across time(s). Overall, my account has implications for two interrelated projects, though the aims of the analysis are especially closely aligned with the first of these: on the one hand, the integration of ideas developed by theorists of narrative into emergent frameworks for studying the richness and complexity of graphic narratives (cf. Bridgeman 2005); on the other hand, the expansion of the corpus of stories on which accounts of narrative have themselves been based, so that those accounts can be adjusted as necessary to accommodate the full range of phenomena encountered in the domain of narrative.

Worldmaking in Multimodal Narratives

This section establishes foundations for the study of narrative worldmaking, discussing how the semiotic cues available in a given storytelling environment afford blueprints for world construction. I also provide some further details about my three case studies: *The Incredible Hulk* comics, Daniel Clowes's *Ghost World,* and Alison Bechdel's graphic memoir, *Fun Home.*

Reclaiming the Referent

The structuralists' failure to investigate issues of narrative worldmaking can be traced back to aspects of the Saussurean language theory that the early narratologists treated as a "pilot-science." Pertinent aspects include Saussure's bipartite analysis of the linguistic sign into signifier and signified (to the exclusion of the referent), and, relatedly, his focus on code instead of message, or the foregrounding of the structural constituents and combinatory principles of the semiotic system of language over situated uses of that system. By contrast, convergent research developments across multiple fields in the years since structuralism—including discourse analysis, cognitive linguistics, philosophy, and social and cognitive psychology—have revealed the importance of studying how people deploy various kinds of symbol systems to refer to, and constitute, aspects of their experience.

Thus, in concert with other recent studies by narrative analysts (e.g., Doležel 1998; Duchan, Bruder, and Hewitt 1995; Gerrig 1993; Pavel 1986; Ryan 1991; Werth 1999), I assume in my work (Herman 2002, 2009, forthcoming b) that a root function of narrative is world creation, that is, the (re)construction of worlds evoked through the telling and interpretation of stories. Further, as is underscored in Tomasello's (1999, 2003) research on the sociointeractional dimensions of language acquisition and use, reference to discourse entities in general is an intersubjective achievement, a collaborative process of identifying discourse referents via a mutual cross-referencing of communicative intentions in specific contexts of talk (see Brown 1995). By extension, story analysts need to study how practices of narrative worldmaking both shape and are shaped by the communicative environments in which they unfold—in other words, how the process of building narrative worlds is at once made possible by and reciprocally impinges upon the contexts in which such worlds are made.

Mode versus Medium

By the same token, other research developments that postdate structuralist narratology can throw light on how multimodal storytelling affects the process of worldmaking. For example, Kress and van Leeuwen (2001, 22) draw a distinction between modes and media. In their account, modes are semiotic channels (or better, environments) that can be viewed as a resource for the *design* of a representation formulated within a particular type of discourse, which is in turn embedded in a specific kind of communicative interaction. By contrast, media can be viewed as means for the dissemination or production of what is being represented in a given mode; thus media "are the material resources used in the production of semiotic products and events, including both the tools and the materials used."

Conversational storytellers, for instance, typically use two semiotic modes to design verbal as well as visual (gestural) representations in narratively organized discourse. In turn, spoken language and gesture constitute expressive media, by virtue of which the representations at issue can be produced and distributed in a more or less localized way—more localized if there is no secondary recording apparatus to disseminate the story in, for example, the medium of video accompanied by sound; less localized if the storytelling process is video-recorded. Further when communicative interactions are remediated in this way, the medium chosen can affect whether the original multimodality of the interactions is preserved or lost. Thus an audio recording of a face-to-face storytelling situation not only remediates the interaction but also transforms it into a monomodal representation. The reverse is true when a novel or short story is remediated as a movie.

The Case Studies

My case studies consist of pages (= sequences of individual panels) taken from three graphic narratives, the first two involving fictional scenarios and the third a nonfictional, autobiographical account. I begin with a panel sequence from *The Incredible Hulk* comics (Lee 1972), exploring how narration via multiple semiotic channels affects the process of assigning a modal status (actual, imagined, projected, hoped-for, etc.) to characters' experiences. I then turn to Daniel Clowes's 1997 graphic novel *Ghost World,* considering how the text uses a verbal-visual logic to position characters in (social) space. Finally, I draw on Alison Bechdel's 2006 memoir *Fun Home* to explore how, in retrospective graphic accounts like Bechdel's, word-image combinations can be used not just to situate stages of the self along a timeline but also to suggest a more complex model of identity—a model according to which the self is a temporally distributed structure, involving a network of relationships among multiple time frames. (In my analysis of *Fun Home,* I use "Alison" to refer to the protagonist and "Bechdel" to refer to the narrator whom that protagonist eventually became.)

Centering on a character originally created in 1962, *The Incredible Hulk* portrays the experiences of Robert Bruce Banner, a nuclear physicist from Dayton, Ohio, who grew up in an abusive home.[3] Banner's exposure to gamma radiation has led to his bifurcation into the normal human Banner and his alter ego, the creature known as the Hulk. Sudden surges of adrenaline transform Banner into this creature, a green behemoth who can lift 100 tons and withstand up to 3,000 degrees of heat (Fahrenheit).

My discussion of the Hulk focuses on the final page of issue 155 of volume 2 of *The Incredible Hulk* comic book series, published in September 1972. In this issue, Banner/Hulk—having been shrunken to subatomic proportions by a serum that sends him careening through a microverse consisting of ever tinier worlds within worlds—comes to rest in a world controlled by a Shaper who transforms dreams—in this case, the dreams of an ex-Nazi scientist—into a pseudo-reality. Here U.S. and Nazi troops battle for the streets of New York City.

Ghost World, meanwhile, centers on two teenage girls trying to navigate the transition from high school to post-high-school life; the text thus stands out contrastively against the backdrop afforded by the tradition of superhero comics like the Hulk. Far from possessing superhuman powers, Enid Coleslaw and Rebecca Doppelmeyer struggle with familial and romantic relationships; resist (with different degrees of assiduousness) the stereotypes their peers try to impose on them; and are brought face to face, on more than one occasion, with the fragility and tenuousness of their own friendship. In this way, *Ghost World,* closer in spirit to the female Bildungsroman than action-adventure narratives, overlays a graphic format on content matter that helped extend the scope and range of comics storytelling generally.[4]

Finally, Bechdel's graphic memoir *Fun Home* draws on the autobiographical energies of texts such as Spiegelman's *Maus* I and II and Satrapi's *Persepolis* but harnesses those energies (and the resources of graphic narration more broadly) to the genre of the coming-out story. As Gutenberg (2005, 73) notes, coming-out stories typically involve a kind of reverse-Bildungsroman pattern, in which "the coming-out protagonist has to make an effort to 'unlearn' gender-specific norms of behaviour in order to survive in a homophobic culture." Likewise, the story of Alison's formation is in large measure the story of her learning to resist dominant norms and expectations about (e.g., sexual) identity. These norms and expectations lead, early in her life, to modes of self-representation that—as *Fun Home* reflexively explores—fail to capture the felt, subjective truth of her experiences.[5] At the same time, in telling her own story, the narrator-protagonist comes to recognize how those same homophobic norms and expectations had damaging effects on her father's life (and thus, in yet another way, on her own).

Identity Construction in Graphic Narratives

This section discusses how my three case studies use word-image combinations to cue several kinds of inferences about agents in narrative worlds. In *Hulk,* I focus on inferences about whether the characters' experiences are real or imagined; in *Ghost World,* on inferences concerning how characters are positioned with respect to one another, interpreters of the story, and broader master narratives; and in *Fun Home,* on inferences about where to locate events on the time line stretching between Alison's past experiences and the present moment of narration.

Assigning a Modal Status to Characters' Experiences: **The Incredible Hulk**

Story analysts such as Doležel (1998), Pavel (1986), Ryan (1991), and Werth (1999) have drawn on ideas from analytic philosophy and modal logic to show how assessments of the actuality status of situations and events bear crucially on narrative understanding. Thus Ryan (1991) argues that narrative universes (= constellations of public as well as character-relative worlds) are recognizable because of a shared modal structure; this structure consists of a central world that counts as actual and various satellite worlds that can be accessed through counterfactual constructions voiced by a narrator or by the characters, and also through what the characters think, dream, read, and otherwise do.

At issue here are the possible worlds that orbit around what is presented as what Ryan calls the "text actual world" (= TAW), or world assumed as actual within the narrative. Narratives typically feature a range of private worlds or subworlds inhabited or at least imagined by characters; these satellite worlds include knowledge-worlds, obligation-worlds, intention-worlds, wish-worlds, pretend-worlds, and so on (cf. Werth 1999, 210–58). Further, the plot of any narrative can be redefined as "the trace left by the movement of these worlds within the textual universe. [For] participants, the goal of the narrative game . . . is to make TAW coincide with as many as possible of their [private worlds]. . . . The moves of the game are the actions through which characters attempt to alter relations between worlds" (Ryan 1991, 119–20). Of course, not every narrative faithfully exemplifies this structure; indeed, as McHale (1987) has shown, a hallmark of postmodern literary narratives is their refusal to adhere to ontological boundaries and hierarchies of precisely this sort. Yet even in the case of texts like Borges's "Tlön, Uqbar, Orbis Tertius," where a world initially construed as a far-flung satellite ultimately merges with the baseline reality of the story, this ontological subversiveness can be registered because of how such texts deviate from the default template for worldmaking.

In parallel with broader, contemporaneous developments in art and culture, the Hulk comic uses word-image combinations to foreground issues of modality. For one thing, the premise of an infinite layering of ever-smaller worlds embedded one within another (visually evoked by Banner's free fall through the microverse in the opening pages of the issue) poses the problem of what ontological level constitutes the baseline reality relative to which the other world levels might be viewed as satellites. Further, in connection with the focal world in which most of the action takes place, the text exhibits a garden-path structure that requires the discourse-level equivalent of the repair mechanisms set into play by garden pathing at the sentence level (cf. Jahn 1999). When Banner arrives on the world controlled by the Shaper, before being strafed by Nazi planes and then transforming into the Hulk, what he takes to be the actual world is in fact situated on an embedded ontological level; it is a state of affairs imagined by the ex-Nazi Otto Kronsteig that has been converted to quasi-reality by the dream-stealing Shaper.

An initial clue that all is not what it seems occurs early on, when a dead Nazi soldier himself transforms into a lizard-like creature before Hulk's eyes (p. 7). A few pages later, an American soldier provides the Hulk with a verbal explanation, presented in speech balloons: "This is the world of the *Shaper,* greenskin. . . . He sorta *rules* us, . . . takes our dreams an' *shapes* 'em . . . gives 'em *life*" (p. 14). Subsequently, when the Shaper uses a beam of light to transport Kronsteig into his moonlike spaceship, that environment is confirmed as the TAW of which the world represented in the previous pages constitutes a (manufactured) satellite. The text thereby suggests how the domain of the real, and not just fictional plots, emerges from the conflict of worlds—from the more or less extensive domination of one possible world over others.

In the sequence reproduced as figure 16.1, words and images conspire to signal the modal status of situations and events experienced by the Hulk during this phase of the unfolding action.

As the Hulk struggles with and gets the better of "Captain Axis," a being who occupied one of Kronsteig's intention-worlds in the form of a scientific experiment during the war, and whom the Shaper has now extracted from Kronsteig's mind, the nonactuality of Captain Axis begins to obtrude into the pseudo-reality created by the Shaper, exposing that world as constructed and contingent versus natural and inevitable. Both the visual track and the Hulk's comments accentuate the contrast between this powerful figment of Kronsteig's imagination and the "shriveled old man" himself. Likewise, as the streets and buildings in the subworld passing itself off as reality begin to shimmer, like illusions in a desert, the subsequent panel portrays the

Figure 16.1 Text Actual World versus Satellite Worlds in *The Incredible Hulk*
Hulk © 2008 Marvel. Used with permission.

Shaper "shrieking from his satellite stronghold," with the narration presented in unframed text above the panel, further underscoring the difference between the TAW and the Nazi-inhabited subworld lifted from Kronsteig's warped imagination. The Hulk's violent opposition to the Shaper's attempt to create a new pseudo-reality from the "muddled brute's" own brain suggests an anti-postmodern resistance to ontological play, a refusal of subversive strategies for worldmaking—in contrast with the Byzantine narrative universe modeled in the comic itself. The text thus reflexively critiques the very structures it exemplifies; the Hulk's preference for "something *real*" is at odds with the bottomless stratification of the microuniverse in which he is trapped.

Situating Identities in (Social) Space: Ghost World

In Harré and van Langenhove's account (1999, 1–31), one can position oneself or be positioned in discourse as powerful or powerless, admirable or blameworthy, and the like. In turn, a position can be specified by characterizing how a speaker's contributions are taken as bearing on these and other "polarities of character" in the context of an overarching storyline—a narrative of self and other(s) being jointly elaborated (or disputed) by participants, via self-positioning and other-positioning speech acts. Hence positions are selections made by participants in discourse, who use position-assigning speech acts to build "story lines" in terms of which the assignments make sense. Reciprocally, the story lines provide context in terms of which speech acts can be construed as having a position-assigning force.

Bamberg (2004, 2005) extends this work on positioning to distinguish among three aspects or dimensions of narrative positioning, which can be visualized as concentric circles spreading outward from the storyworld evoked by the act of telling a story (cf. Moisinnac 2008): first, how the characters are positioned with respect to one another in the represented situations and events; second, how storytellers position themselves vis-à-vis their interlocutors in the context of the speech event through which the narrative is presented; and third, how the storyteller's discourse relates to more or less dominant story lines about the way the world is. However, positioning theory was originally developed to account for discourse in contexts of face-to-face interaction. To what extent can the theory be mapped onto graphic narratives like *Ghost World,* and conversely how might expanding the corpus of narrative data necessitate modifications to the theory itself?

Graphic narratives like Clowes's afford a range of expressive resources by means of which interpreters of the text can be positioned—and through which, in the storyworld evoked by the narrative, characters' own attempts at self- and other-positioning can be represented. Likewise, both visual and verbal elements of the text serve to position Clowes's account vis-à-vis dominant story lines or master narratives circulating in the culture at large. Consider, for example, the positioning logic at work in figure 16.2.

The verbal-visual organization of the page shown as figure 16.2 aligns readers with Rebecca and Enid, while distancing them from the backgrounded male characters about whom the two friends converse (or argue). Here Clowes deploys the multimodal equivalent of a print text's use of third-person or heterodiegetic narration that moves along a spectrum from relatively more external to relatively more internal views—that is, from external focalization, where the vantage point on events is not associated with a character in the storyworld, to internal focalization, where the vantage point is in fact a character's. For instance, readers can use the context established by the design of first two panels to draw an inference concerning the status of the image represented in the third panel. Specifically, it can be inferred that this image of the former bass player is mediated through the perceptions of one of the two main characters—most probably Rebecca, given her physical location and the orientation of her torso and gaze in the preceding panel. That inference is reinforced by the absence of a speech balloon in the third panel, even though the bass player is shown talking on the phone. Readers can assume that, because of the male character's location at the far side of the restaurant, Rebecca cannot hear what he is saying on the phone. By contrast, in the case of the (self-incriminating) utterance that is represented by means of a speech balloon in the second panel, readers can assume that this remark ("You guys up for some reggae tonight") was made within Rebecca's and Enid's perceptual range and is therefore included in the report of their perceptions at this point in the unfolding action. Both the organization of individual panels and sequential links across panels thus align readers with particular vantage points on the storyworld, and prevent or at least inhibit other identifications and alignments.

At the same time, the page uses the modulation between relatively more external and relatively more internal perspectives to present alternating views of Enid's

Figure 16.2 Positioning and Verbal-Visual Designs in Clowes's *Ghost World*
Copyright © 2008 Daniel Clowes; courtesy of Fantagraphics Books (www.fantagraphics.com).

and Rebecca's table as the primary vantage point on the storyworld. Panels 4 and following prompt readers to pull back from the internalized view of the ex-bass player in panel 3 and adopt shifting perspectives during Rebecca's and Enid's debate concerning what Rebecca characterizes as Enid's impossibly high standards for men. In a manner reminiscent of the shot/reverse-shot technique in cinematic narratives, the text first provides, in panel 4, an over-the-shoulder view of Rebecca from Enid's perspective, followed in panel 5 by an over-the-shoulder view of Enid from Rebecca's perspective. Then in panel 6 the perspective shifts again, to a more externalized view that captures Enid's angry expression as she defends her preference for the cartoonist over the "guitar plunkin' moron" (= ex-bass player), to whom Rebecca had alluded favorably. By showing both Enid's angry reaction and the now-discredited male characters in the restaurant, and by attributing to Rebecca the utterance "Still, I just hate anybody who likes cartoons," panel 6 aligns readers with Enid's position, fracturing the global story line concerning the lack of viable male partners into competing story lines about life choices for young women in Enid's and Rebecca's position.

At issue here, in other words, are story lines to which Enid, Rebecca, and the other characters in the storyworld orient as a basis for action and interaction—story lines bearing on gender roles and romantic relationships, among other domains. The verbal and visual details found in individual panels and panel sequences cue readers to attach local textual details to this (emergent) story line, while that story line in turn provides context for interpreting the actions, postures, and speech productions of characters represented within a given panel or across panels. In this way, the scene portrayed in figure 16.2 can be connected to an overarching narrative about the divergent life courses of the two main characters, caused in part by Rebecca's growing willingness to accommodate to dominant story lines versus Enid's continued resistance to those same story lines. More generally, making sense of individual panels and panel sequences requires situating them in a broader logic, whereby selves are positioned and counterpositioned in social space—with Clowes's text exploiting both visual and verbal designs to provide interpreters with orienting clues about the positioning process as it unfolds.

Situating Identities in Time: **Fun Home**

In previous studies (e.g., Herman 2007) I have examined how retrospective first-person accounts can set into play a kind of distributed temporality, with an older, narrating-I seeking to come terms with events involving a younger version of himself or herself, the experiencing-I—and thereby constructing, from the vantage point of the present moment of narration, the earlier self *as* one that in fact had the experiences in question. Similarly, at some points in *Fun Home,* attempts to parse the temporal logic of the text generate an unresolvable question: Exactly where along the time line of the story can the narrator-protagonist's perception of—or affective response to—the represented events be situated? In other words, whereas some verbal-visual cues allow events to be situated at definite increments along the time line stretching between past and present, others index a fusion or blending of time frames, and a distribution of the self across those frames (cf. Fauconnier and Turner 2002; Herman 2007, 320–21).

Fun Home does represent Alison's family experiences as playing a formative role, suggesting that they help explain how she became who she is. Engaging in retrospective first-person narration, the text establishes a time line whose distal end is the period in which the younger-experiencing-I lived in the house that her father built, worked at the funeral home, came out during college, and the like, and whose proximal end is the time frame of the present narration, through which Bechdel, in her role as the older, narrating-I, assesses the impact of those earlier experiences on her current sense of self (cf. Lejeune 1989).

Yet by exploiting the semiotic potentials of graphic narrative, *Fun Home* deploys another, different temporal logic as well. In this double logic, time is not only a forward-directed arrow, with earlier moments incrementally giving way to (and impinging on) later ones, but also a loop linking events assumed to have been separated by time's passing. In consequence, experiential knowledge of life-transforming events is less a thing of the past, bracketed off from the here and now, than a process that flows across time frames and is in fact defined by how those time frames are juxtaposed in discourse. Likewise the emotional effects of prior events are temporally distributed; their impact derives both from the profile of the storyworld and from the process of narration by which it is made to live again.

The specific semiotic resource that Bechdel uses to "delocalize" events—that is, to prompt interpreters to construe them as being anchored in more than one time frame—consists of descriptive tags inserted into individual panels; these tags provide information that might not otherwise be inferred about the objects, situations, or events being portrayed visually. The tails of the tags are shaped like arrowheads (see figure 16.3), to differentiate them from the speech balloons used to represent utterances produced in the storyworld; but their format also distinguishes them from the unframed blocks of text that are placed above individual panels and that correspond to the speech productions of the narrating-I, which postdate the verbal and nonverbal acts represented in the panels themselves. The tags thus have a dual or hybrid status; they parallel the narrator's ex-post-facto speech productions, insofar as they

Figure 16.3 Descriptive Tags and Temporal Ambiguity in Alison Bechdel's *Fun Home*

From *Fun Home: A Family Tragicomic* by Alison Bechdel.

comment on elements of the scenes being portrayed, but their placement inside panels aligns them with the utterances and thoughts of the characters within the scenes.

Further, whereas some of the tags can be straightforwardly interpreted as emanating from the vantage point of the older, narrating-I, in other cases it is not clear what "timestamp" should be placed on the information given in the tags. In a panel that shows Alison polishing a mirror with a can of furniture polish to which the tag "incipient yellow lung disease" is affixed (p. 16), the present moment of narration constitutes the temporal frame of reference; that is, it can be assumed that the experiencing-I did not know about the health risks of the polish at the time that she was using it. The same goes for another panel that portrays Bruce Bechdel angrily hurling a plate against a linoleum surface and that contains a tag that reads "permanent linoleum scar"; only with the advantage of hindsight could the narrating-I attest to the permanence of this scar. In the case of figure 16.3, however, it is unclear when the attribution of elation to the father in the fourth panel on the page occurs. Did Alison recognize Bruce's elation on the occasion of her visit, or is the ascription made possible by the act of narration itself—an act that brings the past and present into dialogue and generates this attribution as a result of the interplay between time frames? The same questions could be asked about another, earlier moment in the narrative, when Alison (or is it the narrating-I?) attributes to herself "marker envy" when she sees row upon row of magic markers owned by one of her father's artist friends in New York (p. 191).

In short, because of the way it laminates words and images, (re)constructing the storyworld of *Fun Home* requires not just establishing a chronology of events that separates earlier from later phases of the narrator-protagonist's life but also recognizing how her sense of self is shaped precisely by its fuzzy or indeterminate situation in time (Herman 2002, 211–61). Revealing the limits of linear models of the life story as a chain of causes and effects stretched end to end from past to present, Bechdel exploits the resources of graphic narrative to suggest that it is not always possible to know exactly where in time one's own experiences, inferences, or affective responses should be located.

Conclusion

This chapter has tried to bring together two approaches to postclassical scholarship on stories: cognitive narratology and transmedial narratology. As I hope I have demonstrated, coordinating these two approaches can generate productive new research questions—questions that could not even have been formulated, let alone addressed, within classical, structuralist frameworks for narrative inquiry. What sense-making possibilities do multimodal storytelling practices afford that are not afforded by monomodal or single-channel narrative practices, and vice versa? Further, in narratives exploiting more than one semiotic channel, how is information about the storyworld distributed between the various channels or tracks—and with what effect? Why, in graphic narratives, are some elements of the storyworld represented visually and others verbally, and to what extent would the texts cue different worldmaking strategies if the information were parceled out differently? For that matter, are there differences among the worldmaking strategies required for multimodal narratives that exploit different semiotic channels, for example, words and images in graphic narratives versus utterances and gestures in face-to-face interaction? To explore these and related issues—issues situated at the interface of research on narrative and inquiry into the scope and nature of human intelligence—story analysts would do well to build on the collaborative, cross-disciplinary impulses very much in evidence both at the Georgetown University Round Table 2008 and in the present volume.

NOTES

I thank Michael Bamberg and Barbara Johnstone for their helpful comments about the Georgetown University Round Table presentation on which this chapter is based. I am also grateful for the Arts and Humanities Seed Grant from Ohio State University that supported my work on this project.

Figure 16.3, "Descriptive Tags and Temporal Ambiguity in Alison Bechdel's *Fun Home,*" is from *Fun Home: A Family Tragicomic* by Alison Bechdel, © 2006. Reprinted with permission of Houghton Mifflin Publishing Company.

1. In parallel with Herman (2009, forthcoming b), in focusing on narrative ways of worldmaking I build on Goodman's (1978) pioneering account but adapt it for the purpose of analyzing distinctively narrative methods of world creation.
2. Hence, as discussed in Herman (2002, 9–22), the notion *storyworld* is consonant with a range of other concepts—including *deictic center, mental model, situation model, discourse model, contextual frame,* and *possible world*—designed to explain how interpreters rely on inferences triggered by textual cues to build up representations of the overall situation or world evoked but not necessarily explicitly characterized in narrative discourse.
3. I am grateful to my Ohio State colleague Jared Gardner for his generous assistance with my research on *The Incredible Hulk.*
4. Clowes's text was originally published in serial installments in the tradition of underground comics and subsequently assembled into a novel. My discussion of the text below builds on analyses sketched in Herman (2009).
5. For further discussion of *Fun Home*'s self-reflexivity about processes of self-narration, see Watson's (2008, 27) account of the text as "a memoir about memoir, memory, and acts of storytelling" and "at all times an ironic and self-conscious life narrative."

REFERENCES

Bamberg, Michael. 2004. Positioning with Davie Hogan: Stories, tellings, and identities. In *Narrative analysis: Studying the development of individuals in society,* ed. Colette Daiute and Cynthia Lightfoot, 133–57. London: Sage.

———. 2005. Positioning. In *Routledge Encyclopedia of Narrative Theory,* ed. David Herman, Manfred Jahn, and Marie-Laure Ryan, 445–46. London: Routledge.

Bechdel, Alison. 2006. *Fun home: A family tragicomic.* Boston: Houghton Mifflin.

Bridgeman, Teresa. 2005. Figuration and configuration: Mapping imaginary worlds in *bande dessinée.* In *The francophone bande dessinée,* ed. Charles Forsdick, Laurence Grove, and Libbie McQuillan, 115–36. Amsterdam: Rodopi.

Brown, Gillian. 1995. *Speakers, listeners and communication: Explorations in discourse analysis.* Cambridge: Cambridge University Press.

Clowes, Daniel. 1997. *Ghost world.* Seattle: Fantagraphics Books.

Doležel, Lubomír. 1998. *Heterocosmica: Fiction and possible worlds.* Baltimore: Johns Hopkins University Press.

Duchan, Judith F., Gail A. Bruder, and Lynne E. Hewitt, eds. 1995. *Deixis in narrative: A cognitive science perspective.* Hillsdale, NJ: Lawrence Erlbaum.

Fauconnier, Gilles, and Mark Turner. 2002. *The way we think: Conceptual blending and the mind's hidden complexities.* New York: Basic Books.

Gerrig, Richard J. 1993. *Experiencing narrative worlds: On the psychological activities of reading.* New Haven, CT: Yale University Press.

Goodman, Nelson. 1978. *Ways of worldmaking.* Indianapolis: Hackett.

Gutenberg, Andrea. 2005. Coming-out story. In *Routledge encyclopedia of narrative theory,* ed. David Herman, Manfred Jahn, and Marie-Laure Ryan, 73–74. London: Routledge.

Harré, Rom, and Luk van Langenhove, eds. 1999. *Positioning theory: Moral contexts of intentional action.* Oxford: Blackwell.

Herman, David. 1999. Introduction. In *Narratologies: New Perspectives on narrative analysis,* ed. David Herman, 1–30. Columbus: Ohio State University Press.

———. 2002. *Story logic: Problems and possibilities of narrative.* Lincoln: University of Nebraska Press.

———. 2004. Toward a transmedial narratology. In *Narrative across media: The languages of storytelling,* ed. Marie-Laure Ryan, 47–75. Lincoln: University of Nebraska Press.

———. 2007. Storytelling and the sciences of mind: Cognitive narratology, discursive psychology, and narratives in face-to-face interaction. *Narrative* 15:306–34.

———. 2009. *Basic elements of narrative.* Oxford: Wiley-Blackwell.

———. Forthcoming a. Cognitive narratology. In *The living handbook of narratology,* ed. John Pier, Wolf Schmid, Jörg Schönert, and Peter Hühn. Berlin: De Gruyter.

———. Forthcoming b. Narrative ways of worldmaking. In *Narratology in the age of interdisciplinary narrative research,* ed. Sandra Heinen and Roy Sommer. Berlin: De Gruyter.

Jahn, Manfred. 1999. "Speak, friend, and enter": Garden paths, artificial intelligence, and cognitive narratology. In *Narratologies: New perspectives on narrative analysis,* ed. David Herman, 167–94. Columbus: Ohio State University Press.

Kress, Gunther, and Theo van Leeuwen. 2001. *Multimodal discourse: The modes and media of contemporary communication.* London: Arnold.

Lee, Stan, creator. 1972. *The Incredible Hulk.* Vol. 2, issue 155, September. Written by Archie Goodwin, inked by Herb Trimpe and John Severin, ed. Roy Thomas. New York: Marvel Comics.

Lejeune, Philippe. 1989. *On autobiography.* Trans. Katherine Leary. Minneapolis: University of Minnesota Press.

McHale, Brian. 1987. *Postmodernist fiction.* London: Methuen.

Moisinnac, Luke. 2008. Positioning in conversational stories: Advances in theory and practice. Prospectus of Panel Discussion held at the Georgetown University Round Table 2008.

Pavel, Thomas G. 1986. *Fictional worlds.* Cambridge, MA: Harvard University Press.

Ryan, Marie-Laure. 1991. *Possible worlds, artificial intelligence and narrative theory.* Bloomington: Indiana University Press.

Tomasello, Michael. 1999. *The cultural origins of human cognition.* Cambridge, MA: Harvard University Press.

———. 2003. *Constructing a language: A usage-based theory of language acquisition.* Cambridge, MA: Harvard University Press.

Watson, Julia. 2008. Autographic disclosures and genealogies of desire in Alison Bechdel's *Fun Home. Biography* 31:27–58.

Werth, Paul. 1999. *Text worlds: Representing conceptual space in discourse,* ed. Michael Short. London: Longman.

17

The Role of Style Shifting in the Functions and Purposes of Storytelling: Detective Stories in Anime

FUMIKO NAZIKIAN
Columbia University

ANIME IS A STYLE OF ANIMATION, commonly referred to as Japanese animation, that is popular not only in Japan but around the world. This popularity is in part due to the intriguing stories and the interesting roles played by anime characters. Using a discourse-based microanalysis, this chapter examines the role of speech styles in the context of storytelling, especially focusing on the role of style shifting in Japanese. Using anime as data, I attempt to show how people choose certain linguistic resources to present various images of themselves or others to fulfill various communicative goals. More specifically, I investigate a very popular Japanese anime, *Detective Conan,* to depict the intricate mechanisms of style shifting between the two verb ending forms, the plain *da* and *desu/masu,* by analyzing their use in the discourse of a particular character.

Norrick (2000) indicates that in storytelling every story can be told in different ways to achieve different communicative purposes and that such purposes may be achieved by deploying particular linguistic devices. For example, fantasy stories may display their unreality using conditional clauses and verb phrases with the modals *would* and *could.* Jokes or humorous stories can be displayed with linguistic tones or structure like "build-up-pivot-punch lines" (Norrick 2000, 131, 171). What about other types of stories, such as detective stories, where mystery solving is the key element of the narrative? How can the storyteller's objective of solving a mystery and convincing the audience of his or her deduction be achieved? How can the realistic and yet hypothetical nature of mystery stories be displayed linguistically? This study seeks to explore the interpersonal and discourse functions of the plain *da* and *desu/masu* forms in a detective anime.

The plain *da* and *desu/masu* forms in Japanese appear in the main clause predicate position (e.g., Cook 2002) and are recognized as the dominant verb ending forms. *Desu* forms mark morphologically nouns and adjectives, as in *gakusei desu,* "am/is a student," or *takai desu,* "is/are expensive"; *masu* forms mark verb stems, as in *ikimasu,* "(someone) goes." The *desu/masu* and the *da* forms are generally identified as indexing different social contexts, such as social distance and relative social status between interlocutors, determined by their different status and/or their degree of intimacy (e.g., Ikuta 1983; Maynard 1993). For instance, the *desu/masu* form marks socially formal and polite contexts; the *da* form marks socially informal and casual contexts.

However, recent discourse-based studies indicate that such characteristics as polite, formal, informal, casual are insufficient to explain various functions of the two forms in ongoing discourse or diverse contexts, where the style shifting of the *desu/masu* and the *da* forms occurs (Cook 1996, 1998, 1999, 2002; Makino 2002; Maynard 1993; Okamoto 1997, 1998, 1999). Instead of characterizing the style shifting as associated with the sociocultural features, these studies identify motivations for the style shifting in dynamic, ongoing discourse. Moreover, Cook (2002) characterizes two uses or styles of the plain *da* forms, (1) the informal (IF) and (2) impersonal (IP), depending on the contexts where the *da* form is used. She illustrates how interpretations of *da* forms can be distinguished by the absence or the presence of "affect keys," such as final particles, rising intonation, and the like.[1] Cook maintains that "if the plain form co-occurs with affect keys, it foregrounds the speaker's affective stance towards the addressee or the referent" such as intimacy or in-group relationship of the speakers; when the form occurs with no affect keys, it then foregrounds the content of the information or the referential meaning (Cook 2002, 162).

Although previous studies have advanced the understanding of style shifting, these studies have focused on the shift from the formal (F) to the informal speech style (IF). Little attention has been paid to the role of style shifting between the F and the IP. Drawing on Cook's characterizations of the plain *da* forms, this study seeks to identify the discourse functions associated with the style switching between the *desu/masu*/formal and *da*/IP through the unfolding of interaction in the detective anime series *Detective Conan*. I became interested in this series because in all episodes I saw, there was a predictable scene where the switching takes place from the *desu/masu* verb ending form to the *da* form at the climax of the episode. I found it interesting to investigate style shifts as resources for the participants to build shared images or information in the unfolding of the mystery. By briefly reviewing previous studies, I describe the characteristics of the two forms *da* and *desu/masu* in some detail.

Studies on Style Shifts and the Two Functions of the Plain Forms

It is generally held that speech styles are represented by two verb ending forms in Japanese. These are *desu/masu* form (which is also known as the polite form) and *da* form (known as the plain form, the abrupt form, the naked form), and their variations. The shift between the *desu/masu* and the *da* verb ending forms is one of the most interesting linguistic phenomena in Japanese and has been studied by many linguists. The style represented by *desu/masu* forms and its variations is often characterized as "polite," "formal," or "*desu/masu* style"; the style represented by *da* forms is known as "informal," "casual," or "*da* style."

Cook (1998, 2002) characterizes *desu/masu* as representing deference toward the addressee or as representing the speaker "on stage" or "playing in social role." Regarding the *da* plain form, Cook (2002, 162) characterizes two uses or styles of the plain *da* forms as IF and IP. The IP is depicted as "devoid of affect" or lacking in "affect keys," such as final particles, postposed information, rising intonation, or a lengthened vowel. She claims that "if the plain form co-occurs with affect keys, it foregrounds the speaker's affective stance towards the addressee or the referent," such as "intimacy" or in-group relationship of the speakers; when the form occurs with no affect keys, it then foregrounds the content of the information or the referential meaning. According to Cook, the IP occurs mainly in three different contexts, (1) inward communicative direction; (2) certain written genres, such as newspaper articles, textbooks, and academic writing; and (3) specific turns in institutional talk, such as summary or evaluation turns. These descriptions of IP and IF are useful; however, there is still an issue as to how the foregrounding function of the impersonal style works in interactional activities such as storytelling.

Motivation for Style Shifts: Discourse-Based Studies

Cook's classifications suggest that there are two possible orientations of style shifting. One orientation is from the F to IF style. The other orientation is from the F to the IP style. Because both the F and IF styles index social or interpersonal meanings, it is reasonable to assume that the shifting from F to IF may represent some changes in social or interpersonal meanings, which are often characterized by terms such as "distant" to "intimate," "formal" to "casual," and "public face" to "private face." What then motivates the shift from F to IP? What sort of communicative end does this switch serve?

Previous studies also dealt mainly with turn-by-turn conversations taken from works of fiction or natural conversations or from written essays where one recalls personal stories. In this study I extend Cook's (2002) classification to the analysis of speech style shifting in the broader context of storytelling. In contrast to previous studies, where IP was characterized as representing "backgrounded" or "appended" information (e.g., Makino 2002), I show that style switching from F to IP has an active effect on engaging the participants in story-building activity.

The Data: Overall Characteristics

Detective Conan, known as *Case Closed* in the United States, has been one of the most popular Japanese TV anime series since 1996, and as such should be considered as reflecting naturally occurring conversation.[2] There are more than 500 anime episodes and more than 50 manga volumes. The anime-wiki summarized the synopsis as: "The anime is about a 16-year-old high school detective Shin'ichi Kudo, who while investigating some suspicious activity, was poisoned and left for dead. But instead of killing him, the poison had the unexpected effect of physically shrinking him back to the form of a 6-year-old. He is hiding his identity and living with Ran Mouri and her private investigator father Kogoro, under the new name of Conan Edogawa."[3] In a recurring feature of the anime, Conan uses a tranquilizer made by his gadget expert friend, Professor Asaga, to knock the inept investigator Kogoro unconscious. Conan uses Professor Asaga's voice-changing bow tie to speak in the unconscious Kogoro's voice to prove his theory and solve the case. For this reason in the examples below, I use "C/K" to indicate when Conan speaks by mimicking the voice of the unconscious Kogoro.

In this anime series, Kogoro is presented as a funny but "hotheaded" middle-aged man, and he speaks in an animated way using the *da* IF style, together with a variety of affect keys. Conan, as a typical six-year-old child, also speaks using the *da* IF style combined with various affect keys. However, in a particular scene, C/K dominantly uses the *desu/masu* and switches back and forth to the *da* IP style. This is the scene where C/K solves the mystery in front of an audience, which includes the culprit of the crime. I became curious as to why the switching from *desu/masu* to *da* always occurs in this particular scene, what effects are generated by the switch, and how the switch contributes to achieving the storyteller's purpose.

The data set shows a dominant use of the *masu* form, with a considerable number of shifts to the IP. The use of *desu/masu* in this particular scene can be explained by the characteristics of the speech setting: C/K's mystery solving in front of a public audience. The dominant use of the *masu* in this setting agrees with the interpretation in previous studies of the form as public presentation of self (Cook 1996, 1998, 1999), because C/K needs to present himself as a person of authority, as a capable private detective. Speaking in the capacity of an authority figure in front of a group of people is a kind of public speaking. This also corresponds to Makino's (1983) claim that the *masu* form is predominantly used in utterances addressed to others, whereas the plain form is used in self-addressed utterances (e.g., when the speaker mutters to himself or herself). So when and how does the style shift to IP take place?

First, consider the following, which is taken from an episode about a stalker. In this scene the detective Conan solves the mystery in front of the audience, and, as usual, the culprit is in the audience. A woman, who had been stalked by a man, ends up killing him by allowing him to consume a poisoned drink. Conan solves the mystery of how the woman did it. Pay attention to the verb ending forms, which come at the end of sentences. The shaded words and underlined words indicate the *da* and *desu/masu* forms, respectively, and the abbreviations used are listed at the end of the chapter:

Example 1: "The Stalker"

C/K tells a story of what the woman did on the day when the murder took place. "Gattsuman" is the name of a poisoned drink.

1 C/K: *Ano asa anata wa Nagaisan ga jibun o bikooshiteiru no*
that morning you TOP Mr. Nagai NOM self ACC follow NOML
o shitta ue de ano jidoo-hanbaiki de Gattsuman o katta. [*da*]
ACC knowing that vending machine by Gattsuman ACC bought
"You bought Gattsuman at that vending machine that morning, knowing that Mr. Nagai was following you."

2 *Sore o kari ni A to yobimashoo.* [*masu*]
that ACC provisionally A as let's call

"Let's call that (the drink) A for now."

3 *Anata wa sore o torazuni maemotte yooi shiteoita*
you TOP that ACC without picking in advance prepared
betsu no Gattsuman, B o samo ima hanbaiki kara
another Gattsuman B ACC as if now vending machine from
toridashita yooni Nagai-san ni misete sono ba de
took out as if Mr.Nagai DAT show and on the spot
kyappu o akete arukinagara nonda no desu. [*desu*]
cap ACC open and walking drank NOML COP
"Rather than picking that (Gattsuman A) up, you showed Mr. 'Gattsuman' B, which you had prepared in advance, as if you just took it out of the vending machine, and opened its cap right there and drank it while [you were] walking away."

4 *Soshite kyappu o shita Gattsuman o hei no ue ni oita.* [*da*]
and cap ACC did Gattsuman ACC wall on top placed
"And you left the drink on top of the fence, with the cap put on."

5 *Tadashi, sore wa ima nonda Gattsuman dewa naku*
however that TOP now drank Gattsuman being not
sarani moo ippon yooishite oita betsu no Gattsuman C
further another bottle had prepared another Gattsuman C
datta no desu. [*desu*]
was NOML COP
"However, that was not the one you just drank, but it was another Gattsuman, Gattsuman C, you had prepared."

6 *Tokorode sutookaa niwa sukina aite no mono*
by the way stalker DAT-TOP favorite person POSS thing
o atsumeru to yuu myoona kuse ga arimasu. [*masu*]
ACC collect QT strange habit NOM exist
"By the way, stalkers have a strange habit of collecting items possessed by the person they are stalking."

7 *Toozen no gotoku, Nagai-san wa Gattsuman, C o te*
Natural like Mr. Nagai TOP Gattsuman C ACC hands
ni totta. [*da*]
on took
"Naturally, Mr. Nagai took drink C in his hand."

8 *Suruto, sono bin niwa kanari no ryooo ga nokotte ita.* [*da*]
then that bottle in-TOP a lot POSS amount NOM was left
"But it turned out a lot of the drink was still left in the bottle."

9 *Anata ni kataomoi shite ita Nagai-san wa sore o*
you DAT had feelings Mr. Nagai TOP that ACC

yorokonde nonda no <u>*desu*</u>. [*desu*]
with pleasure drank NOML COP
"Mr. Nagai, who had feelings for you, drank it gladly."

In this particular example, there are four *da* instances and five *desu/masu* instances out of nine. They appear almost in a pattern, as shown in table 17.1.

Here, again consider the example "The Stalker." In this example, five utterances out of nine of C/K's speech are marked with the F, while 4 utterances appear in the *da* form and represent cases of the IP. These utterances in *da* forms are the instances of the IP, because they occur with no affect keys such as final particles, rising intonation, contractions, and the like. Hence, the two styles in example 1 appear in this pattern: IP-F-F-IP-F-F-IP-IP-F. So what does this pattern of the repetition of a particular speech style tell us? To answer this question, it is useful to differentiate two types of events: an ongoing event, which is taking place at the moment of the speech; and a series of events, which constitute C/K's deductions. These events are described in utterances 1, 3, 4, 5, 7, and 8. Among them, utterances 1, 4, 7, and 8 are marked by the IP; and utterances 3 and 5 are marked by the *desu* F style.

The use of the *desu/masu* form to present C/K's official role as a detective as well as a storyteller is exemplified in the suggestion, background information and evaluative comments he makes. Utterances 2 and 6 are marked by the F, and their functions are quite clear. As *mashoo* "let's" (a variation of the *masu* form) is used in utterance 2, C/K is making a suggestion to the audience. Utterance 6 provides background information so that the audience will better understand the behavior of the stalker described in the story. In these utterances the social role of C/K as a detective is foregrounded by his use of the *masu* form. Then what is the difference between utterances 1, 4, 7, and 8 and utterances 3, 5, and 9? Why does the teller use the IP in some cases and the F in other cases to refer to the narrated events of the story? What is particularly noteworthy is the fact that utterances 3, 5, and 9 are marked by the same form, that is, [verb-plain] *n'desu*. The reoccurrence of *n'desu* (a variation of *no desu*) in this context may not be accidental, considering the meaning of the form. *~N'desu* is generally characterized as a marker of "explaining," "asking for an explanation," "emphasizing" or "involving," and so on. C/K uses the *n' desu* form to indicate that he is providing an explanation for the events mentioned in the preceding utterances.

In other words, C/K, as the teller of the story, is securing the understanding of the audience at some major points in his storytelling. Utterance 9 is also framed with the *n'desu* form to describe the victim's last action. Here C/K is concluding his talk by explaining how the victim took poison and was killed. Utterances 1, 4, 7, and 8 are marked by the IP style and serve to create vivid pictures of the events. The sequential structure of the "stalker," 1 to 9, can be demonstrated as in table 17.2.

Table 17.1
The Occurrences of the Two Forms, the *Da* and *Desu/Masu* Forms

Utterances	1	2	3	4	5	6	7	8	9
	da	*desu/masu*	*desu/masu*	*da*	*desu/masu*	*desu/masu*	*da*	*da*	*desu/masu*

Table 17.2
The Sequential Structure of the "Stalker"

1. You bought Drink A in that morning at that vending machine.	<IP>	• *Describing the setting of the story*
2. Let's call the drink "A" for now.	<F>	• *Making a suggestion*
3. You drank B instead of A. (This action is not natural; therefore, there must be some explanation behind it.)	<F>	• *Describing the culprit's action 2 and making a comment*
4. And you left the drink on top of a fence.	<IP>	• *Describing the culprit's action 3*
5. But it was not B, but another drink.	<F>	• *Providing explanation*
6. Stalkers have a strange habit of collecting items possessed by the person they are stalking.	<F>	• *Providing background information*
7. Mr. Nagai picked it up.	<IP>	• *Describing the victim's action 1 as the result of the culprit's action 3*
8. He discovered that a lot of drink was still left in the bottle.	<IP>	• *Describing the victim's discovery*
9. Nagai, who had feelings for you, drank it gladly. (That's how it happened.)	<F>	• *The last action of the victim and concluding of the story*

Note: <F> = formal; <IP> = impersonal.

As table 17.2 shows, the first instance in which the IP is used is when the speaker begins to narrate the setting of the crime scene. It also describes the main actions of the culprit and victim as well as the results of their actions. Example 1 shows how the IP is used in the unfolding of the mystery. In the next section, I examine how the use of the IP invites the audience to participate in the process of puzzle solving.

Engaging the Audience in the Process of Solving the Mystery

Having said that the shift from the F to IP speech style serves to signal a shift from narrating to narrated events, one question is left unanswered. That is, how may the audience respond to such style switching; and what does the response mean in the context of storytelling? In contrast to previous studies, which focused on the type of information marked by the IP (Maynard 1993; Makino 2002), here I focus on the effect of switching to the IP. I argue that the switch to the IP functions to engage the audience in the process of story telling. Previous studies (e.g., Maynard 1993) stated that a writer uses the *da* style (here, IP) to express his inner thoughts in a discourse that is foregrounded by the *desu/masu.* Maynard (1993) explains that the use of the *da* style indicates the writer's vivid recollection of what he felt as if he were present at the scene of the story. However, her study does not explain what effect the switch will have on the audience.

In a similar vein Makino (2002) characterizes the *da* form as expressing subordinate or background information such as facts and the author's personal feelings and convictions. Such information is not addressed to the listener; it is self-addressed or represents a moment where the speaker/writer's awareness of the other is low. This study is useful for explaining the effect of the *da* IP style in *desu/masu* style dominant discourse. However, it does not answer the question of why the speaker/writer does not shift to the IP in some cases to represent facts, personal feelings, and convictions.

Makino (2002, 129) further claims that the information marked by the *da* (UCHI "in-group" forms in Makino's sense; IP in the present study) expresses nonnegotiable information such as the speaker's visual images, which are deeply embedded in the speaker's/writer's consciousness; therefore, "the listener cannot make a turn-taking while the speaker is switching from formal SOTO 'out-group' mode to informal UCHI mode."

However, I found some cases that show the participation of the audience in the process of constructing deductions. This is shown in the following example, where the audience also uses the IP and participates in the storytelling. In this example, C/K and a detective, Megure (M), jointly solve a case where a man called Mr. Sawaki took revenge by killing people who caused him to lose his sense of taste. The audience includes the culprit, Sawaki, and the detective, M. Again, shaded parts and underlined parts indicate the IP and F, respectively:

Example 2: "The Sommelier"

1 C/K: *Sawaki-san wa nokosareta shikaku to kyuukaku dake o*
Mr. Sawaki TOP be left vision and smell only ACC
tayori ni sono go mo somurie o tsudukete imashita. [*masu*]
depending on after that also sommelier ACC continued
"Mr. Sawaki continued to be a sommelier, depending solely on his vision and smell, the only senses left to him"

2 C/K: *Daga, sore wa kanpeki na somurie de aritai to yuu*
But that TOP perfect sommelier want to be QT
Sasaki-san no bigaku ni hansuru koto datta . . . [*da*]
Mr. Sakaki POSS pride go against thing COP
"However, it injured Mr. Sawaki's pride not to be a perfect sommelier."

3 M: *Dakara, Sawaki-san wa somurie no shigoto o sute*
so Mr. Sakaki TOP sommelier POSS career ACC give up
inaka e kaeru koto ni shita . . . [*da*]
countryside to return decided to
"So Mr. Sawaki decided to quit his job and go back to his hometown. . . ."

4 C/K: *Sono mae ni Nana-san o fukumu jibun o mikaku shoogai ni*
before that Nana ACC include himself ACC loss of taste
otoshi-ireta mono tachi e no fukushuu o shite ne . . .
caused people to POSS revenge ACC doing SFP
"But after achieving revenge on people, including Miss Nana, who caused his taste disorder. . . ."

Here C/K switches from the F to IP in utterance 2. And here utterance 3 shows that the use of the IP by M marks the participation of the listener. Clearly, the participants engage in the cognitive activity of solving a mystery. The utterances spoken by C/K and M describe a logical sequence to explain the actions by the culprit. This sequence allows C/K and M to jointly construct a possible scenario.

Conclusion

This study has presented data that offer further insights into the discourse-organizational and interactional effects of style shifts in Japanese. Regarding the discourse organizational function, I have argued that the shift from the F to IP serves to signal a shift from the narrating to narrated events.

First, the IP style of the plain *da* form is used to create two distinct but interrelated functions: to mark a switch from an ongoing event to narrated events, and to create vivid images in the mind of the other participants as if they were in the narrated scene. The function of creating vivid scenes allows the speaker and the listener to participate in shared information-building activity. This function of the impersonal style works jointly with other linguistic features, such as "the lack of affect keys," that is, the absence of interactional sentence final particles *yo* and *ne* and the presence of falling intonation.

Second, the *desu*/*masu* form is also associated with discourse-organizational and interactional effects. The speech setting of the present data—mystery solving in public—accounts for the predominant use of the *desu*/*masu* formal style. C/K constantly shows his official status as a professional detective. The use of the *desu*/*masu* F style functions to institutionalize C/K's role and make his utterances official. By presenting himself as a person of authority—that is, a professional detective—he succeeds in dignifying what he has said and framing it as official.

Finally, the study has examined how a mixture of the *da* IP and the *desu/masu* F styles occurs in the sequential organization of the detective anime story. The setting of the storytelling (when and where the crime took place) is presented first in the *da* IP style. As the narrated story unfolds, C/K switches back and forth between the *da* IP style and the *desu/masu* F style. The *desu/masu* F style is used when the speaker engages in communicative acts, such as making a suggestion, providing supporting information or confirming the understanding of the audience. The *da* IP style is used for a sequence of events that describe how the crime took place.

Having stated that the IP style marks a switch between the narrating and the narrated events, how can the results of the present study contribute to analyzing style shifts in other genres? Nazikian (2005), for example, examines the use of the IP in the *desu/masu* dominant discourse of a TV talk show and indicates that the IP is predominantly used by the TV talk show host in at least four contexts: (1) eliciting information, (2) reformulating/recasting information, (3) extending on an internal scene, and (4) completing what the guest was saying. Among the four contexts, the second and fourth ones, that is, completing and recasting the functions of the IP, are especially relevant to and support the present study. The occurrence of the IP in such contexts marks a meaning-building activity, such as negotiation of meaning between the interactants. When the interactants are focusing on such an activity, their respective official roles as the TV interviewer and the interviewee are backgrounded. The limited samples dealt with in the present study contribute to understanding the diverse contexts where the style shifts between the *desu/masu* and the *da* occur.

List of Abbreviations

ACC	accusative
COP	copula
DAT	dative
NOM	nominative
NOML	nominalizer
POSS	possessive
QT	quotative marker
SFP	sentence final particle
TOP	topic marker

NOTES

I am very grateful for the insights and comments from Yoshiko Matsumoto of Stanford University and Shigeko Okamoto of California State University, Fresno. Special thanks to the anonymous reviewers for insightful comments and suggestions.

1. Drawing on Ochs (1988), Cook (2002, 155) characterizes "affect keys" as elements that index speaker's attitudes, feelings, moods or dispositions towards the addressee or the referent. Such elements in Japanese include sentence final particles, postposing information, rising intonation (indexing uncertainty, request for information), vowel lengthening (emotional intensity marker), and/or coalescence (various affective states) omissions.
2. It is pointed out by Kinsui (2003) that the speech of some of the characters (e.g., Dr. Agasa) represents stereotypical images of "elderly" doctors and may not reflect the actual speech in the natural conversation.
3. See www.anime-wiki.org/index.php/Meitantei_Conan.

REFERENCES

Cook, Haruko M. 1996. The use of addressee honorifics in Japanese elementary school classroom. In *Japanese/Korean Linguistics 5,* ed. N. Akatsuka, S. Iwasaki, and S. Strauss, 67–82. Stanford, CA: Stanford Linguistics Association.

———. 1998. Students' use of the impersonal style in a Japanese elementary school classroom. *Crossroads of language, Interaction, and Culture* 1:43–58.

———. 1999. Language socialization in Japanese elementary schools: Attentive listening and reaction turns. *Journal of Pragmatics* 31:1443–65.

———. 2002. The social meanings of the Japanese plain form. In *Japanese/Korean Linguistics 10,* ed. N. Akatsuka, 150–63. Stanford, CA: Stanford Linguistics Association.

Gooshoo Aoyama. 1997. *Sutookaa satsujin jiken.* Yomiuri TV/Tokyo Movie.

———. 1998. *Juuyon banme no taagetto.* Toho Co. Ltd.

Ikuta, Shoko. 1983. Speech level shift and conversational strategy in Japanese discourse. *Language Science* 5:37–53.

Kinsui, Satoshi. 2003. *Vaacharu Nihongo yakuwarigo no nazo* [Virtual Japanese: Secrets of the role-playing language]. Tokyo: Iwanami Shoten.

Makino, Seiichi. 1983. Speaker/listener-orientation and formality marking in Japanese. *Gengo Kenkyuu* 84:126–45.

———. 2002. When does communication turn mentally inward? A case study of Japanese formal-to-informal switching In *Japanese/Korean Linguistics 10,* ed. N. Akatsuka and S. Strauss, 121–35. CA: Stanford Linguistics Association.

Maynard, Senko. 1993. *Discourse Modality: Subjectivity, emotion and voice in the Japanese language.* Amsterdam: John Benjamins.

Nazikian, Fumiko. 2005. Jotai no danwa kinoo ni tsuite [On the discourse function of *da* verb ending forms]. In *Gengogaku to gengo kyoiku* [Linguistics and language education], 141–56. Tokyo: Kuroshio Press.

Norrick, Neal R. 2000. *Conversational narrative: Storytelling in everyday talk.* Philadelphia: John Benjamins.

Ochs, Elinor. 1988. *Culture and language development.* Cambridge: Cambridge University Press.

Okamoto, Shigeko. 1997. Social context, linguistic ideology, and indexical expressions in Japanese. *Journal of Pragmatics* 28 (6): 795–817.

———. 1998. The use and non-use of honorifics in sales talk in Kyoto and Osaka: Are they rude or friendly? *Japanese/Korean Linguistics 7,* ed. N. Akatsuka, 141–57. Stanford, CA: Center for the Study of Language and Information.

———. 1999. Situated politeness: Manipulating honorific and non-honorific expressions in Japanese conversations. *Pragmatics* 8 (2): 51–74.

www.ingramcontent.com/pod-product-compliance
Lightning Source LLC
LaVergne TN
LVHW090807070826
844660LV00022B/1111
* 9 7 8 1 5 8 9 0 1 6 2 9 3 *